Routledge Revivals

The Marketing of Industrial Products

First Published in 1965, *The Marketing of Industrial Products* is the product of diverse talents and experiences. The first words of Aubrey Wilson's introduction to this book emphasise the importance and relevance of industrial marketing to everyone connected with industry. He goes on to stress the need to set industrial marketing into a wider perspective and, at the same time, to provide for the urgent requirements of students for a basic authoritative book.

Each chapter (with one exception) is an original contribution, especially commissioned for the book which has been devised and edited as an integrated work. The editor comments that there can be few if any people who are able to write with equal authority on each function of marketing. He has therefore invited eighteen leaders in their own particular function to contribute to this book. It immediately establishes itself as a standard work. This is a must read for students of marketing and business management.

The Marketing of Industrial Products

Edited by Aubrey Wilson

Routledge
Taylor & Francis Group

First published in 1965
by Hutchinson & Co Ltd.

This edition first published in 2024 by Routledge
4 Park Square, Milton Park, Abingdon, Oxon, OX14 4RN

and by Routledge
605 Third Avenue, New York, NY 10017

Routledge is an imprint of the Taylor & Francis Group, an informa business

© Aubrey Wilson, 1965

Publisher's Note
The publisher has gone to great lengths to ensure the quality of this reprint but points out that some imperfections in the original copies may be apparent.

Disclaimer
The publisher has made every effort to trace copyright holders and welcomes correspondence from those they have been unable to contact.

A Library of Congress record exists under LCCN: 66008652

ISBN: 978-1-032-87493-7 (hbk)
ISBN: 978-1-003-53290-3 (ebk)
ISBN: 978-1-032-87494-4 (pbk)

Book DOI 10.4324/9781003532903

THE MARKETING OF
INDUSTRIAL PRODUCTS

edited by
Aubrey Wilson

(*Managing Director, Industrial Market Research Limited*)

HUTCHINSON OF LONDON

HUTCHINSON & CO. (*Publishers*) LTD
178–202 Great Portland Street, London W1

London Melbourne Sydney
Auckland Bombay Toronto
Johannesburg New York

★

First published 1965

*This book has been set in Times New Roman,
printed in Great Britain on Antique Wove paper
by The Anchor Press, Ltd., and bound by Wm.
Brendon & Son Ltd., both of Tiptree, Essex.*

CONTENTS

THE EDITOR

Aubrey Wilson, the editor of this book and also the author of Chapter 19, is Managing Director of Industrial Market Research Ltd., and has played a leading role in the emergence of industrial marketing research as an important tool of management. His early career was in marketing in the textile industry with particular emphasis on distribution problems. He received a Ford Foundation-English Speaking Union award to study developments in research techniques in the U.S.A. He is co-author of *The Changing Pattern of Distribution* and *Industrial Marketing Research— Management and Techniques* and a well-known lecturer in many countries on industrial marketing subjects.

THE AUTHORS

Chapter 1. Clive Barwell is General Manager of the marketing services division of Mullard Ltd., with overall responsibility for the advertising, public relations, economic and marketing research and educational service departments. He is one-time Chairman and still a Council member of the Audit Bureau of Circulations, and a member of the Council of the British Industrial Film Association. His services to advertising management were recognised by a Fellowship of the Incorporated Advertising Managers' Association, of which he is a Past President and is now a Vice-President. He is also a member of the Institute of Public Relations, a Fellow of the Royal Society of Arts and a Freeman of the City of London.

Chapter 2. Jacqueline Marrian, B.COM., is Lecturer in Organisation of Industry and Commerce at the University of Edinburgh. After graduating from Edinburgh University she studied advertising, marketing and organisation theory at the Graduate School of Business, Columbia University, on a Rotary Foundation Fellowship, at the same time working with Ogilvy, Benson and Mather, an American advertising agency. Miss Marrian's research interests are concerned with the nature of the relationships between parties in commercial transactions.

Chapter 3. Mary Griffin is Manager of the industrial marketing research department of S. Smith & Sons (England) Ltd. Her training was in chemistry and mathematics before serving in the Superintendencies of Internal Ballistics and Theoretical Research in Armaments in the wartime Ministry of Supply. Following a period with Henry Hughes & Son (later the Kelvin Hughes Division of Smiths) she joined the Central Patents Department of Smiths, where she was responsible for the Kelvin Hughes patent work. Subsequently she was given the responsibility of organising and operating the present industrial marketing research department.

Chapter 4. Margot Newlands, M.A., is Commercial Development Manager of Thomas de la Rue International, where she is responsible for both marketing research and the commercial development of new products and processes. She was a member of the British Export Trade Research Organisation, undertaking assignments in Sweden, Denmark and Czechoslovakia, and later became Market Research Officer of the Industrial Commercial Finance Corporation, and, subsequently, of Formica, also of the De la Rue Group.

Chapter 5.   Gordon T. Brand, B.SC. (ECON.), is Head of Research, Industrial Market Research Ltd. He began his business career as a salesman in the consumer products division of Standard Telephones & Cables and later transferred to industrial selling. Subsequently he was responsible for setting up and operating a marketing research department for the Components Group of Standard Telephones & Cables. Gordon Brand has been responsible for the development of many of the advanced techniques now in use in industrial marketing research and has undertaken extensive research into problems of sampling.

Chapter 6.   Dr. Max K. Adler, D.SC., B.SC., is Adviser on marketing research to the Board of Directors of the General Electric Company Ltd. He received his Doctor of Economics at the University of Vienna and his B.Sc. (Econ.) at London University. He has organised and operated marketing research departments for Osborne Peacock, Odhams Press, Hoover and Standard Telephones & Cables. Dr. Adler has published two books on marketing research, *Modern Market Research* and *A Short Guide to Market Research In Europe.* He also lectures on marketing research in Great Britain and overseas.

Chapter 7.   David Rowe, M.A., Barrister at Law, is Legal Adviser to the British Electrical and Allied Manufacturers' Association. His business career has included service with the Distillers Company as a salesman in their plastics and chemicals division, and the problems of industrial selling remain one of his primary interests. His present work is chiefly concerned with contracts for the sale of engineering equipment—an area where the problems of marketing and law often meet.

Chapter 8.   Michael Desoutter, D.L.C., a founding partner of Evenett & Desoutter was trained as a mechanical engineer. He has worked in the United States in the advertising department of a large insurance company. On his return to Great Britain he was again engaged in engineering, being concerned with both the motor vehicle and contractors plant industries. Subsequently he became a technical copywriter and a senior account executive in an advertising agency before forming his present company which specialises in industrial advertising and associated services.

Chapter 9.   Harry Trigg is a partner in Hertford Public Relations Ltd. He served his apprenticeship in journalism in Australia, coming to the United Kingdom in 1947. After working in Fleet Street he joined the press office of the Ministry of Supply. He entered the public relations field in 1950, becoming a director in a firm of consultants before spending seven years in Sweden as the PR director of Atlas Copco. His experience is largely international and he has been responsible for establishing a PR network in more than twenty markets, including countries as far afield as Mexico and New Zealand.

Chapter 10. Dennis Rose, M.A., A.F.R.AE.S., is an independent marketing consultant specialising in the engineering industries. He has held engineering appointments in the R.A.F. and B.O.A.C. and subsequently was given production engineering and project development responsibilities in the electronics industry. He formed and operated the economic and marketing research unit of Ultra Electronics and later held senior marketing positions with the General Electric Company and Edward High Vacuum International.

Chapter 11. D. John Aylott, M.A., Barrister at Law, is with the Service Department of the Central Electricity Generating Board. He won an honours degree in the mechanical sciences Tripos and also read law and was called to the Bar in 1958. His industrial experience began with English Electric Company as a graduate apprentice and subsequently supply officer to the transformer division. Later he became Production Control and Purchasing Manager with Nicholas Products Ltd. His interests in industrial marketing have been particularly concerned with problems of the organisation of physical distribution.

Chapter 12. Leon A. Smulian, B.SC., M.I.E.R.E., is the Director responsible for the Manufacturing and Automation activities of the James Scott Group of Companies and is Joint Managing Director of James Scott (Electronic Engineering) Ltd. He was Engineer in Charge, Special Products Division of Ultra Electric and later became responsible as Chief Engineer for Radio and Television Research and Development. His interests were subsequently extended to marketing and management by running his own company and by special management assignments to the British Aircraft Corporation and Elliott Automation.

Chapter 13. Fred Davies, M.A., is Head of the North American Department of the Federation of British Industries. His career has included a period as lecturer in a Canadian University and as personal assistant to the Overseas Director of the Federation of British Industries. He was appointed an assistant in the North American Department of the Federation of British Industries and subsequently became Head of the Department. He has been Secretary to a number of overseas trade missions.

Chapter 14. E. A. Lever, B.SC., B.COM., was Marketing Adviser to the British Institute of Management. His business life began as a management trainee in a department store. Later he became publicity manager of an electrical company, sales manager for a radio manufacturer, general manager of a refrigeration division of a company and sales director of three companies concerned in the electrical and electronic industries. He was author of

Advertising and Economic Theory. He devised many marketing education courses for the British Institute of Management and was himself a lecturer on marketing subjects.

Chapter 15. David Burns, B.SC. (ENG.), A.M.I.MECH.E., is a Director, Controls Company of America (UK) Ltd. He is an engineer who has always been concerned with management—particularly marketing management. After serving in the technical branch of the R.A.F. he became a sales engineer and subsequently held marketing executive positions with large British and American companies. He has been a management consultant specialising in industrial marketing problems and has given considerable study to problems of financial control in marketing.

Chapter 16. Franklin A. Colborn, B.LITT., M.A., is Director of the Institute of Marketing. He was Professor of Germanic Philology in the University of Copenhagen before joining Samuel Courtauld & Co. (Overseas), as a director and subsequently became a director of the company in Australia. He has been managing director of France & Son, furniture manufacturers and commercial director of Dalton, Barton & Co., furnishing textile manufacturers and wholesalers. His marketing experience includes activities in Europe, particularly Scandinavia, Australasia, U.S.A., South Africa and the West Indies.

Chapter 17. Peter C. T. Clark is Industrial Corporate Development Adviser to the British affiliates of Corn Products International. His early career was in the brewing industry where he became managing director of his family firm and joined Corn Products on the integration of the two firms where he has worked in industrial manufacturing and commercial departments. His special responsibility now is to intensify all forms of industrial development and growth: this has involved extensive exercises in industrial marketing and in industrial marketing research.

Chapter 18. Theodore Levitt, PH.D., B.A., is a member of the Faculty of the Harvard Business School. His wide business consulting experience ranges from blue chip industries to small service businesses. These activities include such varied aspects as marketing strategy, education and organisation, management organisation, corporate long-range planning, product and distribution planning, executive selection, marketing research, industrial design and site location and advertising. Chapter 18, 'Marketing Myopia', was a prize winning article in the *Harvard Business Review* and set an all-time record of 73,000 copies in reprint sales.

The views and comments expressed by the various authors are entirely their own and do not necessarily represent those of their firms.

INTRODUCTION

Industrial marketing is so broad a subject, so vitally important for individual firms, for industries and for the economy, that it is truly remarkable why so few books specifically on this subject have appeared in the United Kingdom. Even in the United States, where texts on all aspects of marketing appear with astonishing speed, so far only one book has been published on industrial marketing. Thus, a justification for adding this book to business literature is not difficult to make.

It is readily evident why there should be so little published material. In considering writing this book it became apparent that no matter how well a person might understand the theory and pursue the practice of industrial marketing there can be very few people who are able to write with equal authority on each and every function of marketing. There are, of course, marketing chiefs in industry who are well qualified in their subject, but I venture to suggest that there is no one who could practice all the marketing activities covered in this book with equal skill and facility. For the detailed operation of, for example, industrial marketing research or of advertising, they turn, as they must, to their specialist managers.

For a book on industrial marketing, therefore, to be useful for business men and students it must be the product of diverse talents and experience while, nevertheless, devised as an integrated exercise and not merely a series of thematically connected 'readings'. To form a team of individual experts willing to accept and work within this editorial philosophy was the pleasant, if difficult, task with which I was faced.

However, if readers were not to be confused by unresolved conflicts of opinion among the contributors it was necessary to at least agree a common definition of our subject—among marketing men, no mean task in itself. But with this agreement, the decision on what was to be included in the book also became acceptable.

It was apparent early in my preparations why so many writers on marketing omit vital sections. There are few books on marketing which fail to give advertising its due or omit marketing research; but intensive examination of marketing literature failed to produce detailed studies on pricing policies, on supporting services, and on physical distribution and, surprisingly enough, nothing on the problems of integration of marketing activities themselves, as well as marketing within the total corporate complex. Thus, there is no accessible body of knowledge on these topics upon which writers can build.

Hence the decision on what marketing aspects to include was conditioned by three factors: first, the shortage of authoritative texts on a number of industrial marketing functions; second, the need to set industrial marketing into a wider perspective and to prevent it becoming cloistered and esoteric, and, third, the urgent need, of students of industrial marketing in particular, for a basic book that does not require transmutation from consumer goods marketing terms and thinking. My choice has been governed by these considerations and my endeavours have been directed to satisfying these important, if sometimes conflicting, needs.

Perhaps a confession is also in order at this stage; this book is not devoid of nepotism. Every contributor is a personal friend, and many of them close friends for many years. I am delighted that, on examination, I can claim the friendship of those who are regarded as the leading thinkers and doers in their own particular marketing specialities. Moreover, many of the contributors, having completed successful careers within their marketing speciality, have advanced to overall marketing or general management or consultancy and, thus, are in a specially advantageous position to see a total picture. The reader can judge for himself whether or not the authors' wider marketing view combined with experience in a narrow expertise has produced something unique in marketing literature.

This book is the work of very many hands; all of us contributing the various chapters are grateful for help which we have received from our friends and colleagues. As editor of this book, my special thanks are due to Jacqueline Marrian, for clarifying my own thoughts, for suggesting novel lines of thinking and for compiling the classification which appears at the end of her chapter and which gave the other authors guide lines in formulating their own contributions. Her editing of my own chapter has improved it immeasurably.

I want to express my thanks to Thomas Dalby of Hutchinsons, who nurtured the idea of the book and who shepherded it through the various processes publishers adopt before commissioning a work and finally to publication. Knowing the effort this entails, I cannot understand why publishers never tire of authors.

My debt is very great to my colleagues in Industrial Market Research Limited for taking over so much of my day to day work, thus leaving me more time to devote to the editorship of this book.

I would like to acknowledge Violet Baker's contribution for the smooth organisation of the book, for her diplomatic, but firm, nudging of contributors and for her secretarial prowesses. Her creative influence has been important in the preparation of this book. The fact that the manuscript was completed and delivered on time is largely her achievement.

To my fellow contributors I want to pay a special tribute. They cheerfully agreed to collaborate, little knowing how onerous a burden this would prove to be. Good naturedly, they accepted my proddings and even more good naturedly allowed me to mangle their texts under the pretence of editorial authority. I hope their reward might be in the widespread acceptance of this book.

Finally, my thanks are due to my family; they permitted me to go into monastic seclusion for weeks at a time and to abrogate my domestic responsibilities.

AUBREY WILSON

London, March 1965

DEFINITION

INDUSTRIAL MARKETING—All those activities concerned with purchases and sales of goods and services in industrial markets and between organisational buyers and sellers.

1

The Marketing Concept

CLIVE BARWELL

It is more than ten years since the term 'marketing concept' was coined, and it says something for its initial impact in America that it is still in use. In the course of time it has had to withstand a constant buffeting from protagonist and antagonist alike, and it has had to justify its continued existence as a sound business philosophy in a period of unprecedented technological development.

In these conditions marketing techniques tend to change rapidly, and each change usually brings with it some organisational reconstruction. Indeed, if anything has encouraged the antagonists of the marketing concept it has been the endless revolutions in marketing management which appear to plague American big business.

It may be this, perhaps more than anything else, which has accounted for the reluctance in some quarters of British and other European industries to examine seriously American marketing methods. There is still a deep conviction that if the product is good it will sell itself, and that the longer one can keep an article in production without changing its specification or styling, the more profitable it will be.

The fact that the marketing concept is at last beginning to be regarded seriously in this country is, therefore, a matter of considerable significance. There are, of course, many reasons for this awakening, not the least of which is the undoubted presence of the Americans with their marketing techniques in Europe.

But most important is the rate of technological progress which is speeding obsolescence and making buyers more exacting and demanding. The effect of this explosion—for that is what it is—has yet to be appreciated, because we are still, to some extent and by tradition perhaps, cushioned against the shock. The far-sighted in industry, however, will not have failed to see what this means, even if they have not yet decided how to meet the challenge.

First and foremost will be a radical change in manufacturer-customer relationships. The manufacturer is going to be in as much danger of being technologically overtaken by his customers as by his competitors. He will no longer call the tune to the extent to which he has been accustomed. Indeed, unless he can foresee an unending vista of technological break-throughs from his own Research and Development, he may not be able to call the tune at all. He must, therefore, reckon with a far more sophisti-cated market for his products, a market which is already becoming increasingly alert to developments in other countries, and increasingly informed and technically efficient in product development and application.

This tremendous upsurge in technological innovation will not only demand a better understanding of customer needs from the point of view of the product itself but also of supply and services. This latter aspect is well covered in Chapter 10 of this book and the process of discovering these needs, in Chapter 6.

REVOLUTION NOT EVOLUTION

What we are approaching is a revolution in industrial marketing which cannot be dealt with by methods which may have served well enough in the past. And, paradoxically perhaps, the basic challenge which industrial managements must be prepared to meet first is the resistance to change they will find in their own organisations. If we are to cope successfully with the marketing conditions of tomorrow we must begin to make a habit of change today.

It is imperative to realise that the revolution will be permanent, and that it will seriously damage, if not destroy, the organisations which fail to readjust themselves to the new conditions. It will not be a passing phase which can be ridden by temporary expedients of cost cutting until the situation reverts to normality. It will be normality. The classic procedure of axing the advertising or marketing research budgets will offer no solu-tion. On the contrary, these and similar services must assume far greater importance, albeit they will need to be properly integrated and more imaginatively directed. But what management must understand is that change in this context is indivisible. Its need must be recognised and under-stood throughout the organisation. It will apply as much to research, development and production as it will to the rest of the marketing spectrum.

During the decade which has elapsed since General Electric of America belatedly discovered that they had omitted to consider the housewife's needs when they designed a certain electric cooker, a great deal has been said and written about the marketing concept. Some of this vast output of words has contributed enormously to the art. Some has unnecessarily elaborated and embroidered the original notion. And much has done no more than confuse the marketing concept with marketing itself.

A DISTINCTION

At present when some American marketing theorists are saying that the textbooks of 1960 are already obsolete it would take a bold man to offer a new, dogmatic definition of marketing. The definition which was given to each contributor to this book, and which is quoted before this chapter, was deliberately simple and it is not the purpose of this chapter to elaborate it. There are more than enough definitions to go on with. Indeed, one might go so far as to say that 'you pays your price and takes your pick'. What it is hoped to do is help to differentiate between the marketing concept and marketing, to appreciate that there are half-way houses between product orientation and market orientation, and that there are some basic principles and elementary steps which can point an organisation in the right direction.

One must, of course, be warned against the people who have 'tried it, old boy' (they are often the same as those who have 'tried' advertising), as well as those who pay lip service to any innovation or passing fad in order to show that they are 'with it'. Most of all, be warned against those who not only pay lip service to the marketing concept but also re-label their departments and executives.

The marketing concept is a philosophy, not a system of marketing or an organisational structure. It is founded on the belief that profitable sales and satisfactory returns on investment can only be achieved by identifying, anticipating and satisfying customer needs and desires—in that order.

It is an attitude of mind which places the customer at the very centre of a business activity and automatically orients a company towards its markets rather than towards its factories. It is a philosophy which rejects the proposition that production is an end in itself, and that the products, manufactured to the satisfaction of the manufacturer, merely remain to be sold. 'Selling', says Theodore Levitt in Chapter 18, 'focuses on the needs of the seller, marketing on the needs of the buyer. Selling is pre-occupied with the seller's need to convert his product into cash; marketing with the idea of satisfying the needs of the customer by means of the product and the whole cluster of things associated with creating, delivering and finally consuming it.'

Identify, anticipate, satisfy. These three words are the most important in this chapter. They are the basis of the marketing concept. They provide the key to the re-examination of any industrial marketing organisation. They open the doors to the proper integration of marketing elements and the effective employment of marketing services. They point out areas of collaboration and interrelation with research, development and production.

If this is the marketing concept, what then is marketing? As Levitt implies, it is the actual process of integrating and co-ordinating all the functions which serve to identify and anticipate needs, communicate these needs to research, development and production, create and stimulate demand, and transfer the products and services from the supplier to the customer.

So much can usually be readily accepted, and it is up to this point that it is difficult to find anyone in disagreement. But how to do it, and with what, and with whom! This is where the best intentions in the world begin to falter, and it is not surprising that they do. No two organisations are precisely the same, and what may be good for one is not necessarily good for another. The extent to which an organisation can orientate itself towards its markets depends on the nature of its business and the peculiarities of those markets. The more technical an industry, for instance, the more will the customer's needs be influenced by the results of the supplier's own research. In fact, the customer in such industries is often best served by being persuaded to modify his designs to use components or materials which will satisfy his needs more economically than those which he may originally specify.

MARKET AND PRODUCT ORIENTATION

There are, therefore, half-way houses between complete market orientation and complete product orientation, and these can only be established by the most careful and patient study of the problem. One such approach[1] illustrates the opposite poles of market and product orientation by two simple diagrams depicting a company which has three product lines—A, B and C—each being sold to three markets—X, Y and Z. A *product*-oriented structure would be organised as shown in Figure A. Here, each salesman has three markets to service with his specialised product knowledge. Every buyer must see three salesmen to obtain information on all three products.

A *market*-oriented structure, on the other hand, would be set up as illustrated in Figure B. In this situation each salesman carries all three lines and has, theoretically at least, developed a specialised knowledge of the needs of one of the three markets. Each buyer needs to see only one salesman to obtain service on all three products.

'On paper, the market-oriented approach appears to be better suited to the desires of the customer. It should save time in interviewing, telephoning and writing. The buyer can consolidate orders, catalogues, and application data. He deals with a salesman who knows his customer's business in depth. Thus the seller has made it easier for the buyer to do business with him. In fact, however, there are massive complications involved in such an organisational structure. Within a typical company, strong pressures dictate a product-oriented approach to the market place.'[2]

The effective compromise between these two extremes—and to be effective it must not depart from the basic principles of the marketing concept—will depend to a large extent upon a company's size and complexity. There are few problems in an organisation which is small enough to put the control of the total marketing operation in the hands of one executive. In a large company the burden of responsibility may be too great to be borne single-handed. In such cases the key to a successful marketing organisation lies in the grouping of major marketing elements and their integration and co-ordination in the overall corporate operation.

1. Robert W. Lear, 'No Easy Road to Market Orientation', *Harvard Business Review* (Cambridge, Mass., Sept.–Oct. 1963).
2. Ibid.

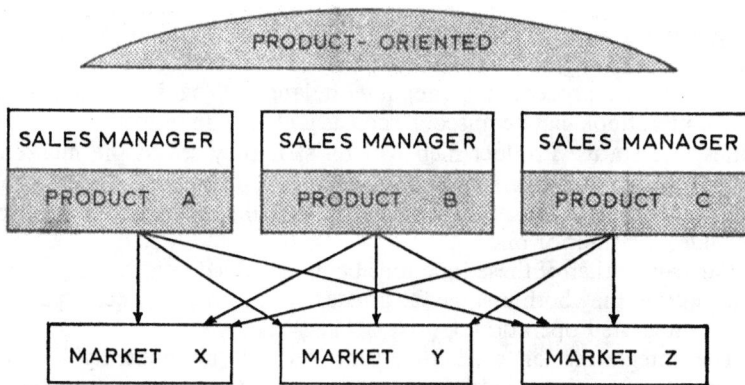

Fig. A

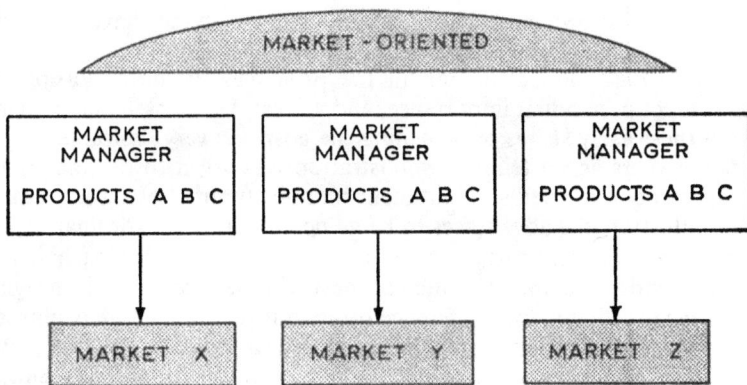

Fig. B

From all this it can be seen that the adoption of the marketing concept and the establishment of an effective marketing structure pose two entirely separate problems. In the case of the former we have what is largely a communications problem; in the case of the latter an organisation problem. It is clear, too, that one can have a marketing structure of sorts without the marketing concept. But the marketing concept without a planned marketing structure is meaningless.

EDUCATION AND INTEGRATION

There is no short or easy path to winning the acceptance of the marketing concept. It may take many months, perhaps years, to permeate an organisation thoroughly with the philosophy. Attitudes of mind do not change easily, and it is precisely this which is involved. No amount of reorganisation or title changing is going to produce the desired results. On the contrary, such a procedure is fraught with danger. What is intended to be a change in outlook can be misconstrued as a change in individual responsibilities and status. Product men will resist if they see in the marketing concept a threat to their own responsibility and status. And the sales function may be seriously weakened if 'marketing' becomes an OK word and 'sales' an inferior one.

Far from either of these functions being devalued in a market oriented organisation, they both assume far greater effectiveness for being part of a totally integrated operation.

The integrating or marketing function will undoubtedly be more important than either product management or sales management, but the marketing manager is most likely to emerge from the ranks of one or the other, provided always that within these ranks are men with sufficient vision, flexibility and capability to absorb the new philosophy and to equip themselves to co-ordinate areas of activity with which they have previously been only remotely associated.

The need for indoctrination in the principles of the philosophy is, therefore, of paramount importance, and a great deal of skill and imagination in these early stages of preaching the gospel is very desirable.

Some years ago a telling demonstration was given to its staff by the management of a Swedish instrument manufacturer. Seeking a dramatic way to illustrate the advantages to be gained by proper co-ordination and integration, they engaged a small orchestra, and labelled each instrumentalist with the name of a different marketing service. At a given signal, the musicians entered the conference room in turn and separately played a little tune on their instruments. When all had assembled and had played their pieces they were asked to play them at the same time. The result, of course, was cacophony. They were then handed their appropriate parts of a piece of music, and conducted in its performance by the marketing manager. The result this time was very different.

Needless to say, the message was not lost on the audience. One business philosophy properly absorbed, integrated and directed produces an impact and a response which cannot be equalled by a mixture of attitudes and unintegrated actions.

Whether such shock methods are necessary or desirable must obviously depend on local conditions, but one thing is certain and that is that a definite plan must be formulated. Furthermore, it must be realised at the outset that success will only come from the careful execution of the plan and that the ideas disseminated must be continuously developed and nourished.

Most industrial organisations find that their biggest difficulties in initiating new thinking arise from the lack of suitable lines of communication. This is one of the reasons why some companies have hurried into reorganisation before thoroughly selling the concept. Far from helping, precipitate action like this frequently hinders progress because busy executives are further burdened by problems arising from the reorganisation.

It is much better to recognise at the outset that one is usually dealing with men who are already fully occupied. Means must therefore be found to help them find time to listen, read, digest and discuss. Most busy executives have a conscience about business reading. Magazines, journals and reports pile up on their desks or shuttle back and forth between office and home. A service of news digests and commentaries is consequently usually welcomed. Such a service is quickly established and becomes a ready vehicle for articles and case histories.

It is equally important to find a suitable area in which the new ideas can be directly related to day-to-day problems. One of the most fertile is the sales and advertising area, for it is still true to say that industrial advertising lags far behind consumer advertising as an integrated part of the overall marketing operation. Nevertheless, sales and advertising departments do come together and when they do some very specific and relevant questions can be posed.

In many industrial organisations the advertising function begins too late and ends too soon. It begins too late because it is felt that the function of the advertising manager (so called) is merely to take a brief from the product or sales manager and make an advertisement. This kind of advertising is all too familiar—trite, superficial and strongly product oriented. Bringing the advertising manager in at the earliest possible stage so that he has time to translate product features into customer benefits not only has the obvious advantages but helps people to think and talk in customer language. The advertising function ends too soon when enquiries are routed directly to the sales department. This deprives the advertising manager of the possibility of measuring results, planning follow-up or taking real care of the customer's needs by ensuring that requested information is presented in the best manner.

A closer integration of advertising and sales will also lead to more objective questioning of a company's knowledge of customers and markets, of sales and advertising objectives and, above all, of the proper place of advertising in the marketing structure.

This is an effective way to begin to apply the principles of the concept. It makes people look outwards, recognise advertising as an essential communications medium, points out deficiencies in market intelligence, encourages the use of essential marketing services.

It is also one of the easiest ways of appreciating the advantages of integrating marketing elements and leading to the adoption of more sophisticated marketing services. Indeed, the term 'marketing services' is already becoming the accepted description of that group of activities which in America are now being called 'marketing communications'. They comprise essentially marketing research, public relations and advertising.

Each of these marketing services and others is treated at length in this book. But because they play so important a role as an integrated operation in the market oriented organisation it is necessary to refer briefly to them in this context.

The idea of integrating marketing research with advertising and public relations may well be considered revolutionary, but on contemplation it is logical enough. One of the reasons why industrial marketing research has developed so slowly in this country is because it has not been properly geared into the overall marketing operation. Consequently, the industrial marketing researcher has had to operate on the periphery of market development activities, being called in on an *ad hoc* basis and being resented when suggesting that sales or product management do not know enough about their customers and their markets. It has almost been a case of his having to be content with crumbs from the rich man's table.

As part of the marketing services package, research is automatically taken into full consideration when marketing plans are being developed. It is, in fact, only in these conditions that it can fulfil its total function and make an optimum contribution. The measurement of market potentials, for example, is quickly seen to be only one of many aspects of marketing research. It can be employed equally effectively in evaluating the corporate or product image, measuring advertising effectiveness and so on. Because it is now a properly integrated function a planned programme becomes possible and this, in turn, makes budgeting that much easier.

Public relations has also suffered because it is not treated as an integrated part of the overall marketing activity. Of course, there are very important public relations' activities which cannot and should not be related to marketing, and in some organisations these are sufficiently predominant as to make the PR manager more appropriately responsible to the chief executive or even the company secretary. But in most industrial organisations PR has a far greater justification for being part of marketing services and centrally controlled as such. There is no reason why the department cannot be 'loaned' for activities extraneous to marketing.

While these are the three basic departments of the marketing services division, a number of organisations are successfully enlarging the scope of the operation and bringing in other facets of marketing communications. Educational services, for example, can be regarded as legitimately within the purview of the marketing concept. They are designed to serve industry as well as educational establishments, and as such can be regarded as an added value to the customer.

More directly involved is the interesting new area of industrial sales promotion which is being developed as a customer relations activity which is broader than the normal person-to-person contact but more intimate than mass communication. Examples are the display and demonstration facilities which are becoming increasingly common in factory and head office.

The ultimate manifestation of the marketing concept must, however, be found in a company's organisational structure. Preoccupation with production has kept marketing out of the industrial board room. Somehow or other it must find its way in. Only in this way can sufficient attention be focused on the problems of reorganisation and all that they entail.

2

Marketing Characteristics of Industrial Goods and Buyers

JACQUELINE MARRIAN, B.Com.

'The broad basic differences between types of goods arise not so much from variations in their physical characteristics as from differences in the ways in which and the purposes for which they are bought.'[1] While initially it may appear to be a fairly simple matter to identify certain goods and services as 'industrial' and others as 'consumer' at any particular time, specific goods and services will only be 'industrial' by virtue of the fact that they are almost exclusively purchased for organisational purposes. It is possible thus for goods and services which have in the past fallen within one of these two categories to be adopted by the other. It is, moreover, the case with many products that they are purchased by members of both markets, either with or without modification. While it has long been accepted that the distinction between industrial goods and consumer goods lies in the different purposes for which goods in these categories are purchased, there has been a notable lack of attention by scholars and business men alike to the extension of this concept into the field of industrial marketing.

In planning selling strategies for the ultimate consumer market it is common practice to seek to identify the characteristics of potential buyers in demographic as well as motivational terms. In the consumer marketing situation it is now accepted that similar products are differently significant to different groups of buyers and to similar groups of buyers in different economic and social situations. The characteristics of buyers in industrial markets in relation to the goods and services they purchase have tended to be neglected as a basis for marketing strategies, product development and presentation. It is true, nevertheless, that the buyer in the industrial market constitutes the ultimate sanction for the seller as does his counterpart in the consumer market. Thus, to classify the vast and heterogeneous range of goods and services which are bought and sold in the industrial market it

1. R. S. Alexander, J. S. Cross and R. M. Cunningham, *Industrial Marketing*, Richard D. Irwin (Homewood, Illinois, Revised Edition), 1961, page 3.

is necessary to understand their significance to purchasing organisations and the perceptions of goods, services, transactions and values of those designated by their organisations as buyers.

ORGANISATIONAL BUYER

It is perhaps appropriate at this initial stage to define and to classify the buyer in industrial markets, who buys on behalf of an organisation rather than for individual or family use or consumption. Since transactions in the industrial market are all those which are not to final or ultimate consumers, the term organisational buyer is used to include those who buy on behalf of commercial, professional and institutional organisations. Organisational buyers are *those buyers of goods and services for the specific purpose of industrial or agricultural production or for use in the operation or conduct of a plant, business, institution, profession or service.* Such buyers act on behalf of organisations for the furtherance of organisational, rather than personal, goals. This is not to imply that they are immune to the influence of personal considerations in performing their organisational tasks. It is rather to stress the duality of their motivation in their purchasing activities.

INDUSTRIAL, INSTITUTIONAL AND INTERMEDIATE BUYERS

Within this broad group of organisational buyers it is possible to make further distinctions as between industrial, institutional and intermediate buyers. Industrial buyers are *those buying goods and services for some tangibly productive and commercially significant purpose*: for example, manufacturers, primary (extractive) producers, agricultural, forestry, fishery and horticultural producers. Institutional buyers are *those buying goods and services for institutional (in the sense of providing a service which is often intangible) and not necessarily commercially significant purposes*: for example, schools, hospitals, armed forces, central and local government, professions, hotels. The third group, intermediate buyers, are *those buying goods and services for resale or for facilitating the resale of other goods, in the industrial or ultimate consumer markets, for commercial purposes*: for example, distributors, dealers, wholesalers, retailers, service trades.

SEGMENTING INDUSTRIAL MARKETS

Further distinctions may be made between organisations of similar economic form, for example, a public company, a partnership, a co-operative venture, and between the different purposes for which organisations are established. The different objectives for which schools, hotels and manufacturing firms are established will dictate in broad, general terms their purchasing needs and behaviour. Organisations performing similar activities to achieve like objectives will tend towards a similarity in buying behaviour. Thus by grouping organisations in terms of like operations it is possible to identify a structure of purchasing behaviour relating to organisational objectives in industrial markets.

It is necessary, however, to carry such an analysis further to draw in such questions as the similarities and dissimilarities in buying behaviour between unlike organisations with respect to like classes of goods and services. Without such an understanding the industrial market remains to the seller, unsegmented and undifferentiated in predictive terms. Differentiation between buying organisations remains at the level of past experience and hunch. As a result assessments for the future which form the basis for marketing operations take the form of 'good' and 'less good' potential. In this, factors which influence organisations in buying and the forces which shape the structure of the market are inferred through trial and error.

The value of identifying and analysing the buying organisation in industrial markets is perhaps less clear in an economy which for many years has emphasised technological and productive factors in relation to goods and services destined for the industrial market. Traditionally, product quality has been problematic to producers, and marketing considerations have tended to be disregarded while product development, innovation, new processes and materials have preoccupied organisations.

In industrial markets the differences which exist between buyers are less apparent than in consumer markets. The majority of organisations are similarly motivated by economic goals, although the strength of this economic motivation will be differently modified between organisations by such other goals as survival, growth, power and social standing. It is this economic criterion which has led scholars and business men alike to assume a profit maximisation goal—implying rationality and perfect knowledge—for buyers in the industrial market.

It is not illogical to assume that the purchasing motives—in broad terms at least—of one industrial organisation will resemble those of another. Nor is it illogical for sellers to assume that their organisational customers will be similarly motivated to themselves, for almost all organisations fulfil the dual role in the market, of buyer and of seller. From these assumptions follows the idea that the buyer, being similarly motivated to the seller, will behave in a manner conducive to the goals of the seller.

The task of the organisational buyer in broad terms has much in common with that of the seller. Both must pursue those activities which will permit them to reach appropriate decisions which are compatible with, and will further the interests of, the organisations they represent. In the case of each the preoccupation will tend to be with the translation of the needs, wishes and aspirations of others, into profitable operations for his own organisation.

Thus the logic of the previous assumptions breaks down, for, although buyers and sellers may be similarly motivated by such organisational goals as profit, growth, survival and power, they will perceive their role in transactions differently depending upon whether they are seeking to enhance those goals as buyers or as sellers.

CONFLICT OF INTERESTS

The differences between them has been summarised by Edmund McGarry, who in discussing the contact between sellers and buyers in marketing transactions has said 'it must be recognised that there is an inevitable conflict between their respective interests [each will] appraise the value of an item, the seller thinking back to past sacrifices will tend to value the item high, while the buyer looking forward to his immediate sacrifices, will discount the satisfactions he will derive and undervalue the item'.[1] Buyers and sellers are thus differently oriented in their dealings with each other, whether or not they occupy similar positions and pursue similar activities in the market. They will, moreover, perceive the goods and services in which they deal, differently. They will place different valuations upon such goods, they will assess their utility differently and assign different priorities to transactions. They may regard associated services, credit, continuity of supplies, delivery dates and reciprocal trading in different ways. The seller, basing his strategies on his own preferences and needs, may find that the incentives he offers to his potential market are less meaningful to their particular organisational needs. Similarly, the seller offering like goods, services and conditions of sale to all types of potential buyers ignores the important differences in policy and operation which exist between different types of organisation.

In strategic transactions particularly, in which the value and importance of the transaction is great and which may form the basis of a continuing association between seller and buyer, it is most vital that the seller understands the purpose and interest of his buying counterpart. The successful outcome of the fully negotiated strategic transaction may be continued, or even reciprocal, dealings between organisations. The appreciation and understanding of the buyer's interests initially will provide a framework for adjustment and flexibility in subsequent routine transactions, so reducing the area of conflict and negotiation and consequently the cost of future transactions.

TWO-WAY PROCESS

A marketing transaction, which is the result of negotiation (implicit or explicit) between a buyer and a seller, is essentially a two-way process. Buyers and sellers interact with each other, each seeking to achieve his own interests through the medium of the transaction. In industrial transactions the contact between buyers and sellers is more clearly seen as an integral step than in the consumer market where the buyer may not actively negotiate regarding the price, quality and nature of goods and services. It is probable in the industrial market that there are as many buyer initiated contacts as those which are seller initiated. Thus, the two parties in negotiation are more clearly seen as being equal participants acting on

1. E. D. McGarry, 'The Contactual Function in Marketing', *Marketing and the Behavioural Sciences*, Ed. Perry Bliss, Allyn & Bacon, Inc. (Boston, 1963), page 381.

behalf of the respective interests of their organisations. The individuals charged with such negotiation are subject to the constraints placed upon their activities by the purpose and policies of their organisations, but they are influenced also by a multiplicity of other factors which should be recognised and understood.

A characterisation which has enjoyed considerable vogue in marketing regarding the industrial and ultimate consumer markets is that of the former consisting of buyers who are rational, expert and possessing complete knowledge of values and substitute products. By contrast, the buyer in the ultimate consumer market has been characterised as irrational, prone to impulse, inexpert and imperfectly knowledgeable regarding values and products available. 'Historically the consumer has been viewed as a fairly free agent with an insatiable appetite and an ambiguous preference system, but somewhat constrained by his income level. The organisational buyer has been viewed as highly constrained by organisation policy leading to an unambiguous preference system.'[1] While there is a grain of truth in such broad generalisations, to regard these characteristics as complete or invariable is to deny the complexity of purchasing behaviour in both groups. Nevertheless it cannot be ignored that the designated organisational buyer, while he is constrained by organisation policy, is subject also to personal goals and aspirations in executing his organisational role. The most valid distinction lies in the different ranges of goods and services bought and in the different purposes which underlie each purchase decision.

BREADTH AND IMPORTANCE OF DECISIONS

The organisational buyer, whether he is specifically designated as buyer, or is also charged with other organisational duties, operates firstly within the general policy framework of his organisation. Thus the assortment of goods he will purchase is dictated by their purposefulness in the operations of his company. Unlike the family as a consuming unit, the business organisation limits its range of interests—and thus the assortment of goods and services which are appropriate to its operations—quite explicitly in its decision to perform a particular type of economic activity. Thus, a buying organisation will typically restrict its purchases to those goods and services which will equip and stock it to carry on particular and declared types of activity, for example to manufacture cotton textiles or to resell furniture. The range of purchases by an organisation will be modified only when the goals of the organisation are extended or modified, or when a new or improved product or service becomes available which will enhance the attainment of its existing goals. By contrast the family or individual buyer is likely to make more frequent and short term modifications to the assortment of goods and services bought.

It follows that the range of goods purchased for industrial purposes by

1. John A. Howard, *Marketing: Executive and Buyer Behaviour*, Columbia University Press (New York, 1963) page 72.

the organisational buyer being typically narrow, enables the buyer to develop a high degree of specialist, technical knowledge which would not be possible were he buying over a wide and ever changing assortment of goods and services. In situations in which organisational buyers do purchase over a wide assortment, in different markets and from widely diverse sources, the reduced opportunity for specialisation is marked and manifests itself in a typically low level of knowledge regarding the nature and limitations of the goods purchased. An excellent illustration of this latter case is that of the one-man or family general retail establishment, carrying a wide assortment of products and brands. In this type of operation the retailer relies increasingly upon whatever information is passed on to him by the seller and upon the effect of direct communication by the seller to the consumer. It is not possible, in such an operation, for the buyer to possess full market and product knowledge over his whole assortment. In large-scale retailing operations in which a larger and more specialised personnel investment is possible, buying has tended increasingly to become subdivided by merchandise lines and markets to enable buying personnel to develop expertise.

While the range of different goods bought may be narrow for the organisational buyer, the volume and value of any one type of commodity bought is generally great. Thus the commitment of the organisational buyer on behalf of his company may represent a considerable investment of resources. This is not to say that all transactions in the industrial market are of large bulk or great value, but that the majority of such transactions will tend to be. The organisational buyer then is responsible for the investment by his organisation in equipment, plant, materials, tools, components, stocks, and so on; for all those goods and services, in fact, upon which other sectors of the organisation depend in order to fulfil their allotted tasks. Upon the actions and decisions of the organisational buyer the activities of the whole or a part of his organisation may depend.

BUYER'S ROLE

This feature of the organisational buyer's role leads on to a major source of influence upon him. While the buyer himself will seek to enhance his own status, prestige and progression in the organisation through the successful performance of his designated role, he has also the responsibility of ensuring the continued operation of other departments and individuals in his organisation. In so far as the buyer constitutes the channel of contact with sources of supply of essential commodities for other parts of the organisation he will tend to be subjected to pressures from a multiplicity of sources in the organisation, many of which may conflict with other demands and with his perception of his own interests. Thus while the buyer's brief may relate to the execution of his function in terms of the overall interests of the organisation he may at the same time be influenced by personal and sectional interests.

These factors emphasise the motivational dimensions of the organisational buyer. Within each section of an organisation there is a tendency for
individuals to compete for status, prestige, recognition and promotion, for
such goals represent the individual's self-interest in his occupation.
Similarly between departments there is a tendency for competition as each
section seeks to enhance its own importance and acceptance in the organisation and to fulfil its part of the organisational task with distinction. Since,
however, organisations comprise interdependent specialist parts of a
whole, even if each part is equally motivated by the organisational goal,
each will, by virtue of its specialisation, contribute to it differently. Competitive sections may even seek to realise their sectional aspirations at the
expense of, or despite the activities of, other departments.

FAVOURABLE BUYING SITUATION

In this context hypothetical cases can be used to illustrate two extreme
situations in which organisational buyers may be placed. In the first case
the position of the organisational buyer who may by virtue of the structure
and philosophy of his organisation and the authority he can command finds
himself able to enhance both his own and the organisational interests
simultaneously, may be studied.

In an organisation of this type the importance of skilled and economic
purchasing is recognised to the extent that the buyer or buyers constitute a
respected and powerful élite in the organisation. In such a case the individual buyer, occupying a position in an organisation which acknowledges
the importance of his role to it, is supported and reinforced in his efforts to
negotiate transactions in favour of his organisation. With such sanctions
the buyer is in a favourable position to develop procedures to ensure the
prompt execution of requisitions; he will be able to institute a system of
priorities which will cater adequately to periodic unusual needs. In addition
to the study of external sources of supply he will be encouraged to study the
internal requirements of his organisation. Such a buyer, supported by the
organisation should be able to develop an equality of interchange between
his department and those other departments initiating orders. Thus he is
likely to be fully informed in advance of changes which affect future
ordering patterns, he may be consulted in the early stages of product or
service development with regard to the price, quality and availability of
certain commodities, and his own participation in specification details may
be sought.

UNFAVOURABLE BUYING SITUATION

In contrast to such a buying situation is that in which the designated
organisational buyer lacks status, recognition and acceptance in his
company. In such a case the buyer may devote much of his energy to
gaining the respect and authority to which he aspires and which by virtue
of the structure of his organisation, for historical or personal reasons, is

denied him. Whether or not the organisational buyer is fulfilling a vital role in his specialism, he will tend to seek recognition for those skills associated with buying. Thus the organisational buyer who is permitted to fulfil little more than an order-placing role, who is restricted by highly detailed specifications of the goods to be purchased and the sources of supply to be patronised is operating in a highly structured job situation, which, if he seeks to exercise buying expertise, denies him opportunities to display his knowledge and judgement.

In this latter situation buyers may well attempt to dictate rigid formal procedures to be followed by those initiating orders to gain a measure of control and initiative. They may in more extreme situations impose 'punishments' upon executives or departments who bypass their procedures, by means of delaying order processing and execution. An electrical industry example illustrates this situation. Source loyalty for fractional horse power motors is high and this makes penetration by a new supplier in the established ranges extremely difficult. It is necessary to obtain acceptance of a motor at the design stage of a new product incorporating the motor and to do this contact with the design engineer is required. This, buyers resist vigorously. The industrial salesman is therefore faced with a situation in which his best chance for obtaining an order lies in establishing a relationship with the design engineer, but in doing this he risks antagonising the buyer. In this sector of the electrical industry a clear pattern emerges of buyers seeking to frustrate direct interaction with design engineers. It is important that sellers develop marketing strategies to enable direct contact to be made with the minimum loss of buyer goodwill.

Restrictionist tactics by buyers can produce inflexibility in the organisation and inhibit its ability to adjust in dynamic conditions. It is clear that an organisation, operating in conditions of change, innovation and competition, will find itself faced periodically with the need to modify production or merchandise lines, production formulae, control procedures and equipment. It is desirable that the organisation while following standard procedures for routine operations has within it the necessary flexibility for rapid adaptation. In the favourable buying situation, in which the buyer is not forced to seek recognition through the imposition of rule-book procedures, it is likely that he will participate fully in innovations and modifications, and that he may even initiate such movements. In the less favourable buying situation, the demands made on the buyer to meet unusual needs may provide him with the opportunity of attempting to gain power and recognition at the expense of the organisational interests. Such demands may, however, be impossible to meet due to the lack of knowledge and communication between the requisitioning and the buying personnel.[1]

1. For a full account of such tactics see George Strauss, 'Tactics of Lateral Relationship: The Purchasing Agent', *Administrative Science Quarterly*, Vol. VII, No. 2, Cornell University (New York, September 1962).

HYPOTHETICAL CASE

To illustrate such situations the role of the buyer in a substantial and production-oriented engineering concern is considered. The pattern for ordering may follow a route through the design, engineering, production scheduling and production departments before reaching the buyer. The personnel in each of these departments may all have their preferences regarding materials, components and equipment which may even lead them to specify particular sources of supply on the requisition. It is quite natural that such preferences should develop through the experience of these specialists as designers and engineers. Their preferences may be influenced also by the direct contact of selling representatives—bypassing the buyer—in seeking to encourage such detailed specification for their goods and services.

While it is true to say that detailed specifications are justified in so far as designers and engineers carry the responsibility for their own work and that they will develop a familiarity with the products of certain sources which may facilitate their own job performance, they will tend, for instance, to emphasise a maximum quality level when a lesser quality of material or component may be sufficient for a particular purpose. The buyer, on the other hand, should be familiar with all alternative and substitute materials and components available, and may thus be in the position to buy more economically for his organisation if given the freedom to select between alternative sources. Such freedom presupposes a level of understanding by the buyer of the usage of materials which may not be possible for him to acquire if his status in the organisation is low.

The buyer, in addition to the fact that highly detailed specifications will further reinforce his lack of status and recognition in the organisation, may find that his performance as a buyer is limited. If he is unable, by virtue of requisitions emanating from many different sources, with short delivery dates and involving a number of different sources of supply, to plan inventory levels and requirements, to rationalise the frequency of orders and to gain bulk ordering advantages by aggregating orders, his own job performance will be at a lower level of efficiency than could be possible. Since the buyer's purchasing efficiency will generally constitute the basis of the organisation's valuation of him, his already unfavourable situation will be further impaired.

The difficulties of the unfavourable buyer situation may be seen quite dramatically when his organisation operates in highly competitive markets for both buying and selling. Where production and selling costs cannot be reduced below the level of those of competitors the organisation may only be able to derive economies through the skilful manipulation of the markets for their basic materials. When these markets are subject to considerable fluctuation in supplies and price, as in certain commodity markets, the buyer lacking scope for developing and exercising purchasing skill will remain frustrated by his own situation and by the knowledge of the saving which could be derived. Some organisations which operate in such markets, assign an executive at Board level for such strategic purchases while leaving less critical and more routine purchases to a more junior member of the organisation.

These buyer situations should be clearly understood as illustrative extremes rather than typical patterns of organisational influence on buying personnel. They do, however, serve to highlight the complex force that buyers constitute in industrial markets and modify the long established stereotype of the rational and economic buyer. Between these two extremes lie the majority of buyer situations. It is situations falling between these two extremes that sellers must learn to recognise and understand.

DEGREE OF ESSENTIALITY

In addition to the differences which exist between organisations with respect to their structure and policies which have been discussed, it should be recognised that for some organisations buying represents a critical element in profitability. In others, price stability and security of supplies, together with an absence of innovation and change in operations, may render buying a more routine activity. In the first instance, where supplies may fluctuate, prices vary considerably in short runs, where judgements regarding fashion are involved, or where markets are highly competitive, the need for authority for the buyer to develop and exercise his skill is clearly seen. In such cases the dangers of denying the authority to negotiate freely for the organisation are self-evident. In the latter case, however, where buying is a routine activity, the status of buying personnel will tend to be lower in the organisational hierarchy, for the needs are for efficient performance of routine ordering rather than the exercise of highly developed skills.

Similarly, it is possible to rank the purchases made by any one organisation according to the significance of particular types of commodities to the purpose of the organisation. Thus at one end of the scale lie those purchases which are essential to the operations of the organisation: for example, raw materials to the manufacturer, merchandise to the distributor, which will be more or less strategically important depending upon the availability of supplies, the levels of inventory held and the market for the resultant products or services. At the other extreme are those items for which the decision to purchase could be, and in less profitable periods will be, deferred. The same item may for one firm represent an essential purchase, while for another firm it represents a postponable expenditure. Moroever, the same item may at different times represent a more or less essential item to the same organisation, as for instance the need for buildings. In the initial setting up of an organisation, buildings will constitute a major and essential item, whereas, until existing buildings become obsolete or inadequate, the same buyer will rank them low on a priority scale of purchases.

SOURCE LOYALTY

While it is easy to comprehend the concept of a continuum of importance of similar goods to different buying organisations, and the changes in priorities which will result from modifications in the needs and objectives of these organisations in connection with generic products, it is also generally true that such perceptions of importance by the buyer will influence his patronage of particular sources of supply. That is, his product and source loyalty or preference. While patronage of a particular source may result from the experience and preference of one or more individuals in the organisation, the basis for continued patronage and reciprocal trading, especially in the case of essential purchases, have more to do with the reduction of uncertainty and risk, than with beliefs regarding the intrinsic differences between products. In essential purchases, that is those which are necessary to the continued operation of the organisation, the possible results of, for example, delayed delivery, termination of supplies and irregular service are grave risks. To reduce uncertainty in this respect there is a strong force operating upon buyers to continue to patronise known sources with which past experience has proved satisfactory. If such continuing relationships can be strengthened by means of reciprocal trading, contracts or informal agreements, the buyer and the seller will reduce the area of their conflict and negotiation and will tend to tolerate periodically higher prices, for instance, in the interests of their mutual security. For less essential or non-recurring purchases, these forces of risk and uncertainty will tend to be less influential, and thus source loyalty and source preferences less developed.

CONCLUSION

Two things have been attempted in this chapter. First, to provide a basis for identifying the similarities and dissimilarities in purchasing behaviour between organisations and the influences which operate in determining the purchasing decisions of designated organisational buyers. Secondly, to develop the concept of the 'degree of essentiality' in the purchasing priorities of organisations and the changes in these priorities as organisational goals are modified. The system of classification which follows is designed to provide a basis for marketers to identify particular products in relation to the buyers purpose and usage in purchasing. Thus sellers may structure their strategies according to whether their products will be utilised as equipment, materials, supplies or services by purchasers. Within these four major usage categories are sub-categories by which sellers may assess their products in terms of essentiality, that is as installation as opposed to accessory equipment, for example.

CLASSIFICATION OF INDUSTRIAL GOODS[1]

All those commodities (goods and services) purchased, hired or leased for use either directly (in the production of) or indirectly (to facilitate the production of) other goods and services destined for either the industrial or ultimate consumer markets (domestic and export) or for rendering services to organisations engaged in serving the industrial or ultimate consumer markets.

There are four broad distinctions to be made initially in this class of goods:

Industrial equipment: goods purchased to fit and equip organisations for their stated purpose as producing, servicing or reselling institutions.

Industrial materials: goods purchased for use in the production of other goods and services, or for resale, which will form a substantial part of such other goods and services.

Industrial supplies: goods purchased for consumption or usage in the production of other goods and services which are not incorporated in their final form, and in which usage the utility of such goods is destroyed.

Industrial services: services purchased to facilitate the production of goods and services, to enhance the organisation purchasing such services, which are only identifiable in terms of intangible criteria, e.g. improved efficiency, skill, productivity, etc., of the organisation and its products.

Within these four major classes of industrial goods, there are a number of important subdivisions.

Note: The term *production* is used in this classification to describe that which organisations produce. It is not used in the more narrow sense of manufacturing output only, but in terms of the whole output of servicing, distributing, etc. organisations.

1. INDUSTRIAL EQUIPMENT

1.1 *Buildings:* permanent constructions on a site to house or enclose equipment and personnel employed in industrial, institutional or commercial activities.

1.2 *Installation equipment:* (capital equipment, plant) essential plant, machinery or other major equipment used directly to produce the goods and services of producing organisations.

1. I am indebted to David Rowe and to Aubrey Wilson for their observations and contribution in formulating this classification.

1.3 *Accessory equipment:* durable major equipment used to facilitate the production of goods and services or to enhance the operations of organisations.

Note: Examples of installation and accessory equipment often coincide, e.g. aircraft, ships, rolling mills, computers, blast furnaces, earth-moving equipment. Aircraft purchased by military organisations or commercial airlines would represent installation equipment, being essential to the performance of the major activity of the organisation. Aircraft purchased by manufacturing concerns for executive use, would represent accessory equipment, facilitating the movement of executive personnel, but not essential to the manufacturing goals of those organisations.

1.4 *Operating equipment:* semi-durable minor equipment which is movable, used in but not generally essential to the production of goods and services; e.g. protective clothing, special footwear, goggles, brushes, brooms, etc.

1.5 *Tools and instruments:* semi-durable or durable portable minor equipment and instruments required for producing, measuring, calculating, etc., associated with the production and distribution of goods and services; e.g. typewriters, all tools, small arms, cameras, surgical instruments, timing devices, cash registers, etc.

1.6 *Furnishings and fittings:* all goods and materials employed to fit buildings for their organisational purposes but not that equipment used specifically in production; e.g. carpets, floor coverings, draperies, furniture, shelving, counters, benches, etc.

2. INDUSTRIAL MATERIALS

2.1 *Raw materials:* basic (primary) material for production which has not been processed or fabricated in any way other than by those processes necessary for its extraction, growth or collection, and which will, after processing, be used to produce other materials or articles; e.g. fish, cattle, wool, copper, iron ore, crude oil, etc.

2.2 *Processed materials:* materials which have undergone one or more processes, for use as a basic material in another productive process, and which will in some form be in the resultant product; e.g. chemicals, plastics, oils, sheet steel, yarns and fibres, glass, etc.

2.3 *Fabricated materials:* (including components): processed articles in a final form and which are used as parts of other manufactured goods, and which undergo only minor, if any, further changes in substance or form. This class includes goods purchased for resale upon which no substantial additional operations are performed; e.g. nuts, bolts, screws, rivets, rope, wire, woven fabrics and all consumer durable and non-durable goods purchased for resale.

2.4 *Fabricating materials:* processed materials and fabricated articles used in the manufacture of other goods and which do not retain their form in usage but which are incorporated in the resultant product; e.g. paint, adhesives, solder, animal feeding stuffs, caprolactam, etc.

3. INDUSTRIAL SUPPLIES

3.1 *Packaging materials:* all those materials and fabricated containers used for packing, encasing and protecting other goods in their final form or in an intermediate form as they are passed on to a further productive process; e.g. cans, boxes, plastic containers and coatings, etc.

3.2 *Operating supplies:* (industrial consumables) all those consumable materials and articles required for the production of goods and services which are consumed in use and which are not incorporated in the resultant product; e.g. lubricants, abrasives, fertilisers, all forms of fuel and power.

3.3 *Spares and replacements:* all those durable, fabricated parts and articles necessary to replace existing parts of all forms of industrial equipment to maintain its operating utility; e.g. drills, cutting blades, hoses, washers, belting, valves, batteries, etc.

4. INDUSTRIAL SERVICES

4.1 *Equipment services:* all services associated with the installation, running, maintenance and repair of installation, accessory and operating equipment, tools, instruments, furnishings and fittings.

4.2 *Facilitating services:* all those services offered to facilitate the productive operations of organisations including the provision of finance, storage, transport, promotion, insurance, etc.

4.3 *Advisory and consultative services:* all services to provide general or specific technical expertise and intelligence including advice on the use of equipment and materials, research, education, etc.

3

Generation of New Product Ideas

MARY GRIFFIN

REASONS FOR NEW PRODUCTS

Successful business depends on the maintenance and growth of profits. Here, then, is the motive behind the search for new products, the need for which arises in connection with the expansion of business and the replacement of obsolete and obsolescent products. There is nowhere an inherent requirement for an established industrial product, currently profitable and likely to remain so, to be replaced by another which has as its only additional attraction, that of novelty. This appears to be a truism: in practice it is a consideration often overlooked in the trance induced by the novel. Only uneconomic deployment of management skills and tools is likely to result if new product searching and planning is divorced from the overall development of existing products.

One way to avoid this hazard is to draw the definition of 'new products' as widely as possible so that they may be construed as coming within one of the following categories: second and subsequent generation products; products new to a manufacturer's product line or product mix but in basic functional form already available on the market he is serving with his current products; products already in a manufacturer's range but adapted to suit another market; and completely new products, that is products which are novel in the patentable sense.

EVOLUTION OF NEW PRODUCT IDEAS

Once the definition of what constitutes a new product has been formulated, consideration of the ways in which each type may evolve has value in that it enables the boundaries of searching to be set. 'Open-mind' searching, lacking a focal point or confines, risks waste in the examination of search areas which have no relevance.

New products from old
In the history of a product the first technical task following its initial

development is to eliminate the faults which prevent it reaching its expected optimum performance. Ideally, these faults should all disappear as a result of the further development which follows prototype testing, but in practice, they frequently only receive consideration after the product has been marketed. For the purposes of this chapter these 'first order' improvements are not regarded as new products and are not, therefore, discussed.

Once a product has been successfully launched, and all the shortcomings have been largely remedied, there is the possibility that customers will demand improved performance, that is performance in excess of that originally envisaged, or that they will request the provision of additional features. Such customer requirements may well lead to developments which can be regarded as new products. Increased performance requirements, for example, will often entail redesign and the use of superior components, as may the provision of additional features if these are not to appear as mere appendages. In this way a camera with a built-in coupled exposure meter is potentially a more saleable product than one which has a conventional exposure meter fitted to the outside case. All new products which evolve in this way have in common their origin from customer requirements, whether stated or anticipated, and thus an early awareness of the need for them will only result from close contacts with the customer.

Changes in a customer's product designs or manufacturing processes may necessitate the complete redesign of a product sold to him as processed, fabricated or fabricating materials. For example, once the American airlines and aircraft equipment manufacturers had made mandatory the adoption of a special racking system for the mounting of all aircraft equipment, a British aircraft equipment manufacturer who had not foreseen that British aircraft manufacturers would follow this lead and who had not redesigned his equipment accordingly would very soon have found himself excluded from the market. Here more is needed than an ear for the customer's articulated requirements: a supplier needs to be aware of the technological and other changes which will, in the first instance, affect directly only the customer himself. This considerably widens the areas of knowledge which must be under observation but much of the information required can be obtained from an intelligent acquaintance with the customer, his products and his competitors.

New generations of existing products also appear as the result of the exploitation of materials, components and techniques which have evolved since the product was first launched. Such evolutions may lead to reductions in production costs, to more acceptable designs, or to both, and hence to increased market shares, in unit and value terms or perhaps initially only in unit terms where a resultant price reduction makes the product attractive to previously resistant customers. Maximum rewards will only result if there is a realisation of the full capabilities of the new or improved fabricating materials. When reinforced plastic was first adopted in commercial vehicle building, the necessity to design for the new material was not immediately appreciated and the resultant products promised to be as expensive as their steel counterparts. However, once it was realised that the property of plastic which enabled it to be used to produce much larger unit parts should be fully exploited, drastic savings in tooling and assembly costs were achieved.

The results of value engineering ideally should be applied throughout the whole life of a product from its moment of concept but it is when the potentialities of new materials or products come up for consideration that the rewards of continuous value engineering are highlighted because the findings are immediately available for application, with consequent cost savings. Indeed, value engineering properly employed considerably aids smooth product progress and avoids product development which proceeds in a series of jerks. The latter may be more dramatic but the former yields greater benefits.

Systematic value engineering studies and appraisals can also aid in the revival of old, even obsolete, products which, with the advent of new technologies and materials, are capable of redesign to render them once again profitable items. The battery-operated dry shaver is a good example of this. It considerably pre-dates the mains-operated models but was superseded by the latter because of the short life and the bulk of the batteries. The emergence of a completely new race of miniature long-life batteries has led to the revival of an old product which has had a marked impact on the dry-shaver market, and thus on the industries supplying components and materials to the dry shaver manufacturers.

Similarly, human engineering studies contribute both in the initial development stages and in the evolution of new generations of product. Human engineering may perhaps be taken here in its broadest possible connotation so that it also embraces those changes in the attitude of man to overall working conditions which may influence the future of a product. The manufacturers who have turned their attentions to the design and production of prefabricated buildings are motivated not only by the savings which will result in decreasing erection times but also by the realisation that in years to come it will be difficult to find men prepared to carry out heavy labouring tasks and to work in inclement weather conditions.

Constant and methodical investigations to ensure that each product idea is fully exploited to give maximum profits will also yield an additional dividend in the indication they will give of the probable obsolescence life of a product. A manufacturer of ceramic terminals studying his customers' technology would have been alerted by the changes likely to occur in transformer designs once encapsulation techniques were adopted, and would have seen currently large market outlets as disappearing ones. Thus he is led naturally to seek new products for this market with which he is familiar or new markets for his present products or adaptations of them.

These principles of applications engineering, value analysis and human engineering have been combined and further developed in a new approach to the problem of the generation of new product ideas. The method devised, known as the 'systems concept', involves the technical and commercial study of industrial processes and methods to determine whether a new product can be evolved which will improve an existing process either in product quality, production speed and reliability, or profitability. It is the study of the process itself which enables the specification of requirements, including a precise statement of functional requirements, to be formulated for the new product.

The method can perhaps be best illustrated by an example of its application.

A major brewery had traditionally used malt, barley flakes, sugar and hops in the preparation of the 'wort' fed to the fermenting vessels. Figure A is a much simplified flow chart showing the separate operational stages in the preparation of beer. It will be seen that one of these stages is concerned only with the preparation of the sugar solution.

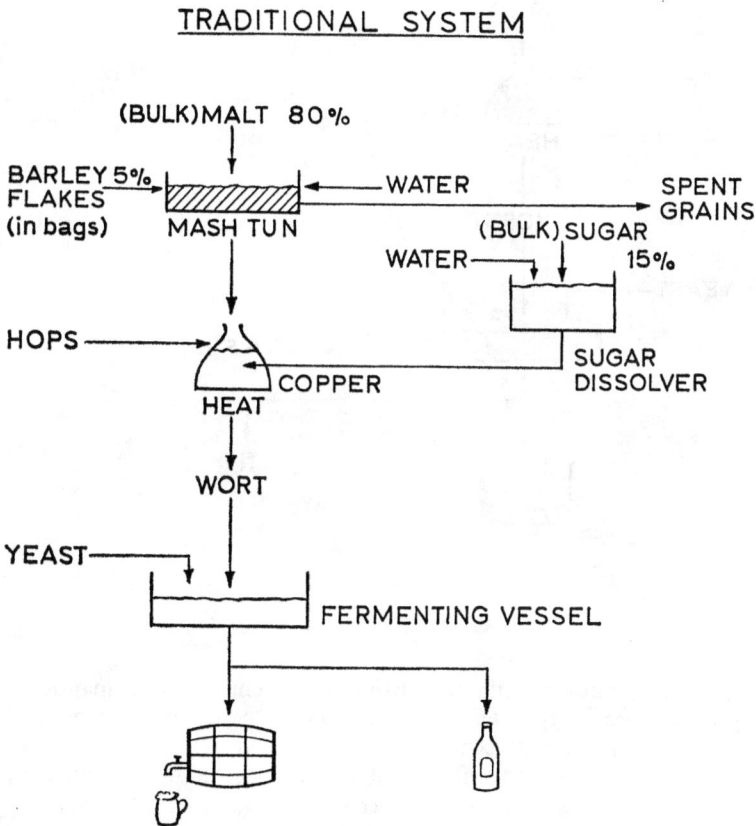

Fig. A

The development of a new product, 'wort syrup', which could be produced relatively cheaply external to the brewing plant, led to its use to replace the flaked barley, the sugar and a proportion of the malt, thus achieving a reduction in the number of raw materials fed into the plant and the elimination of one process stage. This is shown schematically in Figure B.

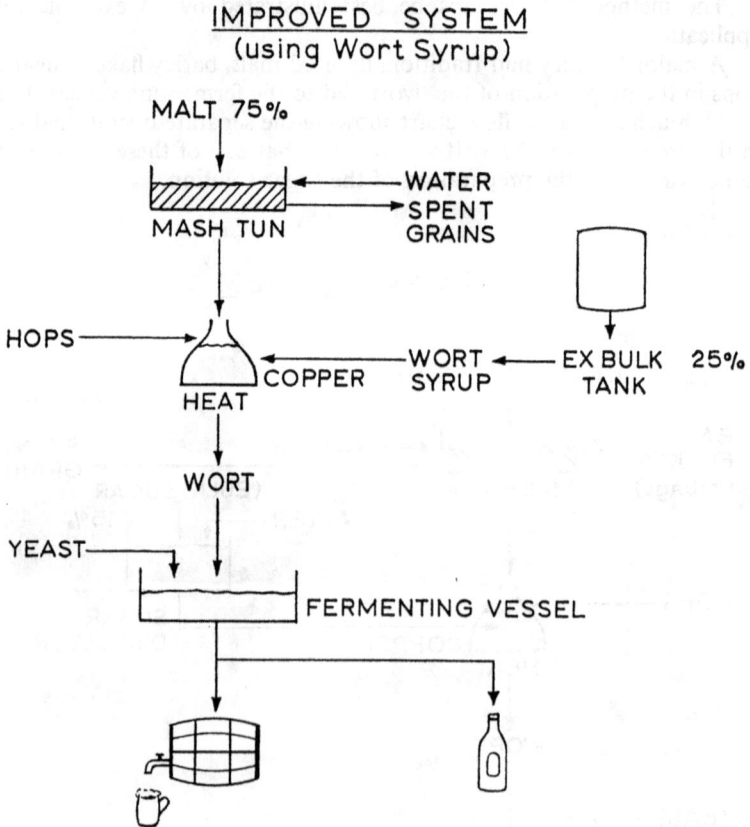

IMPROVED SYSTEM
(using Wort Syrup)

Fig. B

It is possible now to envisage further improvements in the manufacturing process which may be effected by the use of 'wort concentrate', itself a new product directly descended from 'wort syrup'. The use of 'wort concentrate', it is believed, will permit a further decrease in the amount of raw material fed in as malt, will reduce costs at the wort production stage of the brewing process and will result in increased output from a given mashing capacity.

An extension of this line of development has led to a proposed 'blue sky' mode of operation. In this the new product, 'wort concentrate' has been further developed to a form in which it makes the use of malt as such unnecessary in the brewing plant. 'Wort concentrate' replaces completely the malt, flaked barley and sugar traditionally fed into the plant because this new product can be manufactured elsewhere from the same raw materials, more cheaply than the stages of the brewing process it replaces can be operated in the brewery. The brewery as such thus promises to become a fermentation unit using 'wort concentrate' produced elsewhere.

Many of these developments are, of course, coming from within the brewing industry itself, but suppliers outside the industry are studying the processes of their potential customers, are becoming aware of methods for improving brewing efficiency, and are then developing the products needed to achieve this. Thus, new products are evolved which will lead to considerable progress in both the customer and the supplier industries, with each enjoying the benefits accruing from access to the thinking of the other.[1]

New products for present markets

In seeking for natural expansion much can be achieved by aiming to serve present and potential customers over a wider front. Information on customer requirements will be accumulated during studies made to ensure that current products are developed to meet, and to continue to meet, customer needs. Such studies, involving as they do consideration of the overall requirements of present and potential customers, are likely to be productive in their yield of ideas for additional products which, whilst not new in the inventive sense, are new in the context of a manufacturer's current product line or mix. Almost in parallel, information on the needs of peripheral markets is acquired.

Thus such an approach to the search for new product ideas has three major facets which display opportunities for expansion by additions to a current product line, additions to a current product mix, or the development of an entirely new product line to meet other, and perhaps unrelated, customer needs: such opportunities are not, of course, mutually exclusive but may be exploited in parallel. In adopting either of the first two modes of expansion, there is likely to be fuller deployment of current technical skills and marketing facilities, whilst the third will, at least, entail the continued use and possible extension of existing marketing facilities.

Current product lines should first be looked at to ensure that there are no omissions which could be profitably rectified. For example, a pressure gauge manufacturer may have achieved a steady, if not spectacular, growth rate over a period with a range of gauges which has changed little over the years. His growth has, in some measure, kept pace with the increasing requirements in industry for pressure measurement. However, the addition to his product line of the less conventional stainless steel

1. I am indebted to Corn Products (Sales) Ltd. for permission to quote this example of the 'systems concept' approach.

Bourdon tube gauge may capture for him an enhanced market share because he would then be in a position to supply some of the specialist needs of the chemical and food processing industries which would otherwise have been outside his capabilities.

Examination of the natural derivatives of a current product mix will often reveal large areas which can be scanned for new product ideas. Thus the pressure gauge manufacturer, having satisfied himself that he is capturing all he can reasonably expect of the pressure measurement market, finds his attention turned naturally to the whole field of industrial measurement (and ultimately control), where both his present technical skills and marketing techniques can be applied.

The remaining facets of what has been termed the 'industries we serve' concept may involve an appreciable measure of diversification in comparison with the substantially linear modes of expansion so far discussed. Here the constant factor will be a manufacturer's knowledge of his customers, whose additional needs he now proposes to try to meet. New technical skills and new plant may be needed, but because of his established marketing facilities, he is diversifying into a field where he is with some knowledge. In this way recent years have seen, for example, some manufacturers, whose preoccupation hitherto has been with navigational needs, turning their attention to other shipboard requirements, such as those for data logging and engine control.

The problem of defining search areas of the kind envisaged here is essentially similar to that of designing a faceted system for the classification of information. The aim is the fullest exploitation of all the skills and resources associated with a product, a product line or a product mix, whether these be technical or commercial. Each must, therefore, be considered in turn by isolating the generic heading under which it falls and then investigating the potential offered by others coming within the same category.

Old products for new markets
So far the emphasis has been on locating new product ideas resulting from attempts to obtain the maximum return from investments in product development, technical skills and plant, and marketing facilities. There are, however, products whose acceptability in current markets is on the wane but which may meet exactly the requirements of a new market. This is particularly true of overseas markets in countries in a less advanced stage of development than the exporting country. Such an importing area, wishing to manufacture a certain product locally, may often be satisfied with equipment less up-to-date than that currently in use elsewhere. A bottling plant in an underdeveloped country, for example, need not be electronically controlled—simple mechanical or manual controls, whose domestic market may have eroded, will suffice. For such markets less complicated machinery is cheaper, perhaps easier to sell, and almost invariably less costly to maintain.

Other products are capable of adaptation to make them suitable for markets completely new to the manufacturer. There are also techniques involved in the operation of some products which may be used to open up new markets. In certain instances the market will be an existing one whose needs are to some extent met, but it may be one where the demand has hitherto been completely unsatisfied and perhaps unrealised.

Searches for new product ideas of this nature entail envisaging all the possible applications of a product, the techniques embodied in it or those employed in its operation.

An imaginative approach of this kind led to the development in the early years of the Second World War of the ultrasonic flaw detector which is a direct descendant of the echo sounder used in navigation and, today, for fish detection. The value of the echo sounder to a mariner lies in the facility for depth sounding and in its ability to detect obstacles in water. The step required to apply the techniques developed for this purpose to the detection of discontinuities in any medium, for example, flaws in metal parts, may seem a small one to those skilled in the art but it was nevertheless a highly imaginative one and led to a new race of products and, later, to the further applications of these techniques in medical diagnosis.

New uses for radar, microwave and other technologies are currently being researched although a manufacturer with competence in any of them is probably plagued not so much with a dearth of new product ideas as with the problem of creating new markets.

New inventions

Ideas for newly invented products may arise anywhere. Inside a company, their probable origin will be in the research and development department or from the results of marketing research. Alternatively, they may be presented to a company in the offer of manufacturing or sales rights.

An article[1] which deals with inventions and their originators points out the improbability of ordinary technical people or the 'long-range' planners proposing truly visionary or 'blue-sky' products. But, as is implicitly acknowledged in the article, both the invention capable of immediate translation into a saleable product and that which has probably only a 'far-off' future have their place in a company's product planning, and both warrant careful examination.

The problems attending the introduction of newly invented products will probably be more complex than those which will arise from the intro- duction of new products of the kind considered earlier. There is, however, a rule which applies to the study of inventions: first consider those which come somewhere within the company's present competence and only then turn to the consideration of the remainder, whose development and introduction would be tantamount to starting from scratch in a new business.

1. Tom Alexander, 'The Wild Birds Find a Corporate Roost', *Fortune* (Chicago, August 1964).

The probable areas of evolution of new product ideas having been delineated, the specific ones to be examined will, to some extent, be determined by the factors giving rise to the actual need for new products. The requirement may stem from attempts to effect the better employment of capital, research and development resources, plant, labour or marketing facilities, or a combination of any of these. In certain cases, on this basis, it may be possible to restrict searches to one or more of the defined areas but restrictions of this nature have inherent hazards because searching is then by no means exhaustive.

So far as is possible, new product searching should be a continuing operation: one as routine in a company as that of invoicing customers. If a systematic procedure is installed, all the defined areas will be scanned regularly and the findings recorded. It is important that all new product ideas should be classified in accordance with certain of their basic characteristics in order to facilitate the rapid retrieval of those which offer most promise in the light of the special requirements of the firm at any time. In classifying them, therefore, there should be some rough but realistic indication of the capital investment required, the present resources which can be used, the market at which the product is aimed, the time required before launching will be feasible, and the optimum selling price. A full explanation of this process will be found in the next chapter.

The search itself may be conducted in very many fields but there are some sources likely to prove particularly fruitful.

Internal sources
Initially, the objective is to locate the maximum number of ideas as cheaply as possible. This involves the fullest use of information present within a company. The knowledge sought is, therefore, fundamental information on what customers and potential customers want or can be persuaded to want.

The primary source in a company of such information is its sales force. Through their daily contacts with customers, markets and their colleagues in competitive companies, they acquire much useful information, sometimes without any awareness of its true value. This will not be available automatically within a company seeking new product ideas; it will have to be extracted from members of the sales force. Gradually, the interest of sales people in searches for new product ideas will be stimulated and the task of extraction will become less arduous. There are nevertheless some risks in this mode of feed-back and some caution is needed, and can be exercised, to ensure useful results: this problem is dealt with more fully in Chapter 5.

A company's research and development engineers also make useful external contacts in the course of their work in that they meet their colleagues from competitive companies and allied industries at technical meetings, exhibitions and on business occasions. There is less reticence amongst engineers about the work on which they are engaged than is commonly supposed but the information gleaned as a result of such contacts is rarely communicated to quarters where it would have most value. Here is a latent store of information which may usefully be tapped.

Of the other departments in a company which are capable of assisting in new product searching, it is only necessary to refer briefly to the contributions expected from anyone in the company engaged in marketing research. Researchers will, in any event, be very closely associated with any attempts at new product planning.

Today the majority of production engineers are alert for news of any developments of new or improved production techniques, processes or materials, and their knowledge, too, makes a valuable contribution to an accumulation of information destined to be productive of new product ideas.

Service departments are the recipients of all customer complaints and if arrangements can be made for the systematic recording of these, periodic studies of such records can be very revealing, and on some occasions will inspire new product ideas.

Another periodic inspection which may yield results is one of the unexploited patents owned by a company and of the inventions submitted but rejected. This can, of course, be arranged as a once-and-for-all inspection, and the whole information content classified in the form already suggested. It will then be available for instant retrieval and the tedium of repetitive searches will be avoided. Inventions submitted later can then be similarly classified on receipt.

Efforts should be made to involve all the people who are potential sources of key information in the new product planning operation so that all of relevance is communicated automatically, even if this involves much which is irrelevant.

The enthusiasm and interest generated in this way must, however, be maintained. This can only be done if ideas are seen by their originators to receive careful appraisal and evaluation so that when an idea must be rejected or shelved, its originator is told the reasoning behind the decision and, so far as possible, persuaded of its rightness. Equally, accepted new product ideas must bring reward to their originators by some form of recognition, particularly where the generation of such ideas is not part of a man's day-to-day employment as it is in the case of research and development engineers.

Rejections, however soundly based the decisions behind them, inevitably dampen to some extent the enthusiasm of the originators, but their number can be reduced by making product policy clear. Thus, if it is laid down that the direction of new product development must be within the company's existing technology, ideas outside it will neither be sought nor submitted. The more precise the new product policy, the lower will be the rejection rate.

External inventions

There are in the United Kingdom and overseas several organisations concerned with arranging the exploitation of inventions, the development of
some of which they may have sponsored. In the United Kingdom there
are the National Research Development Corporation and Technical
Development Capital Limited, and overseas there are organisations such
as the Battelle Memorial Institute, the Armour Research Foundation and
very many others, particularly in the United States.

Most of these organisations issue newsletters of some kind, and a new
product planning department will make arrangements to ensure that it
receives as many of these as are likely to be of interest.

The universities are also sources of inventions which may be available
for exploitation by industry. In the United Kingdom the National Research
Development Corporation offers some assistance to the universities, as it
does to Ministries and other Government research departments, in their
efforts to obtain exploitation of their inventions.

A company's external patent agent may well be able to help because he
may have private clients who lack the necessary capital for the further
development of their inventions, and the Research Associations may also
be able to give assistance in a similar manner.

Finally, when considering methods of learning of inventions which may
be available for exploitation, the patent department will make an important
contribution. Routine inspection of newly published patent specifications
is a function of any patent department, and any seemingly relevant findings
can be communicated to the product planning department. (Due to the
delays in the British and United States patent offices in the examination of
patent applications it may be more rewarding to study published specifications in certain European countries, such as Belgium, where corresponding
applications may have been filed and where, because examination is
restricted to formalities, the delays in publication are less serious.) An
engineer studying the recent patent specifications of others skilled in the
same art can often observe trends of development thought present in
competitive companies. This has several cross-fertilisation aspects, because
not only will it stimulate his own ideas but the study may also reveal blind
avenues of approach which would otherwise have been explored.

Other published information

It will be a first reaction of anyone concerned with new product planning
to turn for information to the technical and commercial literature in his
fields of interest. The problem is to devise the most thorough means of
scanning all relevant literature in the time available.

Here intelligent use of at least two abstract journals covering any
particular field can be of great assistance in the selection for detailed study
of those articles likely to be of most interest. This will then leave time for
the regular study of the editorial and news content in relevant technical
journals. There is considerable value in the newsletters and similar features

which appear in many technical publications and, in fact, some proportion of the search work of a product planning department is regularly carried out for it by the reporters of the technical press. Newspapers, appearing as they do at short, regular intervals, must hunt very thoroughly for news items sufficiently topical and relevant to warrant inclusion.

These publications, which come from many countries, give information on developments both in the United Kingdom and overseas, but additional overseas information on new products is to be found in the journals and newsletters put out by the commercial departments of overseas Governments, Chambers of Commerce and other bodies with particular territorial interests.

SCREENING NEW PRODUCT IDEAS

Methods of accumulating new product ideas in an orderly, harmonious and logical fashion have been set out. If this can be achieved, there will ultimately be a store of new product ideas classified to make easily retrievable those suitable to meet prevailing circumstances and panic action will be avoided.

In new product planning the circumstances in which new products will be needed are forecasted and the essential requirements to be met by these products are defined. Against this background, the initial retrieval is made from the store of new product ideas and screening follows. Screening occurs at a very early stage in the new product development programme and is carried out in support of the efforts to keep costs at a minimum in these preliminary stages thus leaving more funds available for the detailed studies, such as the feasibility and marketing research exercises, which must follow.

Recently, a qualitative screening process has been devised[1] and the method described is applicable from the moment when the need for retrieval arises because it shows how the circumstances and requirements for new products may be defined. The procedure set out in the article should be studied in detail because the synopsis given here only serves as an outline guide.

Qualitative screening is in essence an information-seeking and appraisal process in which the information sought is not only on a product's characteristics but also on these relative to certain external factors. The object of the process is not to determine in absolute terms whether a proposed product should be added to a company's product mix, but to indicate whether further detailed investigation is justified.

The proposed method of screening has four phases: the preparation of an inventory of the company's resources, the preparation and use of the first coarse screen in which obvious deterrents to the development and marketing of the product are identified, the preparation of the fine screen which comprises a series of questions to which answers must be obtained

1. Aubrey Wilson, 'Selecting New Products for Development', *Scientific Business* (Burnham, Bucks. November, 1963).

for decision-making, and finally the rating of the product in relation to each of the elements of the fine screen and the weighting of the questions relative to each other.

Stress has already been laid on the importance of an accurate audit of a company's total resources in any new product planning programme. This audit, in fact, is the first phase of the proposed screening process and it enables an assessment to be made of a company's strengths and weaknesses so that at the last stage in the screening process, the overall characteristics of a product can be judged against the resources already present within the company.

The second phase is concerned with the identification and evaluation of obvious deterrents: 'factors which, if negative, would be sufficient on their own to warrant discontinuation of, not only the screening process, but any further activities within the firm relating to the product's development'.[1] This coarse screening stage is thus concerned with aspects such as the difficulties of access to essential raw materials, the life of the market for which the product is destined, the ability of the company to operate profitably in the face of existing or potential competition and the product's demands for resources outside the company's competence.

Some product ideas will disappear at this coarse screening stage but those remaining require more detailed study to yield information essential for decision-making. The third phase is concerned with the preparation of the fine screen. The elements of this screen are questions, the answers to which give, for example, an assessment of market stability and growth, the research and development, production and marketing requirements associated with the introduction of the product by the company, and the identification of any factors which give the company a special relationship to the product.

Each of these, market stability, market growth, research and development requirements and others, can best be measured by considering in turn the major factors associated with it. For example, in assessing stability, it is suggested that the group of factors to be considered includes the durability of the market, its breadth, its stability in depressions and in war time, the existence of a captive market, and the monopolistic characteristics of the product.

For each of these groups of factors, and for any other groups which are germane to a particular product, therefore, it is possible to synthesize a series of questions which, for convenience, may be collated in tabular form and grouped generically. Thus is the fine screen prepared.

These questions, once formulated, can be weighted one against the other according to their importance against the background of the company's resources. A simple numerical weighting can be assigned to each to indicate whether it is, in the context mentioned, very important, of average importance or only marginally so: thus, for example, the question could be assigned the value 1, 2 or 3, the highest number indicating a

1. Ibid.

question of most importance. This value is then shown in a column of the table alongside the related question.

The product is now studied in the light of each of the questions and is rated according to the answers received. For example, in the generic group concerned with research and development factors, the question may relate to the use of existing knowledge. If the development of the product promises to make extensive use of this, it would be assigned a high rating. For simplicity, the ratings should be comparatively few: for example, very good; good; average; poor; or very poor. These ratings, too, may be assigned numerical values adopting 'average' as the norm and assigning positive values to ratings above the norm and negative ones to those below. On this basis of quantification, 'very good' would rate $+2$. These ratings, in the cases where a tabular presentation has been adopted, will also be shown in a column alongside the related question.

A product's score must reflect not only the answers to the questions but also the relative importance of the questions. Its score in relation to each question is, therefore, obtained by multiplying the weighting value by the rating value and the scores for all the questions are added to give the product's overall score.

This total score, obtained for all the products concerned, enables them to be compared one with another and also with competitive products which can often be similarly scored.

As well as presenting this information in tabular form, it can also be presented graphically and both the tabular and graphical presentations enable an assessment to be made of whether further detailed investigation is warranted, and whether the product profile, as shown in the graph, can be improved by the company. These presentations also show the product's position, in terms of importance, in the hierarchy of new products under consideration.

The process described is essentially a qualitative one and its main purpose is the elimination of unsuitable ideas. Methodically executed, it can go a long way to ensuring that expenditure on product development and marketing research is confined to those products where there is a high probability of finding a profitable market.

It is not intended here, nor in the article referred to, to lay down rigid methods for screening new products. The purpose has been to indicate the types of processes which may conveniently be adopted to yield optimum results. If screens of the type described are used, their elements will have to be varied from time to time to suit particular circumstances.

NEXT STAGES

All that has gone before has merely been directed to setting the stage for new product planning and development so that from the beginning the irrelevant has been removed.

The routines which have been suggested can be instituted comparatively simply and can be operated inexpensively. The cardinal requirement is that they be carried out systematically, consistently and rigorously.

The planning and development phases which follow involve appreciable expenditure and it is important to ensure, therefore, that none of this is spent on the detailed studies of products which are inherently unsuitable.

4

Organisation of New Product Development

MARGOT NEWLANDS, M.A.

An organisation is only as good as the people who operate it. The first essential of a good new product organisation is, therefore, a team of people who believe in new product development and who have fertile and inventive minds. The organisation should then be designed to stimulate and guide this originality on sound and economic lines.

The organisation should be just sufficient to achieve this end, but not to stifle the company in mountains of paper and daily interdepartmental committees. The recommendations which are made in this chapter are simple, and the paper controls few. They may be adopted without difficulty by the smallest firm, but are, in fact, successfully used by large concerns both in the United Kingdom and in the United States.

AIMS

The organisation should have the following main aims:

Welding together departments contributing
to new product development
Unless this is done, it will be found that the Research and Development department develops products or ideas which interest scientists, but will not sell at a profit. The other danger is that the sales and marketing department will want to sell all the products except the ones the company makes, but will not go to the trouble to say exactly what they want. The financial controllers will bemoan the falling profits of existing lines without pointing out in a constructive manner what is required in terms of turnover and profit earning from the new products. The board itself will complain that its research effort is non-productive and wasteful, that its marketing men lack ideas and that its factory staff are only prepared to make products which are familiar to them. A good new product development organisation will not solve all these problems, but it should lead to identity of purpose and avoid the worst dangers of different departments working in isolation or even in opposition to each other.

Developing an overall company strategy
for new product development
The previous chapter has shown the importance of defining the areas for new product search even before any new product ideas are pursued. This, in some companies, is settled by the board in consultation with individual members of the company, prior to setting up an organisation to deal with the day-to-day business of developing individual products. If no such guidance is available the organisation itself should do the job. A series of individual projects does not in itself make a good programme if they do not fit into an overall plan. This should look considerably further ahead than the development period of any current project.

Ideological involvement in new product development
A good working arrangement between departments and a far seeing programme are both useless unless the board and other prominent members of the company are convinced of the importance of new product development. This means that the people involved in the organisation must be of sufficient weight and have sufficient time to give to the matter, to put the importance of new product development over to their colleagues. These colleagues will not be concerned with new product development directly perhaps, but unless they are convinced of its necessity they can quite easily shrivel it to death by lack of interest.

Setting priorities
Another essential feature of the new product development organisation is the designation of priorities. This should be done in the light of the general strategy of the company and by means of various financial and other measuring devices discussed later. If the techniques for new product idea generation and for screening these ideas which were suggested in the previous chapter are adopted, then an awareness and sensitivity to a new product's potential will develop within the organisation and time-consuming and expensive ideas will be eliminated from the start.

Automatic feed back
At the heart of a good new product development organisation will be automatic feed back. By this is meant the system should be self-checking and activating, like the servo-mechanisms used in automated industrial processes. No researcher must be allowed to start a project without stating its likely cost and time of completion, and no marketing man should be allowed to investigate the market without the same restrictions. There should be regular feed back of information from both sides of the development team and continued reassessment of the viability of the project. It might be argued that this approach would put a strait-jacket on adventurous and creative men. If all new ideas were expected to show an immediate return, in market terms, this would be so. All it means, however, is that

such projects must be assessed on a different basis, but their regular re-appraisal and costing is just as necessary as with more immediately practicable ideas.

THE SCALE OF THE NEW PRODUCT
DEVELOPMENT ORGANISATION

The size and complexity of the organisation devoted to new product development in any given firm do not, as might be expected, depend on the size and complexity of the existing product set-up. They depend upon the rapidity of technological change in the market in which the firm operates, and the degree to which the firm itself keeps up with, or even leads such change. The more rapidly an industry and its products are changing from year to year, the greater the proportion of the firm's time in such an industry which should be devoted to new product development. At one end of the scale there are electronic engineering firms where 75 per cent of the personnel are devoted to new product development; at the opposing end of the scale there were, until recently at least, huge firms in the petroleum and building material industries where very little time, money or thought was devoted to new product development at all.

To say that new product development is typical of rapidly developing industries is not, as might be assumed, a tautology. The implication is rather that industries which in the immediate past have been developing rapidly are likely to continue in such a manner in the short or medium-term future. Firms in such industries cannot rest on their laurels. Last year's invention is next year's obsolete line.

Intense efforts at new product development should also be typical of stagnant and declining industries. Unless the declining trend is recognised quickly, however, a company may find itself forced into a position where the required resources for new product development are lacking at a time when they are needed most.

The only firms who have no strong requirement for a new product development programme are those with a rising demand for their products which have reached a state of absolute perfection. Such products barely exist in the industrial field, but Scotch whisky and French perfume might be quoted from the consumer market. But even these firms are vulnerable to shifts in fashion and taste, as Theodore Levitt shows in Chapter 18.

The speed of technological change which prevails in their own industry is known in a general way to all industrialists. The exact degree to which their own firm is keeping up with or dragging behind general progress is more difficult to establish. Marketing research is often necessary, therefore, before deciding on the level of new product development which is necessary in order to maintain the position of the firm in the market. This will establish not only what share of the existing market is held but what share of the whole market area, new products and old, is still held by the firm in question. A series of such market surveys, coupled with information from the sales department and examination of the sales records over recent years, will provide the company with indicators of the rapidity of techno-logical change in its own industry. This in its turn will offer guidance on the degree of interest which the company should be taking in new product development.

If new product development is regarded more as an offensive, than a defensive, activity, as a means of conquering new fields as yet unapproached by competitors, then a study of the existing markets and market shares will be helpful but not decisive. It will not suggest the appropriate scale of new product development. This will be determined by a study of the overall operations of the company and its long term forecast of the likely profit and return on capital. If this seems satisfactory, both in the light of past experience and by comparison to firms of similar calibre in other industries, then it may be decided that new product development is already adequate and need not be intensified. But if the likely profits and return on capital seem poor in comparison to past experience, then the company would do well to intensify its new product development programme.

It will be obvious from the previous paragraphs that the search for a percentage of company resources which should be devoted to new product development is a vain one, both in a general or even specific sense. One can merely summarise some of the factors which call for an intense effort in the development of new products; rapid technological change in the existing product set-up, replacement of existing product lines by newer products, declining profits in existing business caused by falling demand or falling prices and dependence on one or two lines.

The scale of the new product organisation should be sufficient to provide a solution to the existing product problem whatever it is. A com-pany faced with the prospect of declining profits of £200,000 over a five year period must find new products of a profit earning capacity of at least this amount. This may involve new sales over the same period of £2 million, assuming a net profit prior to tax of 10 per cent. Taking into consideration the uncertainties of forecasting, it may well be that the company should aim for either a higher turnover than £2 million or alternatively a higher profit earning rate than 10 per cent. In any event, it will provide no solution to this company's problem if the research team develops five ingenious new lines with forecast total sales of £500,000 and a net profit of £50,000.

The question of scale must also be considered from another point of view. Large companies tend to have large overheads and senior executives who think in large terms. They probably move more slowly and deliber-ately than their opposite numbers in small firms. Their sales organisations also are large and their technical literature produced on a lavish scale. A proposition which would be perfectly acceptable to a small family business would scarcely justify consideration for five minutes by the main board of any of our larger companies.

It may be helpful, therefore, to lay down certain rules of thumb for the guidance of the new product development team; to instruct them, for example, to consider no new product which seems likely to sell at a rate less than £50,000 in the third year, or, looked at from another point of view, no product which makes a marginal contribution to the recovery of company overheads of less than £5,000 a year.

These rules are purely concerned with the scale of propositions, not, of course, with the return on sales or investment which is considered later in this chapter.

TYPE OF ORGANISATION

The type of organisation chosen will vary according to the size and complexity of the new product development programme. Where there is a distinctly identifiable research and development section, plus a team of economists, market development personnel and accountants, both fully and exclusively occupied with new product development, then there is a case for the setting up of a separate section or company: for example, Company A (Market Development) Ltd.

The advantages of this approach are so great that it should always be considered, if practicable.

There is, first of all, the fixing of responsibility firmly in the hands of those whose sole job it is to push forward new product development. They 'live' new product development. They must take the credit and the blame in the main company for progress or lack of progress in this field. This will act as a powerful spur to effectiveness.

Within a separate section or company the exact cost of new product development will be known, and this can be measured in terms of results over the years. Where responsibilities are split between departments, whose members service the existing selling and production functions, it is sometimes difficult to estimate the cost to the company of new product activities.

Such a separate market development company is likely to have a more pragmatic and spontaneous approach to new product development. Its members are able to experiment, market test and make mistakes without committing the prestige of the whole company to a given product. This is especially valuable to companies who believe nothing is worth doing unless doing well, whose marketing managers believe in full scale national launches, advertising build-ups, public relation introductions and so on.

A market development company may also be welcomed by the sales organisation in the main company. They are only asked to put their full efforts behind fully tested and proved products.

From the production point of view, the same arguments apply—production problems are ironed out in small scale production units, and do not interfere with the main production lines. Production managers are often presented with a new product, required in large quantities for stock-up purposes at the beginning of its life—a time when the sheer business of producing even very small quantities of the item at reasonable scrap rates is at its most acute stage. Subsequent to launch, quite modest replacement orders may come in to maintain a production line, which by now has reached a level of economic production on a large scale. Some of these discrepancies and difficulties can be avoided by separate production facilities being allocated to the market development company.

The main disadvantage of this approach is that the market development company may get isolated from the mainstream of company activities. This can be avoided by properly organised liaison between the boards of the market development and parent company, and similar liaison between production and marketing men in both companies.

EXECUTIVE COMMITTEE

There must be a central body to control the new product development programme. This executive committee may well be the main board in small companies, a specially chosen committee in medium sized ones and its own board in market development companies. Its job must be to settle and put into effect the overall product strategy, agree overall and individual budgets and fix priorities.

The key members are obviously the Research and Development manager and the Market Development manager, but almost equally important are top level representatives of Finance and Production. One of its members should be designated New Products manager; his main job will be to co-ordinate and monitor all new product activities in the company or department. He should also act as secretary to the executive committee.

The committee should meet regularly and for the specific purpose for which it has been set up. If, for example, the main board of a small company doubles up as a new products committee, new product development should not be relegated to a final item on the agenda at the monthly board meeting. A special new products meeting once every two months is better than a half-hour postscript to the board meeting every four weeks.

The meeting should decide on action, not facts. This means that the facts needed for the decisions must be collected, written down and circulated prior to the meeting. This is a commonplace of meetings procedure, but is of particular importance in the management of new product development, since the facts may be involved and quite impossible to assimilate if presented verbally to non-technical persons. They must have a chance to discuss the data prior to the meeting. Scientists will need to read the market survey with particular care, the accountant to read the research report, and the whole committee must digest the financial figures if the meeting is to be worth while.

Where there are a very large number of research projects the subsidiary data collected on each project cannot possibly be shown even to the members of the executive committee. They should be available, however, and should be consulted by the committee, particularly if they feel that bias is creeping into the recommendations of those working on the project.

Normally, the committee will need only a summarised report, presented by a team leader. The executive committee will consider these reports and decide in the light of the facts presented whether the project should be accelerated, slowed down, allowed to go on as planned or totally suppressed. It will also approve or disallow requests for further development expenditure. Important product policy questions which emerge during the course of the project development will be decided by the executive committee and conveyed to the team leader.

This combination of a number of compact teams reporting regularly to a small executive committee has the advantage of delegating the actual management of new product development to the technical and marketing experts, without losing budgetary or policy control of the projects at any point in their life history. The main danger to be guarded against is a too great dispersal of responsibility and loss of impetus down the line. This can only be avoided by setting agreed target dates for the completion of each stage of development and employing both marketing and scientific research staff who will honour such dates.

NEW PRODUCT TEAMS

The team technique is at the heart of properly organised new product development. It is almost invariably employed in scientific and technological research and development, but its extension to include marketing, production and financial personnel for new product development is more unusual.

The members of the team will vary according both to the nature of the project, and the stage in its development which has been reached. Initially, it may consist of two persons, the person in charge of the project in Research and Development and the Market Development executive most closely identified with the area of the market for which the project is destined. Later the team may be joined by personnel from Production and Sales. Outside assistance and advice from Finance and Marketing Research will also be called for, but representatives from these departments are unlikely to be needed for each meeting of the team.

Each team leader should send in a regular report to the new products manager, prior to the meeting of the executive committee. These reports should briefly summarise the stage of development which has been reached in the project and compare budgeted with actual expenditure. The date of commencement and scheduled dates of completion for the various stages in the development of the product should also be stated at the head of each progress report as a constant reminder of the passage of time. Unless this is done, the executive committee, and even the research team itself, can easily forget how long the project has been in the pipeline.

The main job of the new product team leader is to turn ideas into profit making products. An equally important job is to recommend the abandonment of projects which seem likely to fail.

DEVELOPMENT STAGES

During the course of its life each new product will need to pass through a number of stages.

Screening
This process has been covered in detail in the preceding chapter and can be summarised as separating the wheat from the chaff: identifying product ideas which fall within the scope of the company's new product development programme and seem in themselves to have a promising future.

Business analysis
Once the product has passed through the screening process, it is subjected to business analysis. This activity, in its early stages, involves consultation between scientific research and marketing personnel within the company and customers and expert sources from outside the company, to establish a firmer and more detailed factual basis for the product idea than was provided in the original screening report. Its purpose is to provide data on which a decision to sanction the expenditure of money and time on the development of the product can be based.

Its second and equally important purpose is to provide guidance to the research staff engaged on the project on specification, design, pricing, packaging, timing and likely volume of sales.

A series of business analyses will be completed during the development of a new product, each of which brings up to date the information which has been collected since the last review. The form in which the data may be summarised is described later in the chapter under the heading 'new product justification'.

The business analyses themselves will contain information in support of the figures contained in the new product justifications, and will include: *forecast sales*, that is the proportion of the total market likely to be captured by the new product, the likely reaction of competitors and the effect of new product on sales of existing lines made by the company; *prices*, the average price likely to be obtained for the product for each year for which the forecast is made; *costs of production*, the product specification and cost changes likely to come about as a result of change in sales volume, changes in raw material prices, improved manufacturing techniques; *capital costs*; *promotion expenditure* and *development expenditure*.

The business analyses should also contain some assessment of the degree of certainty which may be attributed to the various forecasts made under the headings. As the product moves forward to its point of launch, the degree of certainty should rise to a point where the margin of uncertainty is of manageable proportions. That is to say, on the basis of the worst of the figures presented, the product still remains likely to prove profitable.

Development

After the completion of the first favourable business analysis, development of the product is likely to begin. It will continue throughout the life of the product up to the point at which the project leaves the development department and is handed over to the production department. There are two main stages in development—laboratory and product development. It is important to realise that the responsibility of the new product development team does not end until a production type product and a fully economic production process has been evolved.

Testing

As soon as the product exists in prototype form, it goes out for test. It will be necessary to distinguish in the test reports between comments, whether favourable or unfavourable, which relate to the peculiarities of the test samples and those which are likely to be relevant to the factory made product.

After receiving test reports the product is likely to go back for further development. The data will also be examined by Marketing and any necessary alterations made in the business analysis and the new product justification.

Commercialisation

As soon as a satisfactory series of test reports has been received, a final business analysis must be made. If this is favourable, the team will recommend that the product proceed to commercialisation. If the capital investment is large, this will be the most difficult and decisive point in the history of the project, but by this time all the relevant facts should have been collected and the areas of doubt largely eliminated.

Test marketing

This marketing approach is used more frequently for consumer than industrial goods. It is only appropriate when the item is one widely and frequently used. In such cases it may be possible to test launch a new industrial product in a given industrial area and receive meaningful sales and customer reports within a reasonable time. Such cases rarely occur. More commonly it is found that the cost of waiting until the results of the test marketing come through is greater than the possible loss, should the product prove a failure.

A phased launch is different from a test launch in that areas of the market are taken one by one, and the whole attention of the marketing and sales departments concentrated in that area before moving on to the next. For example, a new type of pump might be sold initially to the chemical industry, then to the foodstuffs industry, brewing and so on.

Launch plans

The transfer of new products from Market Development to the existing products marketing organisation is most easily accomplished after an introductory period during which the product is 'on probation', under the eye of the marketing development company or department. Nearly all new products suffer from some defect or other, which can be spotted and dealt with more quickly if the product has not received a full-scale launch treatment.

Whether this intermediate marketing and production stage takes place or not there will be a point when the product is ready to be handed over to line management to take its place in the existing product range. Unless the sales, service and marketing managers and the production personnel have been intimately involved in the last stages of development it may well be found that unacceptable decisions have been made by the market development company or department, for which later no one is prepared to take responsibility. The product may fail through misunderstanding or indifference within the firm, rather than lack of acceptance by the market.

Such misunderstanding can be largely avoided by making certain that the final decisions are joint ones, line management making a contribution at least as weighty as that of the market development team.

DOCUMENTATION

Each of the stages through which new products pass requires its own documentation. Drawing up the appropriate reporting forms should be one of the first tasks of the new products manager. Once accepted the forms should be generally applicable within the company or operating group. The new products manager must then make certain that they are used by all product teams.

The exact design of these forms will depend on the nature and range of projects under development: there is no universally acceptable layout. Of general relevance, however, are that the forms should be printed and widely distributed, the paper used should be suitable for writing on or use in duplicating machines and the layout should be simple and encouraging rather than impressive and inhibiting.

If these rules are followed it will be found that the forms are welcomed, used as everyday working documents, subject to constant revision, and not as repositories of ultimate truth.

However simple and well laid out the reports are relating to technical and marketing research, product testing, customer trials, marketing and pricing plans, and so on, the commercial prospects for a new product will be impossible to gauge unless these various categories of information are summarised and translated into a brief series of figures in one document.

NEW PRODUCT JUSTIFICATION FORM

A method by which such a summary may be achieved, is the 'new product justification form'. It will be seen that this form has three pages. The first one, Figure A, summariess the data which are contained in Figures B and C.

FIGURE A   NEW PRODUCT JUSTIFICATION

REPORT NO.

PRODUCT	STAGE REACHED									
	Business Analysis	Develop-ment	Testing	Commercial-isation	Follow-up					
	Year 1	Year 2	Year 3	Year 4	Year 5					

I   *DISCOUNTED CASH FLOW RATE*   % *PAY BACK*   Years

II   *PRODUCT CONTRIBUTION*

    SALES   A

    CONTRIBUTION TO COMPANY OVERHEADS   B

    RETURN ON SALES $\left(\dfrac{B}{A} \times 100\right)$ C   %   %   %   %   %

III   *RETURN ON INVESTMENT*

    (CUMULATIVE)

    TOTAL INVESTMENT ON NEW PRODUCT

      Fixed

      Working Capital

      Introduction Expenses

            TOTAL   D

    RETURN ON INVESTMENT $\left(\dfrac{B}{D} \times 100\right)$ E   %   %   %   %   %

    (Before Tax)

   BASIC DATA

     Volume

     Selling price per unit

     Contribution per unit

FIGURE B

NEW PRODUCT JUSTIFICATION
(Supplementary Schedules)

REPORT NO.

PRODUCT		Year 1	Year 2	Year 3	Year 4	Year 5
II	*PRODUCT CONTRIBUTION*					
	Unit: Volume per annum:					
	Selling Price per Unit:	A				
	SALES (A × B)	B				
	Variable Cost per Unit	C				
	Raw Materials					
	Labour					
	Overheads					
	Distribution					
	TOTAL	D				
	VARIABLE COST (A × D)	E				
	CONTRIBUTION TO PRODUCT					
	FIXED EXPENSES (C − E)	F				
	Product Fixed Expenses (1)					
	Depreciation					
	Factory Overheads					
	Selling					
	Advertising (2)					
	Marketing Research (2)					
	Research and Development (2)					
	TOTAL	G				
	Loss of Contribution by other Products (3)	H				
	CONTRIBUTION TO COMPANY OVERHEADS					
	AND PROFITS (F − G − H)	I				

(1) Additional fixed expenses arising solely due to introduction of new product. No allocation of existing fixed expenses.
(2) Excluding special introduction expenses treated as part of initial investment.
(3) Calculated identically to the contribution by this product.

FIGURE C   **NEW PRODUCT JUSTIFICATION**
(Supplementary Schedules)

PRODUCT		REPORT NO.

	Year 1	Year 2	Year 3	Year 4	Year 5
III TOTAL INVESTMENT					
Fixed Assets					
Land and Buildings					
Plant and Machinery					
Patents, etc.					
Future Obligations (Fifth Year)					
Less Recovery of existing plant no longer required					
TOTAL					
Working Capital					
Stocks					
Debtors					
Less Creditors					
Less Working capital released on any product discontinued or reduced					
TOTAL					
Introduction Expenses					
Development Expenditure					
Special launching expenses (advertising)					
Marketing Research prior to commencement					
Losses in early years					
Other (specified)					
TOTAL					
TOTAL INVESTMENT ON NEW PRODUCT					

It gives the essential facts relating to turnover, marginal profits, return on investment, pay-back period and discounted cash flow rate.

Figure B contains detailed calculations on variable costs of production and product fixed expenses; from these the cash contribution the product is likely to make to company overheads and profits can be deduced.

Figure C analyses investment both in terms of fixed assets and working capital, and also in relation to introduction expenses, the most important of which is likely to be development expenditure. Included in this figure must be machine development and the cost of running in production prior to achieving satisfactory production rates and costs.

The forms cover forecasts for only the first five years of a product's life, but may be extended for as long into the future as the forecasting skill of the company's executive extends. Five years is normally considered sufficiently long, both in terms of market expectations and return on capital. If a product does not look promising by the end of five years after launch and if a substantial return, if not total pay back, on capital has not been obtained, by then, the chances of ultimate success are probably remote.

The basis of return on sales is a marginal one. That is to say, profits on the new product are calculated as an existing contribution towards meeting general company overheads, not after a proportion of existing company overheads has been allocated to the product. Charges directly related to the product, such as scientific and marketing research and the time of market development, sales and advertising personnel, are so attributed, but an allowance is not made for general company fixed overheads, such as personnel, accounts and company management.

If the new product calls for an entirely new company with its own general management structure, then the cost of this item can easily be inserted under 'fixed expenses' in Figure B. The resultant 'contribution to company overheads' will then represent the profits before tax of the new company attributable to the parent company.

The production of a 'new product justification' sheet should precede the expenditure of any substantial sum of money by the company on marketing or scientific research.

The difficulty in obtaining accurate data for the 'new product justification' form in the early stages of a project is admitted, but this is no reason for abandoning the use of the form until a time when all the facts are available.

The form is designed to eliminate the ideas that can never pay, for example products which will never sell in sufficient quantities to justify their research expenditure, to spotlight the ideas which seem worth pursuing and monitor their progress up to launch date, and to provide a comparison between various new project ideas, so as to assign priorities to the most profitable ones.

If the combined skill of Marketing and Research and Development cannot produce the vital figures for this form, even as a very broad estimate, the chances are either that the project is ill-advised or that it represents an idea rather than a product. In both cases the attempt to fill up the form will isolate the main areas of ignorance. The cost of filling the gaps in knowledge should be more easily estimated. The company must then decide whether it is prepared to spend the required sums in order to obtain the basic facts.

For example, the research department may say that they cannot estimate how much time and money they require to develop the product. If this is the main gap in the form, and the outlook in other respects seems promising and it may then be worth while approaching the problem from the other end and saying, 'How much Research and Development expenditure could this product stand and still make a good profit?' If the reply is '£50,000 and two years' time' then it may be agreed to allow the expenditure of £5,000 and six months as speculation. The project can then be re-examined to see how much progress has been made. By this time, the researchers will be in a far better position to size up the situation themselves.

Costs of production are also extremely difficult to estimate in advance of actual production, particularly in a technologically unfamiliar field. Unit quantities of material are fairly easily established, but scrap rates, speeds of operation on machines as yet uninvented, and labour can only be guessed. Here again, more accurate estimates may only be obtained by setting up a small-scale production line. The cost of this can be estimated. The company must then judge whether the sum seems worth spending.

Volume forecasts can only be established by marketing research or by examination of the sales of competing products, where the product already exists. In the case of completely new products, indications of likely sales can be obtained by examining areas of need (as distinct from demand) and by test marketing small quantities of the new product or material, prior to full-scale production.

Likely prices should be established by reference to the market, and not to the costs of production. There is a tendency on the part of some marketing men concerned with new products to try to escape responsibility for pricing by asking for estimates of unit costs and then fixing their prices in relation to these. This is the wrong way round. The marketing man should establish at what price he thinks he could sell his product and then give guidance to his research colleague on the approximate area of cost, at which the company could make good profits at various levels of sales. In practice, both sets of calculation should proceed independently in the initial stages, with constant reference and consultation between Marketing and Research and Development[1].

During the development period of a new product, a series of new product justifications will be completed, each one refining the estimates made in the one preceding it. The final estimate will be made just prior to the point at which the product leaves the market development company or

1. See Chapter 12.

department, and is accepted by the marketing and production departments in the existing products organisation of the company.[1]

FOLLOW-UP

It is just as important for market development staff to follow progress of new products after launch, as it is for line managers to take an active interest in new products prior to launch. One year after hand-over, a brief review should be made of the history of the product since launch. Actual and forecast figures on volume, price, costs of production, capital investment and profits should be compared and reasons given for discrepancies. In this manner, lessons may be learned by the market development staff which will enable them to do their next new product development assignment more efficiently.

PROFITABILITY YARDSTICKS

Net profit percentage on turnover
This can be calculated both on a marginal basis, as suggested in the 'new product justification' sheets, or after allocation of a necessarily somewhat arbitrary proportion of the general company overheads to the new product. This yardstick has little to recommend it, except its simplicity and familiarity. Its main disadvantage is that it takes no account of the level of investment in the project.

Percentage return on investment
This goes one better, but suffers from the disadvantage that no distinction is made between fixed and working capital, and thus does not measure the true level of risk. Furthermore, it is expressed before tax and does not give sufficient weight to the vitally important effects of tax regulations on plant write-off in different areas of the country.

Both percentage profit on turnover and return on investment suffer from the fault that neither take account of timing. Further, they are expressed in annual terms, which makes it difficult to compare one investment with another. What, for example, is one to make of the following three examples:

	% Return on Capital		
	Product 1	*Product 2*	*Product 3*
Year I	—	5	25
Year II	15	15	5
Year III	25	15	—

Which of these products is the most profitable? Product 1 because the profits earned are higher in Year II and III, or Product 2 because the profits are moderate and spread through the three years' forecast? Or perhaps Product 3 because high profits are earned in Year I?

1. Further comments on product justification from the financial viewpoint will be found in Chapter 15.

Discounted cash flow

The discounted cash flow method of judging the likely profitability of various investment decisions, including those involving new product development, is now increasingly used. Its advantages are that it provides one figure by which the profitability of the investment over the whole life of the project can be judged. This makes comparison between different investments a simple matter. It also takes account of timing and of the cash flow.[1]

Pay back period

The sole disadvantage of the discounted cash flow method of calculating profitability is that it takes no account of risk. This important factor is indicated by the pay back period. This is the amount of time the cash flow (net profit after tax and before depreciation) takes to equal the total fixed investment in the project.

The pay back concept is of no use by itself since it does not take the whole project life into account. It is useful, however, when considered in conjunction with the discounted cash flow yardstick.

A discounted cash flow of 15 per cent and pay back period of up to five years are both considered good. There are firms, however, where such figures would be considered the minimum, and a discounted cash flow rate of 20 per cent and a pay back period of three years is the norm.

Break even point

The break even point is not so much a yardstick of profitability as one by which the level of sales the product is likely to earn any profits at all may be judged.

Its calculation is a useful first stage in the business analysis of a new product. This may be defined as the number of units which need to be sold in order to cover costs. This volume is established by analysing how total revenue and total costs vary at different sales volumes, as follows:

		Case I	Case II	Case III
	Unit Price	£1	15/–d.	£1 5s.
	Variable Cost per Unit	12/–d.	12/–d.	12/–d.
A.	Unit Contribution to Fixed Costs	8/–d.	3/–d.	13/–d.
	Fixed Costs			
	Depreciation on Fixed Investment	£500	£500	£500
	Advertising	£500	£500	£1,100
	Selling	£1,000	£500	£1,000
B.	Total Fixed Costs	£2,000	£1,500	£2,600
	Break even point (B ÷ A) =	5,000 units	10,000 units	4,000 units

1. Detailed explanation of the principles behind discounted cash flow and the mathematics involved in its calculation are given in the Merrett and Sykes book, *The Finance and Analysis of Capital Projects*. A brief explanation will be found in 'New Frontiers in Profit Forecasting,' *Business*, by Nigel Farrow (London, December, 1964).

The table not only illustrates the way in which the break even point may be worked out, but it also shows how it may vary with changes in the price charged and the level of expenditure in selling and promotion. It does not, of course, represent a forecast of the volumes which would *actually* be achieved. It is merely an attempt at establishing the sensitivity of the break even point to changes in price and marketing mix decisions.

If the company decides that Case 1 represents the minimum fixed expenditure that can be envisaged for the new product, then clearly 5,000 units have to be sold before one penny profit or contribution to general company overheads is achieved. Whether Case I, II or III is chosen will depend on actual forecasts of volume likely to be achieved at prices of £1, 15s. and £1 5s. 0d.

LICENCES, KNOW-HOW AGREEMENTS

The organisation of new product development has been discussed mainly in terms of research and development conducted within the firm itself, and not in relation to the buying-in of ideas and products by means of licences, know-how agreements or even the acquisition of whole companies.

The same techniques of investigation and analysis may be employed in this quite different context. The business analysis and new product justification are still required. The team technique may also find application. However, the time available before a decision has to be made is likely to be much less. This factor can lead to unwise commitments and purchases, unless the same questions are asked as would be asked were the product about to be made into a research assignment within the firm's own organisation.

The organisation of new product development has been considered in this chapter in relation to the people who run it, the way in which they work together and the basis on which they make business decisions.

The organisation will be a good one if it learns to identify, at the idea stage, products which can be made, can be sold and can make profits for the company. Equally important, it must acquire the opposite talent of recognising potential failures before they even become the object of technical or marketing research.

Only if these two gifts are developed will money and time be concentrated on the successful products and not be spread equally over a range of product ideas, good, bad and indifferent.

The organisation itself will not produce these powers of discrimination, but it will provide a framework within which they can grow and flourish. Endowed with these powers, the new product development department will form one of the most useful and profitable tools of industrial marketing.

5

Industrial Marketing Research—
Management Aspects

G. T. BRAND, B.Sc. (Econ)

NEED FOR INDUSTRIAL MARKETING RESEARCH

During the time set aside for discussion at the end of a lecture on marketing research the question was put by a member of the group, a sales manager, 'What can marketing research do to help me sell an industrial product now being developed by my company, and which will be put on the market in two years' time'? Inherent in the question was the assumption that once the product had been decided on, developed and manufactured, it was then up to the sales department to do as best they could with it. By stressing the industrial nature of the product, the questioner also implied that difficulties existed which were not applicable in consumer markets, but which prevented the successful investigation of industrial markets.

Comparison is frequently made between the late development of industrial marketing research and the longer established consumer marketing research. Such comparisons, although of possible interest to those concerned in the development of marketing thought, are now only academic. Consistently successful enterprises appear to have isolated the importance of research into markets long before marketing research became more generally recognised. But even if industrial marketing research was a late developer, it is now completely established and is proving itself a valuable aid to industrial marketing management. Each year the numbers of personnel employed in studying industrial markets increases, and at the present rate of growth the amount of money spent on industrial marketing research by United Kingdom manufacturers may well, within a year or two, exceed that spent on consumer marketing research.

The growth in industrial marketing research is not altogether surprising. The need for marketing research into goods and services sold to industry is just as necessary as for consumer goods and services. The need springs from the necessity to fill the gulf in knowledge which has grown up in modern industrial activity between the producer and the ultimate consumer or user. This gulf became apparent with the introduction of mass production techniques for consumer goods, and the widening of markets from local to a national scale and from a national to an international scale.

We live in an atmosphere of growth in which it is assumed that production and wealth will be increased each year. Shareholders are not immune from this atmosphere and in competitive conditions there is a heavy responsibility on management to ensure that the resources of the company —capital, labour and physical assets—are employed in such a manner as to afford the greatest profit return. Scrutiny of nationalised industries has also brought a similar pressure on management in public enterprises.

The rapidity of technological development has affected the solidity and permanency of industrial markets. Traditional suppliers to the railways, for example, have seen their markets dwindle with the competitive growth of road transport. Manufacturers of aircraft may have their turnover decimated by changing government policy. In order to maintain profitability during these fluctuating conditions, companies have sought to diversify their interests. This has involved entering new markets in which the traditional knowledge of management may no longer apply. The management hunch is being replaced by a demand for facts.

Firms not diversifying have been forced into a new awareness of competition from alternative materials and methods. Manufacturers of glass containers do not operate solely in the glass container market. They must also consider cardboard and plastic containers. Ideally they should see themselves as members of the packaging industry if they are to ensure that they are in a position to profit from the changing demands of their customers.

A firm may relax in the comfort of a rising sales curve, unaware of the fact that the total market is increasing at an even greater rate, leaving them with a reducing market share. This is particularly dangerous in an expanding economy in which increases in national production are achieved every year. If the economy should be deflated, the company is in a weak position to ride out the increased competition from relatively stronger rivals fully aware of the market situation.

Conversely a firm may not realise that sales are increasing because competitors are withdrawing from a market which is about to disappear. Unaware of the market facts, the firm may even increase production facilities to cope with the temporary expansion and then be left with expensive but redundant equipment when the market finally collapses.

These examples give a background against which the value of industrial marketing research can be assessed, and they underline the importance of industrial marketing research as a means of producing vital management information relative not only to the marketing effort but also to the total corporate aims. It is useful, however, to pinpoint a number of typical marketing research objectives which can be achieved by the application of the techniques which are explained in Chapter 6.

MARKET SIZE AND OTHER QUANTITATIVE ASPECTS

There is always a need for information on market size, both for a firm proposing to enter a new market and a company seeking a greater exploitation of an existing market. Knowledge of the total market size enables a realistic assessment to be made of the penetration which the company might hope to achieve. Further, the magnitude and intensity of all the other marketing activities can be linked to the total market figure to prevent over or under investment in market development.

Along with market size for a company already in a market, information on market share is vital. Not only does the market share data—either in the form of percentages or 'league tables'—enable a manufacturer to assess the untapped potential, it also provides him with important basic marketing data in relation to his competitors. Such market share estimates, repeated at intervals, give a benchmark against which progress can be measured.

The third aspect of the quantitative data which can be produced by industrial marketing research is of course, market forecasts. Here again, accurate forecasts are a most valuable contribution which an industrial marketing research project can yield. These forecasts, taking account as they do of both historical and current situations can, with the knowledge of developing trends practices and attitudes within competitive firms, users and ultimate users, provide a company with realistic marketing and production targets, direction for research and development.

TECHNICAL FEATURES

A second important function of industrial marketing research is to obtain information on the types of materials or products or services required by users, broken down by characteristics or performance. Opinions within the company will almost invariably differ as to what these requirements are. Without guidance, design staff are always likely to incorporate features into a product which are more liable to reflect their past experience and physical research endeavours than the users' real requirements.

Production personnel naturally tend to judge a product on the ease with which it can be made or its suitability for incorporation into the production programme. The salesman may easily fall into the rut of serving current requirements without taking interest in how the company's products are eventually used, and thus fail to report back on what are the real and emerging needs of his customers. Elsewhere in the company there will be other individuals and departments with their own ideas on what might be the ideal product or service profile.

It is clear from Chapter 1 that a company which has adopted the marketing concept will be motivated by the requirements of its customers. Marketing research can uncover precisely and objectively what these requirements are.

The effectiveness of an industrial sales force is immeasurably improved if an element of precision can be introduced into the sales operation by the accurate designation of the best areas of potential sales opportunities, the best form of sales structure and the most suitable types of salesmen to employ. The division of a market on a geographical basis is an essential preliminary to the effective deployment of a sales force. This can be followed by an analysis of data—both internal and external—upon which key customer itineraries can be based. The majority of industrial markets in the United Kingdom follow a pattern in which it is usual for as much as 80 per cent of the output of an industry to be concentrated in the hands of as few as 20 per cent or less of the supplying firms. The remainder form a long tail on the distribution chart, sharing the smaller proportion of demand.

It is evident that to give each customer or potential customer the same amount of attention would dilute the effectiveness of a sales force. The exact degree of concentration needed by each particular sales force should be deduced from the results of an analysis based on the facts provided by the internal records rather than by asking the representatives to spend more time with their 'best' customers. To relate the selling pattern entirely to the company's existing sales performance could, however, merely repeat past mistakes. The exercise becomes more useful if a detailed documentation of the representative's area is made. The number of user firms of the products or services sold can be listed; the size of these companies (using various criteria) their associations with other companies and developments and expansion planned in the area affecting the use of the product noted to build up a picture of the potential. This information may then be compared with the sales analyses and important non-customer companies added to the key-customer list.

The structuring of the sales force is another facet of research which materially assists the objective gathering of information in the field. A study of users' attitudes and preferences, of competitors' activities, of the strengths and weaknesses of distributors, the location of warehouses and availability of transport are among the factors which assist industrial sales managers to decide on the form which their sales force shall take. Other decisions are materially assisted by an examination of industrial selling, for example, whether the sales force should be divided on a product basis or on a trade basis, or whether a combination of both might meet the particular requirements of the company.

The decision whether to employ technical, semi-technical or non-technical salesmen is also assisted by obtaining information from the field. Further, the support which such salesmen need and can usefully take advantage of can be decided on against the background of the research findings.

PURCHASING INFLUENCES

A great deal of work has still to be done in the study of purchasing influences in industry. The exploitation of industrial marketing skill is still to a great extent hampered by the lack of information on how industry buys. Chapter 2 will have left no doubts as to the complexity of the problem. Industrial marketing research techniques can be adapted to uncover the intricate channels of decision making involved in the purchase of industrial materials, equipment and services.

The buying operation is never as simple as it seems. It varies from the entrepreneurial type of operation in which the proprietor or managing director is virtually responsible for all purchasing decisions to those in which the buyer is only the mechanical means of implementing the decision of others, perhaps design engineers, accountants and research and development personnel. It presents a complex and, to most firms, an unexplored area of marketing activity.

In the past, firms have relied upon the salesmen's contacts and interpersonal relationships with customers. These may be sufficient in themselves within customer companies, but for as yet untapped marketing areas the saleman's knowledge adds less to the sales effort than that of the marketing researcher's enquiries.

While in industrial selling the emphasis is still on purchaser's profit rather than on personal gratification, this latter is now gaining acceptance as a factor of importance.[1] However, the most fundamental problem faced by industrial sellers is still seen to be the manner in which the product can be shown to increase the buyer's profitability. The industrial product which does not hold out eventual improved profit is difficult if not impossible to sell.

But the marketing researcher can, while accepting 'profit' as a rationalised basis of purchase, also help to determine the unconscious decision factors. A loading shovel may make a significant contribution to profits but between Smith's and Jones's loading shovels there may be no observable difference. How and why does the buyer decide? It is in the isolation of the decision factors that marketing research provides a considerable aid to the sales department.

ADVERTISING RESEARCH

Industrial marketing research contributes to improved advertising techniques in three ways. First by the collection and analysis of marketing data which enables suitable advertising strategy to be devised. Second, since, as is clearly shown in Chapter 8, the emphasis in most good industrial advertising is on information, data can be provided which most effectively

1. Hector Lazo, 'Emotional Aspects of Industrial Buying', *Dynamic Marketing in a Changing World*, Robert S. Hancock (Ed.) American Marketing Association (Chicago, Illinois, 1960).

meets users' informational needs. Third, the conflicting and sometimes unsubstantiated claims of advertising media can be probed.

Despite these important areas of assistance the marketing researcher is called upon to provide, there remains the greatest problem of marketing research still to be solved; namely the measurement of advertising effectiveness. While it is possible to measure 'impact' and 'recall' no one has yet succeeded in isolating the effect of the advertising from the total marketing effort. Thus it has been impossible to attribute, except in the most general way, any particular market phenomenon, to specific advertising. It is here that industrial marketing research will make perhaps its most significant contribution in the future to marketing management.

DISTRIBUTIVE CHANNELS AND
DISTRIBUTIVE RELATIONSHIPS

A study carried out in 1962 by the British Institute of Management revealed that the average selling and distribution costs for industrial goods were 8.7 per cent. These are lower than the costs experienced by consumer goods manufacturers, but with the growth of the manufacturing unit, the increasing uniformity of production methods and raw material costs, the distributive process is receiving increased attention as an area with cost reduction opportunities.

Marketing research is often employed to study how the users of a product can best be served, for example, in stock availability, timing of deliveries, order handling and shipment methods. This external information is then used with internal analyses of sales variations and costs involved in stock-holding to develop an optimum distribution policy. The internal analyses are the province of the company accountant but industrial marketing research has an important role to play in the provision of representative and validated information on the distributive needs of customers.

This summary of major research objectives is by no means a full one. There are very many other areas indeed in which marketing researchers can provide important information for management decisions. Some of these areas will be specific to individual firms while others will be of a general nature and applicable across the whole of industry.

SALESMEN OR RESEARCHERS?

To whom should management turn for obtaining information needed for key management decisions? Should the task of collection be allocated to specialist marketing researchers or should the information be obtained through the sales force who after all are in daily contact with the customers? There are numerous reasons why the former should be preferred to the latter.

A fundamental principle of marketing research is that its operation should be completely unbiased. This applies not only in the planning of the marketing research approach, but also to the personnel collecting the marketing information. Industrial selling affords greater opportunities than consumer selling for the detached or realistic approach. But even so, a salesman of industrial goods should be just as enthusiastic as his consumer goods colleague about the product he sells and he should be highly biased in their favour. If he is able to step outside his job and take a detached view too frequently, he will be falling down in his task of selling. If he is a competent salesman he will have the ability to influence a customer in order to put him in a mood conducive to buying. If requested to put marketing research questions to a buyer, the good salesman will find it difficult not to influence his respondent by putting words into his mouth. The average respondent is easily influenced by an untrained interviewer.

The possibility of bias does not end with the influence of salesmen on the respondent, but also exists in the salesman's interpretation of what he has heard. An outside salesman will necessarily be detached from the real purpose of the market investigation however good the channels of communication within the firm. He may well believe that the questions are a method of checking on his own performance, as indeed they might be, and he will be influenced consciously or unconsciously to alter the emphasis of the respondent's replies in a way to present his own position in the best light or to support the views he may have already expressed to management. This danger is particularly true in new product development where salesmen tend to take positive attitudes for or against a new product.

In the absence of official statistics one of the alternative methods of market size calculation is to aggregate user uptake of a commodity and in certain cases heavy emphasis will be put on the reliability of information obtained from key respondents regarding annual consumption. Here a deliberate error may be introduced in the answers of buyers interrogated by salesmen. These errors will stem from psychological factors. Buyers often feel that information given by them in good faith during the marketing research inquiry will lead to sales pressure by the company concerned. The buyer, therefore, tends to give a reply which is less than his real total consumption figures. The salesman being aware of his own sales to the customer will calculate that he has a much larger share of the customer's business than is in fact the case.

Another drawback in using the sales force for marketing research is the preservation of good relations between the salesman and buyer. There must be an atmosphere of trust which inspires confidence to purchase. It would be unfortunate if through poor interviewing techniques a resentment should be built up to spoil a sales association which may have developed over years.

All these arguments and others mitigate against the successful use of salesmen as marketing researchers. It is obvious from the techniques involved that industrial marketing research is no area in which the amateur can dabble or a dilettante play without the grave risk of serious damage to his company. As with most things, if marketing research is worth doing it is worth doing properly, and the only way in which it can be done properly is to be sure that the marketing researchers are skilful and experienced as it is possible for them to be.

LOCATION OF THE MARKETING
RESEARCH DEPARTMENT

If the firm has a marketing director, the marketing research section should report to him thus avoiding the bias whether conscious or unconscious, associated with a sales department. Where the marketing research section reports to the sales manager there is a danger that the surveys conducted may concentrate too much on details at the expense of the broader requirements of marketing planning. More dangerous still, there may be a clash between the marketing research findings and the wishes of the sales manager. In short, the sales manager should not be both judge and jury of the research findings. Where there is no marketing director, the internal marketing research unit should report to the chief executive or to a non-functional director.

The necessity to be absolutely free from all possible bias and internal influence is so fundamental to good marketing research that an inappropriate location of the department can vitiate its use from the outset.

Wherever the industrial marketing research department is located it should be in a strategic position to enable it to provide a link between the technical and commercial aspects of marketing. In controlling the direction of the firm the management should be reviewing objectively the merits of various alternatives. These may vary from the technical 'brain child' of the engineer out of touch with the market to the 'hunch' of the sales manager convinced, but without proof, that large opportunities exist in certain markets. In deciding between two or more methods, management is best served by the facts upon which decisions can be made.

Top management in an organisation can benefit the most from efficient marketing research and no obstacles should be put in their way to prevent their free and direct access to marketing research information. Unless marketing research is given high status within the firm it runs a risk of being regarded as simply marketing intelligence—that is the collection of published material and statistics.

DEVELOPMENT OF THE MARKETING RESEARCH
FUNCTION WITHIN THE FIRM

Four broad stages of development mark the growth of the marketing research function within the firm. The first stage of marketing research is that in which the analysis of sales statistics is undertaken to determine, for example, the distribution of sales between the various users or sectors or between large and small customers. The second step occurs when the department becomes involved in the collection of relevant market information from all forms of published material and from representatives' report. An analysis of information gained from both internal and external sources provides a great deal of market information but it will be found that gaps exist in market knowledge as the material used for desk research is neither sufficiently detailed nor sufficiently representative to permit a correct presentation of the market situation. These gaps need to be filled by field surveys which represent the third stage of development. The fourth stage is reached when the market research unit or department is fully accepted as part of the marketing team, to be consulted on all new projects and probably initiating its own projects and commissioning research from outside agencies.

In the early stages of development of market research within the firm, before the establishment of an internal department, field surveys are better placed in the hands of an experienced agency which can carry out the entire survey from the definition of the problem, the proposal stage and preparation of the terms of reference through to the presentation of the report and the guidance of management as to the implications of the survey's findings and to the means of implementing any recommendations given.

The appointment of a qualified marketing research executive will relieve top management of the liaison function with the outside agency. The internal researcher's task is to appreciate requirements of the firm and translate them into research terms. It is unlikely that at this stage the services of the agency can be dispensed with as one internal researcher is limited in the amount of work he can undertake. A better return will be obtained from the money spent with the agency, as the internal researcher is in the position to isolate the true research needs and to provide a detailed research brief. If he undertakes the desk research and internal analyses the agency can concentrate on field interviewing which it is not normally possible for the internal researcher working on his own to undertake.

As the staff of the marketing research department is increased, the demand for outside assistance does not necessarily diminish. Increased marketing research activity draws attention of others within the firm to worthwhile opportunities of using research. Nothing succeeds like success, and once a department has begun to prove its worth it is likely to be inundated with requests for surveys by divisional or departmental managers who had previously believed that marketing research was not applicable to their problems. The greater part of the work of the leading industrial marketing research agencies in the United Kingdom is, in fact, carried out on behalf of firms with internal departments.

Care should be taken in the selection of an outside agency to ensure that a firm specialising in industrial marketing research is chosen. Consumer marketing research agencies, dependent as they are on samples involving many hundreds of interviews, are organised on a very different basis from the industrial agency in which the emphasis is placed not on the number of interviews but on their quality and depth. Enquiries among housewives and among top management, probably highly technical, obviously require different levels of skill.

The application of marketing research techniques, beginning with sampling and ending with interview methods is so different between the consumer and industrial field that researchers trained in one sector have the greatest difficulty in working in another and, indeed, some are never able to change at all. The ethos, organisation and activities within an agency concentrating on consumer research mitigate against the possibility of producing good industrial marketing research. The opposite is also true and very few, if any, industrial marketing research specialists are successful in the consumer field.

There are of course pros and cons to the employment of specialised agencies. The main advantage of the outside and specialist agency can be summarised under six headings.

First, *objectivity*. It is claimed that an outside agency with 'no axe to grind' can preserve a far higher degree of objectivity than could possibly be obtained inside a firm where, even with the best will in the world, political pressures are generated and self-aggrandisement inevitably leads to animosity.

Second, *anonymity*. No company can ethically conduct marketing research on its own behalf while disguising its identity, particularly if its competitors are included in the enquiries. It cannot have recourse to the standard approach of the outside agency which can, and does, refuse to reveal the identity of a research sponsor but does not disguise the fact that the sponsor is a competitor. When a new product development is under consideration it is usually advisable not to give advance notice to users or competitors of the interest of the firm in the product or industrial sector. Under these circumstances the outside agency has a clear advantage over the internal department.

Third, *cross industry experience*. Agencies are able to make useful economies by applying the solution of a research problem developed in one industry to that of another. Although it is true that for some very large industrial concerns, cross industry experience for the marketing research department is possible, it nevertheless rarely covers the same spectrum as that of the independent agency.

Fourth, *specialisation*. Where an agency makes no claim to cross industry experience, but bases itself upon a narrow specialisation it is also possible for a research sponsor to obtain economies, particularly where the specialisation is one not possessed by the sponsoring firm. These specialisations may be by industry, or may be by techniques. Thus, some agencies concentrate their activities within the chemical or electrical industry. Others devote themselves entirely to the preparation of internal sales analyses or the use of psychological techniques.

Fifth, *cost*. There are many circumstances in which it is cheaper to use an outside agency than to undertake the work internally. Superior techniques can lead to economies in operation, but the existence of information on file relative to the research project could enable an agency to complete a project within less time input and interviewing than would be possible for an internal department starting 'cold'. Both experience and specialisation tend to reduce the disadvantages of the agencies' costs as compared with the internal department. However, if truly accurate costing is made of internal research, that is to include more than just direct time and out of pocket expenses, but making correct allowances for overheads, it will very often be found that there is no real cost advantage to the internal department.

Sixth, *time*. Once again, the existence of superior techniques, internal records, permanent interview forces and contacts can lead to a considerable time advantage in using agencies. This is particularly so when no internal department exists and the marketing research is being carried out as an additional function by some other member of the management team. Very often it is possible for the agency to interlock a project with one that is already taking place and thereby saving further time in the total length of the project.

None of the foregoing is intended to imply that there are not considerable advantages in undertaking the research internally. First, there is the familiarity of the researcher with the firm, its products and with the personnel involved. Second, there is the probably unlimited access to technical know-how within the company. Third, there may well be a considerable volume of information which can be yielded from internal data which it would not be considered advisable to release to any external personnel. Fourth, 'natural' sampling lists in the form of return guarantee cards, customer analyses, enquiries, shareholders and suppliers may exist.

In deciding between 'do it yourself' and the specialist agency it is necessary for all these considerations to be taken into account. Just as with the marketing research itself decisions should be taken objectively, the criteria for a decision should be a comparison of the internal department and external agency in relation to the resources available, the time required for completion, the cost of the projects, and, of course, the research objectives themselves.

APPROPRIATIONS

There are, by and large, three methods of allocating research appropriations for marketing research. The first is where the marketing research department has its own budget and undertakes research as it is required or as it is instructed. With the second method a marketing research executive is employed with no budget but who advises departments sponsoring marketing research—the research being paid for by the sponsoring group. A third and increasingly popular method is for the marketing research department to have a budget of its own and to meet part or all of the costs of research for those projects which meet with the approval of the central marketing department and which fall within the broad marketing strategy of the firm. Thus the marketing research department is in a position to discourage some research and to encourage other projects.

Marketing research survey appropriations whether centrally or divisionally paid for should be linked to the divisional budget in order that surveys sponsored have a direct relevance to the division's marketing plans, and the divisional manager's task of making a profit. Without this relevance there is the danger that money will be spent by an autonomous market research department on surveys which although interesting on their own, form no part of the company's marketing plan.

'WHAT'S IN IT FOR ME?'

The opinion has been expressed that it will become increasingly difficult for marketing research in industry to be carried out owing to the amount of time spent by key personnel in firms dealing with enquiries of visiting marketing researchers. Concentration of industrial activity is such that the same firms are used time and time again by many companies researching into the same market and asking the same questions. It is true that owing to the structure of British industry, in many instances a small percentage of firms in an industry account for a large part of that industry's total output. In assessing an industrial market the large firms cannot be ignored and consequently some of them appear frequently on the lists of companies to be interviewed. However, although a firm's name may appear many times the number of respondents within these companies, which are by definition very large, is also considerable and even within the smaller divisions there are usually many respondents equally capable of answering the questions of the marketing researchers.

A company approached by an interviewer who wishes to spend two or three hours discussing a project to obtain marketing research information may well ask 'What's in it for me?' Some companies have been known to charge for a marketing research interview, a practice which would soon deter the potential users of marketing research on a cost basis alone. But this is a two-edged weapon in attempting to discourage marketing research interviewers. Such firms, in carrying out their own marketing research, would very soon find themselves on the receiving end of interview charges from the companies they themselves have charged.

Nevertheless the question 'What's in it for me?' must be answered. Apart from the obvious advantage of reciprocal facilities for research being offered, there is a great deal to be gained by a visit from a marketing researcher. A trained interviewer will not expect to get something for nothing, but will be in a position through the knowledge of the market he is surveying to exchange information. An interviewer, after all, has a wider and more recent view of the market than the great majority of his respondents and has information, not confidential to the project, which he can give in exchange for the data provided by the respondent. That this practice has its merits is borne out by the fact that competitors are normally interviewed during a survey by interviewers who are known to represent a competitor. These interviews are certainly not all one way, and most are conducted with satisfaction to both sides.

Industrial marketing research will unquestionably be used much more extensively in the future, as both the range of its accomplishments and improvements in techniques bring it into the prominence which is its due. Any attempt to stem the increasing flow of industrial marketing research activity has the air of Canute about it and will meet with a similar lack of success. If industrial marketing research is to be restricted in any way then the future of a country's prosperity will be threatened. The benefits of the scientific approach to marketing are becoming increasingly clear and industrial marketing research is a necessary platform on which marketing policies must be based.

Industrial Marketing Research—Techniques

MAX K. ADLER, D.Sc. (Pol.), B.Sc. (Econ.)

THE PROBLEM POSED

The techniques of industrial marketing research do not vary fundamentally from those used in consumer marketing research. The major differences are in their application and in the problems of sampling and interviewing. The differences which do occur are not just sophistry or an attempt by the practitioners of industrial marketing research to create a new and separate discipline from that of the longer established activity of consumer marketing research. The underlying reason stems from the characteristics of industrial products and services, their markets and the role of the individuals who control and operate the marketing functions.

The first step in the process to complete a piece of industrial marketing research efficiently and economically, and by no means the least important, is to establish, what the problem really is. This is a question which must be put to the sponsor of the survey, that is a member of the management team who has been entrusted in commissioning the research.[1] Whoever is going to undertake the survey, must be properly and thoroughly briefed.

It is vital for the researcher or the research team to obtain water-tight definitions from the sponsors of the product or services to be surveyed, a precise statement of the aims of the survey and details of the information to be sought. To do this is often very difficult for several reasons. Industrial goods which fulfil many purposes and mean different things to different users are complex and not easy to define, as will have already been seen from Chapter 2. A spring balancer may be a machine tool to the firm using spot welders, but it is a mechanical handling device in an abattoir. Which types in the product range or a general group, should be included, and which excluded from the survey? A survey on compressors could include small machinery for refrigerators and very large centrifugal blowers used in the distribution of town gas. Where is the line to be drawn? As if these

---

1. The term 'sponsor' is used in this chapter irrespective of whether the company has its own marketing research department which will eventually undertake the research, or whether an outside agency is commissioned for the purpose.

were not complications enough, language is a poor tool for conveying information. A term can mean this to one person and that to another. Nevertheless, definitions must be agreed upon in order to produce a sound piece of research.

It is sometimes too great a mental effort for the sponsor to devote himself to these definitions and to the terms of reference. In such circumstances there is only one way out of the situation: the marketing researcher himself has to attempt both definitions and the terms of reference and to submit them to the sponsor. In any case, it is absolutely essential that the sponsor should not only agree the terms of reference but approve them in writing. When this is not observed, the great danger exists that the sponsor may complain, after the completion of the survey, that he really meant something else; the research covers too narrow a field and the researcher omitted to delve into one or several important problems.

The possibility of this happening can be prevented. If the sponsor is not willing to agree in writing the definitions adopted and the terms of reference, it is much better not to attempt the survey at all. Such an attitude on the part of the sponsor indicates that he really does not want the research and probably that he is negotiating only because he has been ordered to do so. Any result would be a failure and cannot possibly satisfy the sponsoring company. In addition, it can be assumed, with good reason, that the results of the survey will not be incorporated into the business plan at all.

However, one of the principal skills of the marketing researcher is to be able to assist the research sponsor to isolate his research objectives. The marketing researcher must involve himself deeply in the technical side of the product or service and he must gain sufficient understanding of it in order to produce an acceptable research design. He need not be an expert in the subject matter of the proposed survey. That would be asking too much of a researcher, who has to work on many and widely different products. He must, however, have sufficient general knowledge to be able to appreciate the significance of what the technical experts tell him and he must have the ability to obtain information from them which is vital for the project.

On the strength of this preliminary work, the research team will be able to produce proposals for the agreement of the sponsor. These proposals, which are the terms of reference, will include the research parameters and definitions, they will indicate step by step the details of the research procedure, the expected research yield, and will contain estimates of time and of cost.

An industrial marketing research survey can often take many months or even a year before it is completed. It is a common complaint by management that research takes too long. The research team must, however, resist being hurried, for they can produce a good study only if they have sufficient time to conduct it properly. Researchers should try to educate management in such a way that surveys are commissioned in sufficient time to obtain the information when it is needed. It is a sign of good management to foresee its needs. Research is a case in point. Forward looking management can often come to the conclusion they need more facts long before the decision has been taken.

Although evaluating the cost of industrial market research can be a straightforward addition for those who know the respective cost elements, the important criteria are those relative to the business investment decisions which will arise out of the research. It is much more meaningful to discover the cost of a wrong business decision, which might arise because the research was not commissioned, or the value of the right decision, which could be made if all the informational needs are met. It is not a matter of 'How much does it cost?' but of 'Can we afford not to have research done on these problems?'

DESK RESEARCH

Nevertheless there is no doubt that industrial marketing research can be unnecessarily expensive. It is the obvious duty of the research team to minimise the cost as much as possible. There is always a risk that the over-enthusiastic researcher will rush into the field and conduct expensive interviews when he could have obtained either the whole of the information needed, or at least part of it, by much cheaper and sometimes more reliable means.

Desk research is essentially the search for secondary information—that is, statistical and other material already compiled in some form or another. It must include bibliographical search but it is by no means confined to such sources. Indeed, the most valuable elements of secondary information are very frequently already within the firm although they may not be available in the form which makes them immediately usable without re-processing.

The first step in conducting desk research therefore, is an agreement with the sponsor that he will provide all relevant information available in the company. It is surprising, considering how many records exist in the accountancy and other departments of the company, that so little effort is made to make use of these records for the purpose of marketing research. Perhaps this situation exists because it is not always easy to obtain the internal data for analysis purposes.

It may even be the case that the sponsor does not trust the researchers with the information which is considered a business secret. Under these circumstances the researchers might well refuse to carry out the work for the sponsor. Absolute confidence is essential for the successful conclusion of any study.

Even when free access is assured, the information is very often available only in a form which makes it unusable to the research team. They must, therefore, transform it for their own purposes and this can take a long time and need considerable effort. Whether the effort is invariably worth while depends upon the skill of the research team in extracting the vital information in the shortest possible time.

For internal records a competent statistician is a necessity. Statistics is the art of comparison. One figure does not mean anything at all. Only when it is brought into contact with another figure does it come to life and often reveals a most interesting and important story. One of the characteristics of a good marketing researcher is that he can see trends and correlations where the layman sees a forest of figures only and that he has the skill of showing these connections in a form which is easily understood and recognised.

It is perhaps useful to list some of the types of internal analyses which can be conducted apart from the ubiquitous sales analyses: *ratios*; studies such as financial marketing and cost ratios; *correlations*; a method of measuring the relationship of two or more variables; *historical trends*; an examination of past performances of the company under differing circumstances; *actuarial techniques*; predicting life expectancies of physical equipment.

Desk research must continue outside the firm where very many important sources of information exist. The skill of the researcher will be proved by what he will omit rather than include in his study. Libraries are full to overflowing with the most esoteric information. It is contained in books, in newspapers, in periodicals, in pamphlets, directories, catalogues and in many other documents. The internal marketing research department has a considerable advantage over the marketing research agency in that an internal department can, and should, collect information on all aspects of the activities of the company, irrespective of whether this information is needed immediately or not. Marketing research agencies' interests are so widespread that it is virtually impossible for them to collect all information which might at some time be of use. More important for both internal and external departments than the actual collection and creation of archives is the accumulation of knowledge as to where to look for information when it is needed.

No truly adequate and concise book giving reference sources exists. Often information on sources is more complex and devious than the information they purport to lead to. A number of source books are, however, listed in the Bibliography.

Deciding where to look for information is something that cannot be learned from textbooks. Long experience and the mind of a detective are the assets in this respect. To be on good terms with the creators of the data, such as the statisticians in various government departments, is very useful. To be discerning as to the reliability and validity of the data produced, is even more so.

One useful short cut is worth mentioning. An annual subscription to Aslib (Associations of Special Libraries and Information Bureau) not only gives access to almost all the important specialised libraries in the country, but provides a bibliographical research service without additional charge. A request for bibliographical material on any subject matter will bring, in about four to six weeks, a very full list of references. Similarly, a subscription to the *British Technology Index* can be a considerable time-saver. The index, which is issued ten times a year, plus a cumulative index, gives references to a very large range of subjects covering many hundreds of technical journals and newspapers, both British and foreign.

FIELD SURVEYS

In certain favourable circumstances, desk research will provide all the data required because the facts which cover the terms of reference will have been unearthed. There remains only their evaluation and presentation in the research report. To end an industrial marketing research project here, however, will be the exception rather than the rule. More often than not, desk research will have covered only part of the ground and it will have provided the framework within which those questions which cannot be answered by it, can be formulated.

The research team must be absolutely sure that they have exhausted their internal and external sources of information. They then have to decide how best to uncover the information still missing. It is at this point that field research can be considered.

Field research must be the sole responsibility of an executive experienced in this work. Naturally, he must also have the right to draw on the knowledge of other members of the research department or organisation. He should direct the research effort and in doing so no one ought to interfere with his decisions.

His is then the responsibility for producing a field research schedule. He will have to decide which of the many ways in which marketing research can be undertaken, is the best for the particular study. He will either ask for a certain sum of money or, more often, he will know how much he is allowed to spend. Whichever is the case the sponsor should be made quite aware of the fact that he will obtain as much research as he pays for. It is not good business procedure to try to obtain marketing research on the cheap. There are many actions the researcher can take in order to obtain his results. Among these actions there are also short cuts. If he has not sufficient money to produce a first class piece of work, he will produce a second class one.

The principle must be that either the research study can be commissioned for a certain outlay of money, or it cannot. It is much better not to undertake the study at all in the second case, for poor research is worse than none. By providing facts, marketing research assists in obtaining a higher proportion of correct decisions than would otherwise be possible. Poor research will produce incorrect information and the process of decision making will become more hazardous.

Time is an important factor. The research executive in charge of a survey must be able to calculate the time for the field work, taking all factors into consideration, which will help or hinder him to finish the study. All this he will incorporate into his research proposals after he has completed his desk research. He will also have to establish finally the facts which must be discovered by means of field research. This needs not only experience, but also creative imagination, for the good researcher will have the final report in mind during the whole period of the field work.

UNIVERSE AND SAMPLING

The first of the problems with which the researcher has to grapple is to decide which are the companies to be selected for interview and within those companies, who are the people who should be interviewed. This question is often easier posed than answered. In order to come to the right conclusions, it is necessary to discover who uses the product or service to be researched, and who might use it if made aware of its characteristics, who manufactures or provides it, and who influences decisions to purchase or use it.

When the universe is defined, the next problem is to discover whether any exhaustive lists exist of companies and individuals comprising the universe. This is the sampling frame and its completeness is a condition of successful field research. In most cases a ready made list does not exist or, if it does, it is not complete. Thus the researcher is compelled to compile his own list; this is often a tiresome task in which directories (more often than not incomplete and misleading), membership lists of trade associations, rating lists and other sources, both obvious and obscure, are used. Only in very rare circumstances can a ready made sampling frame be found, as in the case of activities for which membership of a recognised professional organisation is a requirement of practice. Even these lists will have to be scrutinised carefully in order to eliminate organisations or individuals who do not come within the definition of the universe.

Having established the universe, the researcher will then have to decide on the best way of sampling it. It is a statistical law that a sample will represent the whole—that is, the universe—faithfully, only if all members of the universe have the same chance of being selected for the sample. In industrial marketing research, sampling may be abandoned altogether and a complete census taken. That is, every member of the universe will be included. This is the practice when the number of units of which the universe consists is small. In other cases, the industry to be surveyed will be composed of a small number of large companies and a comparatively large number of small ones. In these circumstances it would be a mistake to apply the normal sampling procedures, for it could happen that important parts of the universe will not get into the sample. It is much better to interview all large companies and sample a proportion of the small ones. If data are available, with which to establish the size of the companies concerned, stratified sampling can be used by first dividing the universe into say large, medium sized and small companies and sample these strata disproportionately to their numbers, but proportionately to their size. Similarly, criteria other than size can be adopted, provided it is relevant to the research objectives. For example, types of equipment installed, geographical locations and types of markets supplied.

There are many other problems connected with sampling and only a few can be mentioned. A certain product may be used by smaller companies more frequently than by larger ones. Since this distribution may not be known beforehand, the whole sampling procedure may have to be reconsidered during the survey, and a sequential approach to interviewing adopted. Some products may be used by more than one industry. The universe then consists of several sub-universes. The problem here is how to combine them in order to achieve a balanced sample. Official statistics, like the Census of Production, can be of great assistance for this purpose, but an intimate knowledge of industry is also necessary.

Thus the ingenuity of the marketing researcher will often be heavily taxed in order to arrive at a representative sample, but it must be based on the sound knowledge of the statistical principles of sampling.

INTERVIEWING TECHNIQUES

The marketing research executive will still have to decide which method of interviewing to use in the survey. Sometimes he will come to the conclusion that more than one method can be usefully employed. There are several recognised ways in which interviews can be conducted. The decision which to adopt will hinge on two factors: which is the most appropriate method and is this method possible within the framework of the budget?

The personal interview is in almost every case the most expensive technique. In spite of this, it is still the most often used because it is generally accepted that it yields the best results although its deficiencies are also well known. There are two ingredients for the successful conduct of personal interviews: the interviewer and the interview brief.

What sort of interviewer should be employed in industrial marketing research? Opinions differ in this respect. One interviewer can do an excellent job for one type of survey, but not for another. Generally speaking, the interviewer must have a thorough training. It is of little value for someone with a knowledge of the subject matter of the study to carry out the field interview, if he has not been trained in the art of interviewing. This training has many aspects from being shown the correct way to approach a respondent to dealing with the tensions of the interview and the development of rapport with the respondent to concluding the interview in a manner which leaves the way open for further approaches. However, the foremost training objective is to get the interviewer to appreciate his own attitude to the research project.

It is a very difficult task indeed not to give indications of personal opinions about the subject matter of the interview. The more technically expert the interviewer is, the more firmly will he have made up his own mind what the correct answers to his questions should be. Unless he is trained not to disclose his opinions, the interview will be invalid because of the bias exerted by the interviewer. If the interviewer cannot suppress his own ideas, he will tend to record only those answers, or the parts of those answers, which conform with his own opinions. Repeated experiments have shown that respondents will carefully watch the interviewer in order to discover what he wants them to say. They do this consciously or unconsciously in order not to lose face and also in order to please the person with whom they are having the discussion.

But while technical expertise can be a disadvantage, interviewers in industrial marketing research must have a sound knowledge of the subject matter. They will be interviewing all types of respondents—engineers, scientists, accountants and others from board level down to the shop floor. Unless respondents in the interview feel that the interviewer has a good knowledge of the subject which he is discussing, they will tend to lose interest in the interview and to seek to terminate it at the earliest possible moment.

Because not every word that is being said can be recorded in the interview situation, it is essential for the interviewer to assess quickly what the salient points are. However, all this does not mean to say that the interviewer must be a specialist in the narrow field of the research study. It is sufficient for him to have a broad knowledge of the industry concerned, to understand the product or service surveyed, and to be intelligent enough to profit by a thorough briefing of the details of the investigation.

The most important interviewing tool is the formulation of the interview objectives which is the basis of the brief for the interviewer. Interviews can be broken down into three types—structured, semi-structured and unstructured (or non-directive). For the first and second types of interview a questionnaire is necessary. It takes long experience in order to construct a questionnaire which will fulfil its purpose—to elicit correct answers to specific questions which, in the aggregate, cover the subject matter of the survey. Most words of every language are ambiguous and people misinterpret questions which seem, at first glance, perfectly simple and straightforward. Moreover there are many psychological aspects to be considered for even the sequence in which questions are asked can falsify the answers given. Thus, the questionnaire should be tested with a few respondents before the bulk of the field work starts. This is not always possible because the number of interviews may be too small to allow for such pilot investigations. That is why it often takes many hours of discussions among several people before the questionnaire is finalised.

There are several types of questionnaires. The formal questionnaire—not often encountered in industrial marketing research—where the question wording must not be changed nor the sequence in which the questions are incorporated into the questionnaire. Free questionnaires are found more frequently. No formalised questions are devised and the interviewer is at liberty to change from one subject to another according to the situation in which he finds himself during the interview.

The third type of interview, and the one which is most commonly used in industrial marketing research, the non-directive interview, is not based upon a questionnaire at all, but upon a thorough briefing for the interviewer in both the research objectives and the objectives of the particular interview. It is left to the interviewer to work his way towards the research objectives by whatever routes he thinks are most appropriate. The great disadvantage of the structured and semi-structured questionnaires is overcome in that the respondent is not forced along a predetermined line of conversation. The interviewer in a non-directive interview can allow the respondent to wander across and about the subject and yet still bring him back to the research objective without in any way turning the interview from a conversation into an examination.

The personal interview is, in most cases, highly successful in industrial marketing research. After all, the conversation turns round the job the respondent is engaged in. Talking shop is a favourite hobby of most people and they will more often than not answer everything and more, even if they have made up their mind beforehand not to allow the conversation to go beyond a certain point.

The major difficulty, perhaps, is gaining entry to busy people. Once in the interviewing situation a problem often arises when to finish the interview because it is the wish of the respondent to go into more detail than is necessary for the purpose of the survey. Hence, the interviewer has to learn how to gain entrance and then the respondent's confidence and finally, the most appropriate way of terminating the interview.

Psychological investigations are also gaining ground in industrial marketing research. These are generally conducted by trained psychologists as depth interviews, in order to discover attitudes which are hidden to the respondents themselves. Answers which could not be obtained by direct questions can often be provided by recourse to depth interviewing.

It can easily be seen that the personal interview can be expensive. The interviewer, whether full time or part-time, has to be paid for his work and the number of really good interviewers is severely restricted. In addition to the length of time an interview might take, further time is required for making appointments and for travelling to and from the locations of the respondents, who may be scattered around the country. Thus, cheaper and quicker means of acquiring facts have had to be devised for use in types of surveys where the advantages stemming from the inter-personal factors of an interview are not required.

One of the alternative techniques is the telephone interview. As every organisation in industry is on the telephone, no additional problems of sampling arise. The difficulty consists in the fact that the telephone interviewers must have a certain personality, the characteristics of which have so far eluded definition. The best that can be said is that they must have a 'telephone manner' which is acceptable to the respondent within a few seconds. Further, the number of questions which can be asked over the telephone, is severely restricted and some questions cannot be asked at all. It is difficult to ask a respondent to look up his files in order to answer certain questions, or to consult a colleague; yet this happens very often in face to face interviewing situations.

Another alternative to the personal interviews are the mail questionnaires. They are not, however, as cheap as is generally supposed. This is because the costs are generally calculated on a 'per thousand' basis, whereas in fact, the real cost is the valid reply rate. Often, to get a substantial response, second and third follow-up letters have to be despatched. Whatever the response rate may be the replies are not representative because those who do reply, differ in some way from those who do not bother. In some cases, personal interviews with a sub-sample of those who did not reply to the original mail questionnaire can be conducted in order to see whether and what the differences are between the two groups.

Mail questionnaires must contain only a very limited number of questions and these must be so simple that they can be answered by ticking the pre-printed reply form. Nevertheless, despite these shortcomings mail questionnaires have proved their worth especially where qualitative information is being sought.

A cheap and simple technique which is often overlooked in industrial marketing research, is that of observation. A considerable volume of information can be obtained merely by visual checks, for example, the incorporation of certain types of components in other products or uses other than that intended by the manufacturer for products. These can be a valuable pointer to the quantities consumed. Very often the interviewer is shown round the building he is visiting. He can obtain a great deal of information by observing the size of the operations, the number of machines and the number of workers. From these observations he can deduce a great deal about the firm. Everything depends on the interviewer himself because he has to know what to look for.

From these several research tools, it is the responsibility of the research executive in charge of the survey to decide upon which are to be utilised and the appropriate mix. His responsibility in this respect is very great because upon the research mix will depend the time, the cost and the information yield of the survey.

ANALYSING AND REPORTING THE RESULTS

After all the research efforts have come to an end and the secondary and primary research data have been gathered, the research team is faced with a large number of documents which have to be combined into a logical whole. The first step is to edit the questionnaires; at this point omissions and contradictory statements will be discovered. Sometimes it is even advisable to contact respondents again, in order to clear up any ambiguities or misunderstandings which may have arisen. Numerical information will have to be assembled and analysed by hand or by machine.

Coding is the second step. This is essential (particularly if punched cards are to be used), in order to compress the information obtained in such a way that it can be assembled on a single card. The coding is followed by punching the cards and then verifying them.

Once the results are obtained, whether from machine or from hand tabulations, it is of utmost importance to verify every figure—the third step. This can be done in various ways. Obvious exaggerations or under-statements can be discovered and rectified. The results of the desk research sometimes contain overall figures in which those of the interviews should fit. The best method of verification, however, lies in the questionnaires themselves. The most significant questions can often be asked in different ways. When the answers are compared it may happen that they are the same for all the questions. If the answers to most of the questions yield the same results then further probing or re-analysis usually shows them to be correct. If a reconciliation cannot be made then something is seriously wrong and the inquiries have to be repeated to probe the cause of the discrepancies.

The fourth activity is the construction of tables where the skill of the statistician comes into play. The answers have to be classified in a meaning-ful way and this is sometimes easier said than done. Class intervals have to be decided on. It depends on the correctness of these intervals whether the results are distorted or not. The tables have to be simple in order to be understood yet, at the same time, they have to contain all the relevant information. Connections between figures referring to different questions have to be detected and cross-tabulations have to be made in order to see whether these connections really exist. Qualitative answers have to be quantified. This always involves a loss of information and it is up to the researcher to minimise this loss.

The figures themselves are meaningless to the unskilled eye. They have to be interpreted and explained. The report has to be organised in a logical way, giving every piece of useful information and eliminating the inessen-tial. Thus, judgement has to be used all the time and the quality of the report depends upon the researcher's skill to extract as much as possible from the raw data and to organise the knowledge thus gained in an orderly and meaningful way.

The fifth and last stage is the writing of the report. The usual form is first to present the findings briefly, then interpret them, and finally draw the conclusions. This must be done without fear or favour. A survey some-times explodes preconceived ideas which is, to say the least, uncomfortable. The reaction sometimes is to blame the researcher for having found facts which show up the deficiencies of a course of action already decided upon, or suggest a change from an existing routine.

Thus it can be seen that in addition to a knowledge of statistical method, a logical mind and a grasp of affairs the researcher has also to be able to withstand pressure from whatever source it may come. He must be convinced that he has approached the study in a completely objective way and that he has presented the findings in the same spirit. Based on this conviction he is in a position to write a report, clear, simple and constructive, not omitting anything of value, nor overloading it with ephemeral matter.

This, however, is not the end, for the report has to be presented and discussed with the sponsor and his responsible staff. In many cases, this presentation meeting takes place before the written report is handed over. This is done in order to avoid the possibility of everybody reading into the report what they wish to see and overlooking the less comforting parts.

CONCLUSION

Industrial marketing research is what the word *research* indicates: a search for the best method of discovering the facts objectively and correctly. There are still only a few general rules which can be applied. The industrial marketing researcher has to rely upon his past experience and on the experience of his colleagues. He has to apply his creative imagination in order to find solutions to problems with which he has not been faced before. Yet industrial marketing research has come to stay. In the last few years its expansion has been remarkable. It is to be hoped that this does not mean a dilution of the effort and that each newcomer to the field will contribute to the general body of knowledge. Much of the success of industrial marketing research and, therefore, of its usefulness to management depends upon the position of the research department in the hierarchy of the company—a fact strongly emphasised in the preceding chapter.

Industrial marketing research can do its job properly for management only when it is free from the pressures developing in almost every business or, at least, when it is in a position to withstand these pressures. There is only *one* truth and it is the task of the marketing researcher to find and to report it.

Industrial Selling

DAVID ROWE, M.A.

Selling is a personal confrontation. The 'oral presentation in a conversation with one or more prospective purchasers for the purpose of making sales'.[1] There is no intrinsic reason why this confrontation should be different in what is called consumer goods selling than in what is called industrial goods selling. The Institute of Marketing, for example, draw the main selling division between 'repeat' selling and 'durable goods' selling and treat consumer goods and industrial goods as sub-categories of each of their two broad classifications.[2]

Another classification of types of selling which does not expressly refer to the consumer goods/industrial goods split at all is 'cold selling', 'development selling', 'missionary selling', 'new product selling', 'service selling', 'systems selling', 'team selling' and 'retail selling'.[3]

One could go on categorising and re-categorising. The fact which emerges is that industrial goods selling is too broad a category to discuss meaningfully without some preliminary narrowing down. The salesman who sells industrial abrasives or nuts and bolts to stockists or the salesman who sells office supplies has very little in common with the man who sells machine tools, chemical raw materials or aircraft. On the other hand the consumer goods salesman who, after years of patient effort, lands a major contract to supply Marks and Spencer may well have had very similar problems and met them in a very similar way to the industrial salesman who wins a contract for the supply of a component to one of the motor car manufacturers.

In spite of all this overlap, however, most industrial goods involve selling problems which are very different from those encountered in the consumer goods field. In general, in industrial markets the number of possible outlets is smaller, sales forces are smaller, selling usually involves a

---

1. *Definition of Terms.* American Marketing Association (Chicago, 1961), page 18.
2. *A Manual of Sales Management,* Institute of Marketing & Sales Management by Pitman (London, 1961).
3. J. P. Matthews, R. B. Buzzell, T. Levitt, R. E. Frank, *Marketing,* McGraw-Hill (New York, 1964), Chapter 16.

detailed technical knowledge, each sales visit is of much longer duration, contacts between buyer and seller tend to be more elaborate involving many other departments in both firms in addition to those concerned with sales and purchasing.

SALESMAN'S QUALITIES

Of course, all selling requires certain basic qualities, although these qualities may be required with varying amounts of emphasis. Drive, determination to go on trying, personality, being a good listener, being conscious of one's prospect's reactions, having a 'feel' of the sales situation. The analysis has recently been carried back to two basic qualities—empathy and ego-drive.[1]

Ego-drive we can all recognise in one form or another. We hear the importance of this particular quality in successful selling beaten out *ad nauseam*—it is equally a quality which any successful line manager must have. But what about empathy? The *Oxford Dictionary* defines it as 'the power of projecting one's personality into, and so fully understanding, the object of contemplation'. No salesman can sell well without this invaluable and irreplaceable ability to get a powerful feedback from his prospect. Unfortunately the two qualities of ego-drive and empathy are not too commonly found together.

Empathy, which should not be confused with sympathy, is particularly important in industrial selling because there is less room for a stereotyped sales approach relying on a statistical chance of success. Theodore Levitt[2] talks of 'sensitivity' as being a key, but rarely recognised, quality and this is essentially the same thing as empathy. Levitt rightly sees sensitivity as a top management quality—equally it must be a salesman's.

The essential distinguishing feature of industrial selling, as we have narrowed it down, is closely related to, indeed is in a sense an extension of, the empathetic quality. It is the explorative function of the salesman. Industrial organisations are much more unlike each other than people. At least people have, barring accidents, the same number of arms and legs, are mostly between five feet and six feet tall, have the same essential needs; and even their differences are capable of statistical treatment. With companies, differences in size, in relationship and control, in product, and in organisation structure, are infinite. And then upon this are superimposed all the problems of individual human preferences and distastes but again involving not just a family group but a whole organisation.

No two firms have quite the same reasons for buying the same product. This is one of the reasons why capital goods and even raw materials manufacturers are permanently under pressure to produce products specially tailored to meet each specific customer's requirements. Where these

1. D. Mayer and H. Greenberg, 'What Makes a Good Salesman', *Harvard Business Review* (Cambridge, Mass., U.S.A. July/Aug. 1964).
2. Theodore Levitt, *Innovation in Marketing*, McGraw-Hill, (New York, 1962), page 36.

kinds of differences exist, it is quite clear that in addition to the overall research into user requirements a further research into each individual prospective user is required. It is no longer safe to take the prospective purchaser's own statement of his requirements on trust. If your company does not supply something which exactly fits the customer's actual rather than imagined needs a competitor will sooner or later take that business from you.

Thus, in the industrial field, each individual prospective customer of any size needs to be researched into. Obviously this cannot be the work of a central marketing research organisation. The marketing researchers can only assess the market as a whole, indicate likely developments and point to overall customer needs. The exploration of each individual firm in depth has to be left to the salesman. He must know his customer's business almost as well as his own. Carl Rieser makes a particularly persuasive case for the role of the new type of salesman.[1]

The man who cannot take this kind of explorative interest in his prospects and their problems, whatever his other attributes, will never succeed in industrial selling for three reasons. He will fail to fit his product range to his prospects' requirements; he will fail to locate the man who takes the buying decision and the people who influence that decision; and over the long period of time involved in creating a new industrial customer his lack of real interest will show through. A deep knowledge of a customer's business is the easiest way to flatter him. Trying to get a company's business without taking the trouble to acquire this knowledge is almost the surest way of insulting it.

Most industrial products call for considerable technical knowledge on the part of the salesman. In some fields it is essential that the salesman should be an engineer. This is perhaps particularly the case where he is dealing with capital goods of the type which are tailor-made to each customer's requirements. It is, however, remarkable how much technical knowledge, in a narrow field, a non-technical salesman can acquire. Perhaps this should not be regarded as too surprising when it is remembered how much detailed technical knowledge an intelligent marketing research assistant can pick up in the course of a market survey. The need for technical knowledge should never be allowed to overrule the absolute necessity for the two basic qualities of empathy and ego-drive.

A worthwhile industrial salesman has got to be promotable material. This follows from the fact that he must mix at management level in the firms he is selling to. He will certainly get nowhere if he imagines that sales of important industrial materials result from interviews with the buyer in the buyer's office during which the salesman occupies a position emotionally similar to an applicant for a job. Somehow he has to obtain for himself a position of equality—this is fundamentally probably the most important reason for the invitation to lunch.

1. Carl Rieser, 'The Salesman Isn't Dead—He's Different', *Fortune* (Chicago November 1962).

Of course, in order to establish the justification for a regular contact at management level the salesman must have something to say which is particularly relevant to his prospects' business. This is one very strong reason for having your salesman specialise more by industries rather than by area. In this way he can become a really important disseminator of non-confidential information about industry developments and, of course, he develops a specialised knowledge of possible applications. Because of the tendency for some industries to be concentrated geographically this industry specialisation is often obtained inside a framework of area representation. The Birmingham representative, for instance, almost inevitably knows about the motor industry.

A salesman must be incisive, able to present his technical case and efficient in seeing that his promises about samples, literature and so forth are carried out. In fact the industrial salesman has more and more to accept that his job involves some element of administration. With increasingly complex products to sell he is unlikely to obtain really important accounts without deploying the whole range of his company's resources. There will be visits from technical service personnel to arrange, works trials, possibly meetings between senior management to organise and possibly a visit to the supplier's factory. These are just a few of the more or less routine details which a salesman must take the initiative in organising and progressing. If they go wrong inevitably the company acquires a reputation for inefficiency. If, however, the salesman organises well, prospects often develop an almost invincible belief in the efficiency and reliability of the whole of the supplier's operation.

It is often argued that a salesman is only productive when he is actually making calls and that, for this reason, the administrative and office content of his job should be kept to a minimum. In the consumer goods field this is probably true. Equally clearly it contains an element of truth for the industrial salesman also, but it ignores three increasingly important facts. First, a salesman who sees his job as involving an administrative element, who knows that it is his job to see that his promises to a customer are turned into facts is also likely to have a deeper appreciation of the potentialities and weaknesses of his own company's organisation. This salesman is more likely to be 'level-headed' and in fact will probably be the sort of person to whom a buyer will respond. Secondly, industrial salesmen must plan not merely their itineraries but also the details of how they propose to set about winning or holding each individual account. This kind of planning involves the collection of facts, the preparation of arguments and may involve discussion with technical colleagues. Salesmen should be encouraged to take planning very seriously indeed and to do this planning in office hours. Here again, the ones who do will find that the time they spend with customers is more productive. Thirdly, in the industrial field the salesman has truly to represent his company. He has to be *the* point of contact with the customer. If he is not actively concerned in guiding all communications between the two organisations there will be no one at the supplier's end who has all the facts, no one who can make really valid recommendations. If this happens the buyer will soon feel that no one in the supplier's firm is in control, and no one is very much concerned about his business.

The industrial salesman has to be a principal—not merely a canvasser. The case for this wider role of the salesman as an administrator has been powerfully advocated in *Fortune Magazine*.[1] Significantly, with I.B.M. as co-sponsor, *Fortune* have now produced a film as a result of the great interest which was shown in the feature.

SALES LITERATURE

Particularly at the beginning of a sales approach, much the most effective way of getting the image of efficiency across is by good sales literature. Today one should certainly add to this technical films.

The value of really good technical sales literature to the salesman cannot be overestimated. If a company's literature is well prepared, technically good and oriented towards the customer's needs he has good reason to assume that the company's product will be these things also. And the reverse is very much the case.

Technical sales literature which represents a genuine and serious attempt to describe the product, its advantages and its applications is an opportunity to display the competence of the selling company. Without it, advertising loses its purpose, because there is no point in getting an enquiry in response to an advertisement if the literature that is sent off in reply does not carry the recipient one stage further. Similarly, good literature gives a point around which a sales argument can be developed. Without good literature a salesman, however competent, has to fit in an apology somewhere.

It is generally true that no one outside the publicity department ever wants to give priority to work on technical literature. Yet if it is to be good it needs the close attention of the best sales and technical personnel. Unfortunately preparing or editing drafts is for them a chore which takes them away from their, apparently, much more important day to day activities. Often it is something they are expected to do in the evenings.

THE BUYER'S OUTLOOK

Having emphasised the importance to the salesman of being able to put himself in the buyer's position it is relevant to examine more closely what the buyer is trying to achieve. This has been dealt with in great detail in Chapter 2 but it is useful to examine at least one aspect of his objectives against the background of a specific problem in selling.

The primary goal of the buyer in a manufacturing company is to assist his firm to produce a cheaper or a better product. This in turn means he is

1. Ibid.

concerned not only with price and quality but also with reliability and service; with maintaining competition between suppliers so that he can have some yardstick for measuring the keenness of prices; with running costs rather than merely initial cost; with economies to be gained from using one supplier's product rather than another's. The emphasis on economies is a particularly noticeable feature of industrial buying when compared with consumer buying. It is very well illustrated by comparing the criteria involved in the purchase of a commercial vehicle and a private car.

Salesmen too often assume that their product is out on price when this is not in fact the case. It can be a very salutory experience to use simulation techniques in training industrial salesmen in which a group of salesmen are given the basic facts on which a buying decision is made and asked to arrive at their decision. In one large company where this technique is used salesmen are often astonished to find that they have, for very good reasons, given part of the business to a supplier whose price, to start with, looked impossibly high.

During the past twenty years the buying function has been brought to a previously unsuspected degree of professionalism and this process is continuing. The work of the Purchasing Officers' Association has been notable in this field. More and more, buyers are attempting to quantify the various factors involved in the purchasing decision. It is, however, easy to underestimate the difficulty of trying to place data which are not readily comparable on a comparable basis giving weight to the various benefits and disadvantages involved. In the modern company the communications problems are very considerable. How is the buyer to know that the works could adjust the specification of a particular component so that a metal pressing could be used rather than a casting? How is he to know that, if necessary, the works can cope quite easily with an increase in impurities in a particular chemical when the last thing the production people may want to do is to admit the fact? Attempts are now being made to deal with these sorts of problems by means of 'value analysis' or 'value engineering'.

In 1964 the British Productivity Council published sixteen case studies in value analysis.[1] It is significant that in seven of these cases reference is made to the advantage to be gained from bringing the supplier's salesman and technical people into the company's discussions. In several of the case studies the actual suggestions for product improvement or cost adjustment which were adopted came from a supplier's representative.

Intra-firm communication will become progressively more difficult as technology becomes more complicated. The buyer must more and more see his professional role in sufficiently understanding the functions and techniques of purchasing. In many large firms he and his staff cannot hope to be experts in all the products the firm buys. He must buy to the specifications drawn up by the company's technical staff and once a specification

1. *Sixteen Case Studies in Value Analysis.* British Productivity Council (London, 1964).

has been drawn up there are many forces inside the firm which are opposed to change. The salesman has a particularly important opportunity in trying to bridge these communications gaps inside the firms he is selling to. Some professional buyers are not unaware of this and, for this reason, after initial contact has been made, encourage salesmen to make contact direct with the company's design staff and engineers. 'Value analysis' affords a most useful way of institutionalising this contact.

BREAKING DOWN BARRIERS

The attempt to win an industrial customer, at least for a major raw material or component usually occupies months and often years. There is no short cut. A firm is either trying to sell an established product which means ousting the competitor in possession, or it is trying to introduce a new product, which usually involves change in the prospect's organisation. Change is always uncomfortable and there will always be conservative forces in any human groups. And, of course, the more revolutionary the advantages the less the salesman is likely to be believed.

In all cases the barriers of distrust and suspicion have to be broken down.[1] In repeat-selling goods such as raw materials and components, it is fair to postulate that you will not often win an important customer until in addition to all the other factors an actual friendship has been created. This is because you cannot expect to have any permanent properties or price advantage over your competitors and particularly over the competitor in possession. If the competitor is doing its job properly it will almost certainly be given some kind of opportunity to match your price unless influential people in the company actually want to place business with you. But they will wish to do this only if the salesman is liked and has created a good impression; if his company has shown itself willing to put itself out to help and if it really looks as if it wants the business.

THE EMPHASIS ON INTANGIBLES

The fact that a company in competitive conditions cannot expect to maintain a product/price advantage for very long has intensified the need to provide non-product advantages. These are generally lumped under the omnibus groupings of 'reliability' and 'service'.

'Reliability' means many things—delivery on time, maintaining a quality standard, a knowledge on the part of the buyer that if something unforeseen does go wrong in manufacture the supplier will not try to cover it up. For instance a buyer who is buying a large forging has a feeling of confidence if he knows that any unforeseen problem in this difficult manufacturing process will be reported and not simply hidden until it appears as an unmet delivery date. With notice of the problem he may have time to suggest a re-organisation of his own company's product schedule.

1. 'The Contactual Function in Marketing', op. cit.

A company which uses a plastic raw material wants to know that everything it gets is in specification not by a hair's breadth but by a fair margin. If a batch is borderline a telephone call from the supplier about the position often produces the reply, 'OK, we will take it and exercise special care in our process'. Sometimes perhaps there may have to be a reduction in price but the openness of the supplier's approach is a powerful sales tool and is not forgotten.

'Service' can mean almost anything, from nothing more than a regular visit from the representative to something approaching free consultancy. Many companies in the raw materials field, metals, plastics, chemicals, will give most comprehensive technical advice which not infrequently involves duplicating the purchasers' manufacturing conditions in their own laboratories and helping to design the purchasers' product. This kind of service, which is more particularly discussed in Chapter 10, can prove very expensive indeed. So much so that it not infrequently happens that the supplier is vulnerable to a new entrant who might be called a 'discount' seller—the industrial equivalent of the discount house.

On the other hand it is surprising how much really appreciated service can be given by just one really intelligent salesman who has attuned his thinking to his customer's requirements. Is the material for instance being ordered in the best available packing? A booklet published in 1964 on the costing of materials handling[1] quotes an example of a small firm which had always ordered sixteen-foot lengths of small diameter steel bars which it then cut into one foot lengths. A consultant discovered that in fact the steel mill cut sixteen-foot lengths specifically for that buyer because he ordered it that way. They were able subsequently to deliver one-foot lengths and make a price reduction because they were able to use offcuts. This story reflects very much against the salesmen of the supplying organisation. They missed a first class opportunity to provide 'service'.

The growth of systems selling is all part of the attempt to sell a complex of qualities which can more easily be differentiated from one's competitors. I.B.M. and I.C.T. do not sell computers, they sell data processing systems. The design of the system, the staff training programme and the computer software matter as much as the choice of the machines themselves. Heating and ventilating contractors sell air conditioning systems, not just the hardware. If you want your plant automated, again it is a system you are sold.

EXTENDING THE SALESMAN'S REACH

The greater duration of an industrial salesman's calls—he will rarely manage more than four or five in a day—makes the problem of getting round a territory in adequate depth extremely difficult. It means that calling merely for the purpose of showing the flag is not easy to fit in. It is

1. First Report of a Study Group convened by the Institute of Production Engineers at the request of the National Joint Council on Materials Handling and in association with the British Institute of Management and the Institute of Materials Handling.

here that direct mail to a carefully selected mailing list can be most valuable. If this technique is properly used it can mean that the difficult opening part of establishing an acceptable contact with a new prospect is very much eased. Well conceived and executed direct mailing establishes the supplier's name with the recipient. Other techniques which can be integrated into the sales programme are of course, the cocktail party, cinema show, and trade fair or exhibition. All these provide opportunities for salesmen to get in what is, effectively, a high rate of calling. Cocktail parties coupled with the showing of a good technical film or with the release of new technical literature or a new product—there has to be a good reason—are hard to beat and need not be expensive. At a provincial centre, a supplier can get people driving in from as far as forty miles around and the true cost is appreciably less than that of an equivalent number of individual calls. At the same time by bringing in the selling firm's higher levels of management and people from the factory and from research one can create a company image in a way which some of the less successful representatives may signally have failed to do.

Trade fairs or exhibitions vary very much in value according to the product one is trying to sell. They suffer from the obvious disadvantage that all one's competitors are also there. One field where exhibitions are of crucial importance is that of machine tools and capital equipment. It is not an accident that it is this sector of industry that has placed most stress on the importance of improving United Kingdom exhibition facilities.

A less obvious technique is the telephone. It is unfortunately true that salesmen are not encouraged to use this means of communication largely because there is always a feeling throughout management that a salesman in the office is wasting time. Telephoning is more and more essential for the administrative aspect of the salesman's job concerned with the organising of visits, samples, works trials, feasibility studies and quotations. Its other uses are discouraged by many managements because a telephone call 'doesn't count'. A twenty-five mile drive resulting in an abortive visit nevertheless goes down as a visit but a telephone call, even a useful one, does not even merit a report form. It may often render a visit unnecessary and so upset the salesman's itinerary in a way he would sooner avoid.

The telephone will often get a salesman further than he would get on foot. Everyone defers to the telephone. The man on the telephone invariably takes precedence over the man in the room. The telephone imparts urgency and efficiency. Its controlled use can tremendously extend salesmen's reach and effectiveness.

CUSTOMERS' CUSTOMERS

Many manufacturers now employ salesmen whose job is specifically to develop the markets for the products in which their materials will be used. This type of 'back selling' is often supported by advertising of the sort which I.C.I. use for plastics, Fibreglass Ltd. for reinforced plastics or the steel industry through its trade association. It can bring great benefits. The company very quickly becomes attuned to the factors which will influence its future sales. It acquires a knowledge of customer problems which can help its sales campaigns. It also receives enquiries for its customers' products which it is able to channel through the area salesmen to its customers. This latter can be a very very useful sales tool indeed. It is often part of the 'service' package.

Sales development representatives can also be used to handle contacts with specifying authorities, with consulting engineers and others. Where an area salesman has a territory which unavoidably has a small number of very important companies to visit and very little else, it is often useful to allow him to do a little sales development of his own. Many enterprising salesmen do in fact do this and so deepen their understanding of customers' problems whilst at the same time just occasionally bringing their customer an enquiry.

MANAGING INDUSTRIAL SALESMEN

In contrast with consumer goods selling, industrial sales forces tend to be very small. In some fields as few as ten salesmen will be enough to cover the whole country. A sales force of fifty to one hundred is large. The nature of the work, however, may involve a relatively sizeable team of sales correspondents in the sales office.

It is, however, almost impossible to generalise about the organisation and position inside the company of the sales team. In engineering companies concerned largely with the manufacture of tailor-made plant the sales force's chief job may be no more than getting enquiries which are then taken over and progressed by powerful product managers who have their own tendering teams and are responsible for such things as pricing and design. In fields where the product is more standardised the sales manager takes the pricing decision and may control a technical service force as well as his salesmen.

The industrial goods sales manager tends to do a great deal of selling himself. This is often inevitable. Important customers often demand special treatment. In fact not infrequently the managing director himself may be their salesman. This can easily be so in the case of the company which is a components supplier to a motor manufacturer. However, whilst the sales manager must undertake some personal selling it is essential that his first job should be that of controlling, motivating and directing his salesmen.

In practice, liaison between salesmen and sales managers often breaks down, even where district sales managers are inserted in the chain of command. Certainly industrial sales force management, as management, lacks the professionalism of the consumer goods field. The most likely reason is that the market is so different. Instead of between several thousand or several hundred thousand outlets of graded ranges of importance there are usually between five and fifty really important potential buyers and then a periphery of a few hundred or a few thousand small firms who can't be ignored because several of them are sure to become important in the next decade. Moreover companies have their liaisons, their cross-relationships and their reciprocal buying arrangements. Such a type of market can impose sudden demands and sudden problems, of what can only be described as a political nature, which can play havoc with the attempt to develop a management system.

The non-homogeneous nature of the industrial market also greatly complicates the problem of finding any acceptable measurement of a salesman's performance. Certainly it is not generally possible to divide territories so that they have a broadly similar potential. For this reason it is too easy to assess salesmen not so much on effectiveness as on how methodical they are and how many calls they make—important qualities but very often not the qualities of the best salesmen.

There is no alternative to a systematic analysis of each salesman's territory account by account, followed by the setting of a forecast target agreed between the salesman and his manager. There must then be a regular review procedure so that difficulties can be examined and strategies worked out. This is particularly important when the salesmen's success inevitably involves the deployment of technical service personnel who may easily be overstretched if too many accounts become active at the same time.

Without a systematic review procedure it is fatally easy for salesmen to develop bad habits, to dilute their efforts over too many prospects and in consequence make an impact on none. Action is no good unless it is based on a plan and salesmen need to be guided towards their plans. 'The sales manager who draws out the conditions at the points of sale, possible buyer's reactions, the needs that might be uncovered and the skills the salesman might need to uncover them, becomes really involved in every salesman's job and can provide the guidance and motivation that will help each salesman get the most out of his territory.'[1]

CHANGING MARKET STRUCTURES

A major issue which cannot be ignored in any examination of industrial selling is the growth of the giant corporation, both public and private. For example, the electrical equipment industry which over much of its product range has substantially only one buyer in the United Kingdom has very different selling problems from those of the same industry in the U.S.A. Similarly concentration in the motor industry creates very special selling problems for component suppliers.

A particular aspect of this problem is the trend towards vertical integration. Selling synthetic fibres to the textile industry is becoming more a matter of buying up outlets rather than of using persuasion. It is note-

1. Frank W. Hankins, *Managing Industrial Salesmen*. Paper given at Indiana University 'First International Seminar on Marketing Management', 5th-18th February 1961.

worthy, however, that I.C.I. appears to favour the buying of a minority interest in textile manufacture rather than outright integration—in fact the formation of a loose alliance.

Almost every merger, if it is a worthwhile one, sooner or later involves a change in suppliers. In fact the merger, or at least the purchase of a minority interest, is becoming a most important sales tool. As the rate at which mergers take place increases every supplier in the industrial field is being obliged to develop its own philosophy on the use of this tool. Equally an industrial salesman needs to acquire a knowledge of interfirm financial relationships. Time can often be wasted trying to sell to a firm which already has a shareholding tie with a competitor. Reciprocal trading, whether stemming from financial connections or other reasons, is un-questionably an important factor which can require adjustment to normal sales methods and structure.

THE SELLING ROLE

The initial effect of the development of the marketing concept in the industrial field was to lead to a demotion of the sales force. The marketing department was set up to establish strategy. The salesman merely had to go out and sell. Marketing was for intellectuals; selling was for primitives. This attitude, which may have validity in the consumer field, has no part to play in the industrial field. An industrial marketing strategy must take into account the precise relations between the supplier and its major customers and prospective customers. This can only be done if the marketing team and the selling team work together as equals and talk the same language. The well-balanced marketing executive should have had experience both in selling and in planning. Only in this way can confidence be built up between the marketing and selling departments.

8

Industrial Advertising

MICHAEL DESOUTTER, D.L.C.

Advertising is almost universally accepted to be an extremely efficient tool in mass distribution. There are, however, three significant differences between the advertising of consumer products to mass markets and that of industrial products to what must be far smaller specialist markets. These differences tend to make industrial advertising more of a skill and an art where, on the other hand, much of the ground work in consumer advertising is a science.

The first of these differences is that the consumer product is usually advertised and sold to an individual, while the industrial product or service must be sold to a group of individuals. The decision to buy, while not actually made by a committee, is influenced by many different people—the buying influences—and it is the combined goodwill of these people that the industrial advertiser must win. Without question these people are far more knowledgeable about the products they buy for their firms than the average consumer is about his personal purchases. The second difference which stems from this is the difficulty already referred to in several previous chapters, of defining these buying influences in an industrial market compared with the relative simplicity of defining a market for a consumer product by age, sex and class. This leads one on immediately to the comparison of media where, in the consumer field, quite comprehensive readership or viewership analyses are available. In the industrial goods sector one is lucky to get an Audit Bureau of Circulation figure. Circulation breakdowns, where they are available, are a far cry from readership research. In the rare cases where readership research is undertaken it is invariably initiated by the publisher and must therefore be viewed with some reserve.

Finally, while industrial advertising budgets are far smaller, the cost of marketing research is higher, and comprehensive and reliable industrial marketing research can represent a disproportionately large percentage of an advertising budget. It is no secret that it is far cheaper to interview a few hundred housewives in a grocer's shop than it is to interview a few dozen works managers of general engineering plants.

In spite of these formidable difficulties there has to be a certain basic ground work and logic behind effective industrial advertising which leads to an advertising brief. From there on it is the job of a creative team to translate this brief into effective advertising.

OBJECTIVES

The basic objectives of industrial advertising cannot be more succinctly put than they have been in the classic McGraw-Hill advertisement which shows a grim-faced buyer seated in a chair, facing out of the page, with the legend:

> 'I don't know who you are.
> I don't know your company.
> I don't know your company's product.
> I don't know what your company stands for.
> I don't know your company's customers.
> I don't know your company's record.
> I don't know your company's reputation.
> Now—what was it you wanted to sell me?'

As a preliminary exercise, the advertiser might well ask himself the question posed above.

Before advertising, a company must consider its objectives and list them. Advertising is a tool of sales policy and it is quite wrong for a company to consider advertising before it has a written and agreed sales policy. From this will come the objectives of its advertising. Much is plain common sense. Obviously, a well established and respected company branching into a new product field has a vastly different problem from that of an entirely new company or a company already established in a product field.

The existence or not of real product differentials, as opposed to those seen only by the designer, will have a great bearing on the problem. Whether these are instantly apparent to users or will require an educational approach is another factor. Unless an educational programme is to be considered, it is essential that the discussions from which objectives are established should be heavily user oriented. Designers, development engineers and production engineers are usually too involved to be objective. Their thinking is also probably three years ahead of the market—that is their job.

It is the manufacturer who finds out what features his market currently considers to be truly significant who will get the most effective advertising. Obviously, one fruitful source of information will be sales reports and the salesmen's own views. There is a danger here of running foul of an excuse for not selling—this is usually oversimplified—rather than the hardcore reasons for sales resistance. It has been pointed out in Chapter 5 that the best salesmen do not make the most penetrating inquisitors.

The object of any advertising in the first instance must be to make clear to the reader what the advertiser does or makes. If it is a complicated service or product, its function must be described and its advantages shown. The next and more sophisticated stage is where there are a number of people making the same product. Provided the market is fully conversant with this type of product and its general advantages, all the emphasis in an advertisement may be put on a particular product plus of the advertised product. It is not always realised that the market seldom knows as much about the product group it buys as its manufacturers imagine it does. They are always rubbing up closest to the user who knows most about the product, and tend to assume this level of knowledge is general. Thus it is not safe to assume that a manufacturer is right when he says that everybody knows that his product now incorporates this or that feature. There are a number of cases of successful campaigns being based on informing the market that the product had a feature that was, in fact, common to all its competitors. However, the advertiser had found out by research that this was the feature that mattered and therefore laid great emphasis on the fact that his product had it. Almost to a man the market assumed that the others did not.

The most successful advertisements are those which put across the simplest message. To a manufacturer of a range of products selling to a wide section of industry and who is introducing a new or improved product with several novel and desirable features, the problem of simplifying the message may seem immense. To him everything is important.

Both long and short term objectives must be considered, and interest may clash. Advertising to bring quick sales of a cheap piece of plant may positively damage the long term objective, which is to be considered the leader in a product field.

The long term objective is almost invariably one of building the correct image; putting over the right character to suit your product field; or perhaps changing an image of a company which is moving out of a declining field of manufacture into a newer and more vigorous market; or presenting a picture of a united, cohesive company when, in fact, it is a multitude of bits and pieces from takeovers. Whatever the short term objective, the advertising which attempts to achieve it will have a secondary effect—an effect on the image of the company which can last a very long time.

The chapter which follows shows that image or prestige advertising is a long term business—images are not changed overnight nor indeed are companies. A company intelligent enough to deliberately set out to identify, develop and burnish its image will be aware that it cannot pretend to be what it is not. It will, along with the advertising that improves its image, improve itself; give better service, restyle its products, reshape its sales force. Honesty is essential if the long term objectives are to be achieved.

People like to know something of the companies with whom they are dealing. The fact that a company advertises establishes its own confidence in itself and its product—it has put this on record. It has also made its audience aware that it values its reputation and is willing to pay good (advertising) money to burnish it. Millions of pounds are spent annually on doing no more than this; putting across a good impression, an image, and at the same time saying what is sold. There is a tendency to belittle this type of advertising, but those who do, ignore the fact that industrial products are sold to people. They may be technicians but they are human beings first with the very human weakness of preferring to do business with people or companies they know and like.

WHO DECIDES?

Given a fair sized company where titles mean just about what they say, the short term objectives should be defined by the sales manager with the help of his team. To 'increase sales by 25 per cent' is not an objective aim any more than one might say, 'I want to be better off'. To say, 'We lost twenty sales we should have got last year to X because the customer likes his after sales service, or because their machine is better-looking or because their plant was made in this country', is constructive. The ideal, short term brief can come equally well from the reasons for sales lost as it can from sales gained.

This is negative—a shortcoming identified, overcome and turned into an advantage. In many instances there will be no such shortcoming; in fact, there will be a 'unique selling proposition' or product plus.

The brief may then be, 'If the market were more widely aware of the advantage of this or that feature fitted to our plant we should sell more'. So much for the short term objectives. Those for the long term are somewhat more difficult. Companies either expand or contract; they do not stay still. Those who are contracting and doing nothing about it should not advertise. To those who have been contracting and are taking remedial measures the long term advertising objectives should be clear from the investigations that have pointed their new course to them. To an expanding company the problem of deciding the long term advertising objectives must fall to the marketing director. He alone must know at what stage his company will have such a percentage of the market as to make further inroads prohibitively expensive. He will know whether his company's heaviest (or hardest to replace) investment is in production or sales and service, and in turn whether further expansion is to be in similar sales fields or is to require similar production capacity.

The final ingredient to the mix which will decide long term objectives should, ideally, be an image survey. Very few companies have anything near a true idea of how their markets and potential markets view them, of what prejudices and grudges they hold, perhaps harking back to the immediate post-war days when a seller's market existed.

PRODUCT DIFFERENTIALS

Too frequently, industrial advertising campaigns for excellent products have been based on product differentials which, while of great interest to other manufacturers of similar products, are considered by the market to have only marginal advantage. The result has been overemphasis on a weak selling point, with the remaining features, which the market really appreciates, being ignored or given a secondary place. If product differentials are to be used as the mainstay of any advertising campaign, it is essential that first the market attitude to those differentials should be gauged. This is an exercise that can be carried out quite cheaply either internally or by an outside research organisation.

With many products there are no tangible product differentials: for example, with an electric motor made to a rigid specification, with plastic pipe to a British Standard, with a raw material, or with nuts and bolts. Products such as these sell on price, delivery, service and emotion—not necessarily in that order. The identification of emotional differentials is one of the keys to success where these conditions of equality prevail.

BUYING INFLUENCE

The establishment of an embracing list of buying influences is essential. This will influence the message, the manner in which the message is presented, and is, of course, all important when it comes to media selection.

The confusion of title and function in industry does not help here, but the widest possible list in order of importance should be made, bearing in mind that in many cases quite important decisions are influenced by an *ad hoc* committee which meets once a day at lunchtime in the management dining-room. Even such unlikely people as visiting advertising agents have been known to join in to air their prejudices on all manner of things.

The managing director and the financial director, particularly if the unit cost of the product is high or the value of orders substantial, must not be forgotten. They prefer to sign large cheques to firms whose names and functions they know.

Similarly, never forget the buyer, or perhaps the foreman, if your product is made to a British or some other standard. Here the technical responsibilities are automatically looked after and the selection of make may be left to quite lowly people.

The designer or the architect must be considered if your product can be incorporated in his design. You will not get immediate results here, but if your product gets put on the drawing you have almost certainly made a sale, though you may not know it for another year.

The plant manager, the chief chemist, the technical director, the operator, the local authority, all may have their place on the list. A survey[1]

1. *Special Report on the Buying and Selling Techniques used in the British Engineering Industry*, McGraw-Hill (London, 1963).

carried out by McGraw-Hill revealed that in companies employing between four hundred and a thousand people there were more than five buying influences, and in companies employing over one thousand, more than six —both very conservative figures.

This is another area where the view of the average salesman tends to be misleading. He has his contact and gets the order from that contact. It is doubtful whether this contact will admit that the buying decision was not his except perhaps when it is unpopular. In many cases the salesman may assume that he is dealing with the sole buying influence.

With products like abrasives, cutting oil and drills, the most powerful buying influence may be quite lowly. To aggravate the situation, the person concerned will probably read none of the trade and technical publications in their field—not even the controlled circulation digests. A situation like this poses an extremely difficult problem, and since there are no published lines of communication the problem may not be solved by space advertising or editorial promotion in technical journals. The prospect could, of course, be reached through the pages of the *Daily Mirror* but this would be both expensive and wasteful since the prospect will represent far less than 1 per cent of the readership. Simple and forceful leaflets delivered by salesman's hand on the shop floor can help, as can premium schemes—for instance collecting blotters off grinding wheels to exchange for a gift. However, such schemes have not been used much in Great Britain. Another fruitful activity in this difficult field is the distribution of samples and technical literature to technical colleges and apprentice schools.

A good source of leads for buying influences are demonstrations where anyone who has anything to contribute to the buying decision will probably turn up. Most manufacturers have their tame customers. In establishing a pattern of buying influence these are likely to be misleading as their 'tameness' is usually due to the personal relationship of some senior man in the selling company with one strong buying influence on the customer side.

Buying influences will vary from market to market. The pattern in a large public body such as the National Coal Board is going to be vastly different to that within a small private firm. Whatever the difficulties, a written list of buying influences should be included with the advertising objectives.

There is a large and important market where the buying influences may be one or two people only. Farmers, garage proprietors, are typical of such markets made up of small entrepreneurs.

BASIC ADVERTISEMENTS

There are six basic types of advertisements. Describing them baldly in a few words, it is difficult not to appear disparaging. This is not the case. There is a useful function for each of these provided that it is effectively executed, can win attention in crowded pages of advertising and conveys the message.

Catalogue page. A three-quarter view of the product, a simple or clever headline with factual, unpretentious copy giving technical details followed by the name style of the company or logotype. This is the easiest type of advertisement to prepare and, perhaps because of this, widely used. Its weakness lies in the fact that it is commonplace, and even the details of the most sensational new product are likely to be overlooked if presented in this form. The headline and lead copy can transform this type of advertisement into something really effective.

Simple reminder. This takes such forms as 'Browns make cranes for every lifting job'. The headline and poster effect are important here. It is a short message and should get read. The remainder of the design should merely increase the attention-getting effect and be suitable in mood for the product. A product may be shown, but it is secondary to the message. This can do a first class job where the field of product application is wide and where there are a large number of manufacturers of the product group. It is also excellent for services and for companies expanding into new product fields.

Testimonial. An actual user or an imagined user benefiting from the product—a very popular form. This establishes user confidence in the product. However, when real customers are used they become sitting targets for the competitors who may cut prices to get in just to have a laugh on the original supplier. This happens remarkably often. Another danger here is that of making the advertisement one for the customer rather than the subject product, or using the idea as a sales aid. 'If you buy we shall feature your firm in our advertising.' This works surprisingly well in some cases but it is not advertising and the space should be paid for from some other budget.

Product differential. This type of advertisement is best if one differential only is featured and dramatised, but all too often much too much material is included, weakening the advertisement. The great problem here is to pick the right differential and unless some really painstaking checking is done beforehand the advertising budget could be gambled on the wrong items. Probably the best type of advertisement for getting intelligent high quality enquiries.

Straightforward prestige. At its worst, a photograph of the factory or the founder, or done in a far more sophisticated way by Vickers with their series of Terence Cuneo drawings. However, this approach would be as appropriate in the next chapter on public relations as in this one. It has an effect on the customer but to be justified the advertiser must have many other publics on whom it is worth while spending money—shareholders, suppliers' workpeople, governments. The number one danger here is pomposity.

Pioneering approach. This approach is to show how a job can be better and more efficiently carried out by using a particular product. Without doubt this is the most interesting and satisfying advertisement to prepare, and, where it is appropriate, most effective. So often the improvement means a lower demand for labour that this aspect must always be extremely tactfully handled.

Perhaps there should be a seventh category, *grand old British advertising humour,* but since the greater part of this type defies analysis it will not be included; but having mentioned it, a warning should be given that it is very difficult to sell with humour. Unless it is extremely well done it can have a definitely adverse effect on the image of a company. There is nothing more boring than a poor joke.

This leads almost automatically to the other controversial subject—sex in industrial advertising. Walk round any factory, drawing office, stores or building site hut and list the subjects of any displayed art you may see. This establishes that for most industrial firms the customers are men. Men are interested in sex and the lower down the socio-economic scale you go the less inhibited they are about displaying this interest. Buying influences are reasonably well up in the socio-economic scale and are much less likely to be favourably impressed with anything that has to rely on sex for attention value. Generally speaking sex is a very unpredicatable ingredient in industrial advertising although excellent for the calendar to be distributed at works floor level.

There are a few advertisements which will not fall into the above categories. A random test run through a few technical publications will show that these are less than 5 per cent. These 5 per cent are, however, frequently the most effective advertisements.

However well thought out and planned an advertisement may be, it will not be effective unless it has the power to draw the attention of the busy reader or flipper. This must be the first consideration in the preparation of any advertisement, and it is the professional expertise in doing this of the ideas man, copywriter and layout artist that is the vital ingredient of an effective advertisement.

There are a number of generalisations about the content and composition of an advertisement which are obvious, frequently ignored and worth noting. The first of these is that the shorter and simpler the message, the larger the number of people who will absorb it. This can be referred to as the poster effect of an advertisement, and it is a sound thing to aim at in nearly all advertisements so that the 'flipper' who must represent the greater part of the page traffic will at least carry with him some message. If this cannot be done, then facing editorial matter space should be considered.

The second is that clutter should be avoided at all costs. It distracts from the message when reading time and space are valuable. The reader may be interested to know that the firm was established in 1870, but unless that is an important part of the selling message it should not just be included as a matter of principle. Where branches are an essential part of the selling service they should obviously be included. Addresses should be the shortest possible allowed by the G.P.O. Logotypes, symbols, and trademarks must be contemporary and used with consistency. Slogans are dangerous and can contradict an advertisement message.

The third is that tear off coupons should be used sparingly and only when there is a direct invitation to 'have a demonstration' or 'send for further information'.

Every advertisement presents an image to the public at which it is directed and it is quite essential that every advertisement should present a good image of the advertiser. Prospects are impressed by neatly dressed, well groomed salesmen, although they may know nothing about tailoring. Similarly, they will be impressed by a neat and well laid out advertisement, although they know nothing of layout or typography.

Series advertisements are popular with advertisers probably because the advertiser himself is one of the few people who will ever see the series complete. If a series is to be considered, each individual advertisement should be a complete selling message in itself and the frequency of the advertisement appearing in the media should be adjusted to accommodate the series. A series of six, running alternate months in a monthly published journal, is going to take far too long to be effective, the first will be forgotten long before the last has been seen. Each must appear at least twice to give it a chance to be read.

Finally all advertisements from the same advertiser should look as if they come from the same stable to give the advantage of apparent advertising weight. This can be done by careful use of type faces, logotypes and trademarks, without becoming boring or detracting from the attention-getting quality.

ENQUIRIES OR IMAGE

For the manufacturer who develops a product which is head and shoulders above his competitors, the advertising problem is a simple one. Show the product, dramatise its advantages in application, and wait for the enquiries. Concern about the image will come later when his competitors have caught up with him. Unfortunately, there are few manufacturers in this enviable position. Most of industrial advertisers are selling their machines, plant, components, materials or services in competition with others whose product or service is, in overall effect, nearly as good as or even better than their own.

Each make or brand will have its own special features, advantages and disadvantages. For most industrial products these features are marginal and are frequently more apparent to their manufacturer than they are to the user; farm tractors, copy turning lathes, steam boilers, compressors, milling cutters, diesel engines, trip switches, PVC, nitric acid, paint—the list of product fields to which this applies is endless.

With the pace of modern development, even a significant breakthrough by a manufacturer is seldom an advantage that lasts more than twelve months, by which time his competitors will have caught up. Sadly enough, if his advantage is not immediately and obviously self-apparent, he may be obliged to educate the market to appreciate and benefit from the new feature, just in time for the pursuing competitors to reap the advantage of this.

Consider the basic ways in which an enquiry may come to be sent to a manufacturer. A need for plant or equipment arises, someone is delegated with the responsibility of finding out models and prices. He may know of three manufacturers to whom he will write, he may ask colleagues, he may look them up in a buyers' guide or he may read the current edition of the appropriate trade journal. The manufacturer who will get the enquiry here is the one who has, by advertising, made this buying influence aware that he makes the product and that it is a good product. The chances that advertising purely for enquiries will bring in this enquiry are remote.

Another case is where the product is a continuing purchase, such as a paint, or twist drills, or even commercial vehicles. The purchaser will go to his established supplier. It is no good waiting for them to let him down to have a chance of getting in. Here the clever advertising of a product differential aimed at the buying influence may well be the only way to get at the purchaser—he may not even be willing to see salesmen from other suppliers. If his interest can be aroused by the product differential, there is a good chance of getting an enquiry and dislodging an established supplier.

A third case, probably the most rewarding and certainly the best moral argument for advertising, is the educational approach. Here one advertises the advantage of doing a job with a new material or new machine, so saving money, increasing efficiency and doing the job better. The prospect sees the advertisement, is persuaded by what it says and makes an enquiry. There are many examples of this 'pioneering' approach. The forklift truck and palletised material handling has improved industrial handling generally. Industrial adhesive tapes have improved and simplified packing. Numerical control is improving the production on machine tools. In each of these cases there are now a number of manufacturers selling competitively, but the markets have a long way to expand and their future lies not so much in the sales they can steal from one another but in the potential markets which do not yet use their products.

Deliberate advertising for enquiries can be a very expensive business if enquiries are to be properly serviced once received. To be successful, the advertisement will have to arouse curiosity and this will bring into the net all sorts of people who have no intention of buying, plus the usual selection of industrial librarians and students; all excellent for the long term image but not very productive in immediate orders.

FIXING THE BUDGET

The classic question is 'How much should we spend on advertising?'

Before any attempt is made to answer this questions it would perhaps be as well to list all the promotional activities, which can wrongly be lumped together under the umbrella words 'advertising and publicity', under their more correct headings. *Advertising and publicity costs:* paid space advertising and production costs, sales leaflets, direct mail and public relations. *Selling costs:* demonstrations, films, exhibitions, Christmas gifts and quotations or speculative schemes. *Manufacturing or first cost:* instruction manuals, spare parts lists.

This division may seem arbitrary but some line has to be drawn and the decision as to whether the activity should be an advertising or a selling cost can be decided by whether the activity requires the salesmen's presence and is in fact *directly* making the salesman more efficient in his function of selling. Thus a salesman is aided in his selling by a demonstration, he may be able to do a cheaper, quicker job by showing a film. Another time he may attend an exhibition seeing twenty prospects in a day rather than his usual half-dozen. Under 'manufacturing or first costs' are items without which a prospect just would not consider buying the product. Perhaps because the 'advertising budget' is such a convenient place for all sorts of items that do not seem to fit anywhere else, many will argue with these divisions.

It has become common practice to express the advertising appropriation as a percentage of turnover; this must be target turnover as opposed to last year's turnover if it is to make sense.

Expressed as a percentage the figure may vary from $\frac{1}{2}$ per cent to about 4 per cent, depending upon the degree of competition in the industry, whether the market is growing, declining or static, and also on what production is available. Obviously, it costs more to establish a new product than to sell an established one, and more to maintain a position in a competitive market than in a less competitive one. With the large number of variables it is impossible to be empirical. It is interesting to note that in the more conservative shipbuilding and heavy engineering industries the percentage is low—well under 1 per cent. In the newer electronics industry, where there is a fast rate of expansion, the percentage is four to five times as high.

All too often the budget is fixed in quite an arbitrary manner. The figure may be based on what competitors are doing or what the chairman thinks he can afford. The only true motive for advertising must be that the advertiser believes that it will substantially help his sales. If this is so he must then do it properly. He would not dream of trying to cover his market with only one salesman; he should no more imagine that an inadequate advertising budget will do the job that needs to be done. If he had only one salesman he would be wise to concentrate the efforts of that man on one section of his market only—the one expected to be the most fruitful. The same applies with advertising where money is very limited. It is a mistake to broadcast the advertising message thinly over the complete market as it will become lost in the mass of other advertisements.

MEDIA

The importance of sound media selection need not be emphasised. The principal red herrings here are the journals read by the manufacturer which are not necessarily read by his customers, but in which he likes to see his own advertisements (a mild form of narcissus complex), choosing publications because the competitors advertise in them and taking space because the publications always give good editorial coverage.

The principal categories of publication are the horizontals, which may cover either a wide cross section of many industries or those which cater for an important but comparatively thin cross sectional strata covering most industries; and the verticals, publications which cover a single or limited number of industries in depth.

Considerable confusion has arisen in recent years because of the high enquiry rates obtained through many controlled circulation publications. It is the gravest mistake to base a schedule of media on enquiry results only. In many cases enquiries are essential, in others they are useful. It must be accepted that in some cases, such as established products of high cost, a large number of enquiries would merely point to past inefficiencies in the marketing. Most industries now have their controlled circulation papers, their '. . . Equipment News'. These are useful digests of information for busy men. They will also have their 'heavies' with more substantial articles directed to the people in that industry who bother to read. To ignore this second category, although it will not pull direct enquiries on little buff cards, is a mistake made today in too many schedules. The schedule should cover all markets in proportion to their potential, rather than last year's sales.

When advertising in vertical publications using product application or testimonial advertisements the subject should be closely related to the market, even if this involves the cost of a number of advertisements for different journals. Thus when advertising boilers in a laundry paper it will reduce the effectiveness to show an installation in a steel works. This sort of error may sound ridiculous but it happens quite frequently.

Where advertising is undertaken with the short term object of getting enquiries four individual quarter pages will pull more than one whole page, though the long term effect of small space advertising may be damaging to a future image. Look in the back pages of any technical publication and the quarter page advertisements tend to be dominated by small companies.

Most publishers charge 20 to 25 per cent extra for facing editorial matter pages; usually this is good value for money. One of the advantages of the controlled circulation digest is that all advertisements are facing editorial matter.

Bleed—that is using the complete area of the page rather than the type area only—is extremely useful for added poster effect, and where one needs the extra space because there is a lot of material to get in. Colour is an expensive item which is not used to full effect in the majority of industrial advertisements. The tendency is to book colour and then having designed a basic black and white advertisement add a few dabs of colour to 'liven it up'. This is wrong and wasteful, colour is expensive and should be used only when the advertisement needs it for clarity of illustration or to increase overall impact. In both cases the advertisement must be designed from the start as a colour advertisement.

Inserts are usually expensive and should only be considered when they can be used later by themselves as promotional literature. They must be bound in to stay with the publication for its full circulation.

The image or prestige effect of advertising is enhanced by weight or the frequency with which a message is seen. This effect will be reduced to a point where it is negligible if the frequency is not at least four in a year in a monthly journal and perhaps ten a year in a weekly journal.

A media plan should always allow a sum for the contingencies which invariably arise in the course of a year. In practice, it is usual to book a twelve-month campaign to obtain the full advantage of a series discounts. This should not necessarily freeze thinking on media for the next twelve months. A lot of changes can take place in that time and the schedule must be adaptable.

By the time the advertiser has seen a layout, two proofs and several voucher copies he may tend to become bored with the advertisement and call for a change of copy. As a rough rule of thumb, to get the best effect from an advertisement it should appear at least four times in 'run of paper' position—that is among the advertisements in the front or back of a journal—or three times in facing editorial position. By this time an effective advertisement should have conveyed its message to a large percentage of those interested.

EVALUATION

If the industrial advertising problem is approached on the lines suggested here, with realistic objectives and with known buying influences, there is no reason why at least some of its effect should not be evaluated with reasonable accuracy. Obviously advertising will not be the only factor influencing the market attitudes and other marketing activities must be taken into consideration.

Within the limitations set out in Chapter 5 the evaluation of the short term objectives, perhaps purely enquiries, is a comparatively simple matter. A further bonus of information may be obtained by the keying of advertisements in individual publications to weigh their comparative performances. In doing this the quality of enquiries is quite as important as the quantity and a careful check should be kept on both perhaps by grading enquiries as they come in. If the product is fairly quick selling it is as well to follow through and establish a sales conversion rate and, further, an advertising cost per thousand pounds worth of order.

On orders of greater value the period of gestation from enquiry to order and delivery may be considerable. In this case evaluation must be by the number of enquiries, though unproductive and lightweight ones from students, industrial librarians and others should not be included. Their enquiries will only help with the long term image of the company.

Where the object is less tangible some form of simple benchmark study may be necessary. The object may be simple, such as 'We wish to be recognised by those who influence buying as one of the top four manufacturers of . . .', or 'We want our market to know that we now do bored piling'.

A telephone survey can in some circumstances establish what percentage of the buying influences is aware of the information today. A further survey in twelve or twenty-four months will show the improvement. As far as the actual survey is concerned, it is certainly better carried out by a specialist marketing researcher, whether employed by the firm or a research agency. A marketing researcher will phrase his 'smokescreen' questions better and avoid loaded questions; he will probably also include in the second survey a percentage of the respondents to the first as a double check on his findings.

Simple, telephone surveys can be most revealing. More than one manufacturer is advertising the most sophisticated details of his product, quite oblivious of the fact that less than a third of those influencing buying are aware that he has moved into the product field. It is common sense that the market must first be told that 'X makes centreless grinders', and become aware of this, before it is going to take an intelligent interest in the details of the spindle bearing.

The majority of campaigns should not require evaluation of this type. It is possible to tell whether the advertising is doing its job from the salesmen's reports, sales correspondence and the general attitude of the market to the advertiser.

In some cases, however, considerably more detailed research should be carried out before the manufacturer spends a penny on advertising.

EXPORT ADVERTISING

Problems of export marketing are more fully covered in Chapter 13. Within the context of advertising it is worth pointing out that although some advertisements translate quite well, the set of conditions which have made them the right advertisement for the moment with the local market will probably not prevail in another country. If what has been set out here is correct for advertising in Great Britain it is obvious that a parallel exercise should be undertaken in any other market where the product is advertised and sold. Such an exercise should be the task of someone familiar with that market. Who better than the selling agent for the country?

It is also true to say that the export markets for many technical products have not reached the degree of sophistication of the home markets, and simpler, almost catalogue-type, advertisements are in many cases the most effective.

It seems that, while accepting the need for advertising to overseas markets, many exporters are not equipped or prepared to put into it the considerable amount of work necessary if it is to be done properly. Too frequently one sees what appears to be a sop to the conscience of the exporter—a general advertisement in a British published export magazine, printed in English and distributed to forty countries.

Trust your selling agent in another country. Give him the money to spend on advertising in his own country, to his own market, in their own language.

SUPPORTING LITERATURE

The advertisement has achieved its aim and the enquiry has arrived. It may not be possible to get a salesman to the prospect for a number of days but it is essential to keep him warm and so, by return post, goes a letter acknowledging the enquiry and enclosing a leaflet, perhaps also promising further details to follow. That leaflet can kill the enquiry or pave the way for the salesman.

In another case a salesman may make a cold call on a prospect, talk about the product and before he goes leave a leaflet.

In both cases when the prospect picks up the leaflet to read it an entirely new set of circumstances prevails. He wants to know about the product—you have his attention. The perfect solution would be for your top salesman to give his most polished sales presentation at that moment. The leaflet must do this using colour, line, type and design in place of voice inflection, gesticulation and expression. The leaflet must be a fairly complete sales story in itself and it should finish with a specification—if not a full one, one that at least gives the most important details. Obviously the sales pitch for different circumstances must vary considerably and it is seldom practical to have a different leaflet for each set of circumstances. The leaflet must therefore contain the basic common selling message. The angling of this must be left to a salesman. In many markets where the unit cost of an order is low the leaflet may have to do the whole selling job as a salesman's time would be too expensive. The carefully thought out and presented leaflet is a vastly different thing to the ubiquitous 'spec' sheet that in so many cases passes for sales literature.

Perhaps even more than space advertising a sales leaflet leaves with the recipient an image of the company that sent it. The man who reads your leaflet is certainly more than half-way along the path to buying in your product field. There could hardly be a more important person.

DIRECT MAIL

Direct mail which was described in the previous Chapter as 'extending the salesman's reach' is a most effective advertising tool all too frequently misused. It can supplement, but never replace, space advertising. It is most effective when telling the recipient something of value to him about the product or service of the sender. Any particularly newsworthy item such as a new product, new service facilities or an increase in the scope of the company's activities should certainly be direct mailed to a full list of interested firms. With space advertising, a press release and direct mail the rate of absorbtion of the information will be high. Where the case for direct mail is weakened is when the word 'regular' is attached to it and it is necessary to scrape the news barrel for subjects to maintain the regular flow. A few contrived mail sheets of little news content will devalue later shots and ease their way straight to the waste paper basket.

Part of the capital assets of any company should be a carefully nurtured direct mail list, keyed for area, size, activity and whether the company is a user or not. This will be built up over the years from enquiries, sales, representatives' reports and news items in the trade Press.

The form the mailing enclosure can take can vary considerably from a straightforward facsimile letter to elaborate piece of print or an ingenious 'gimmick'. Whatever form it takes it is a very good rule to write the piece as a letter first and compare any subsequent elaborations with this letter for cost and effect.

EXHIBITIONS

Although earlier in this chapter exhibitions were placed squarely under the heading of a selling activity they are something that is more often than not looked after by the advertising department and therefore justify further mention. In the last decade the number and variety of exhibitions has increased greatly and the cost both direct and hidden of attending all the 'possibles' can be very substantial.

The reasons for showing at exhibitions are; to announce new products, new models or new services; to demonstrate a product to a large number of people at a low cost per head; to make contact with a large number of customers and potential customers at a low cost per head. If attendance at an exhibition will not fulfil one or more of these it should not be considered.

A subsidiary advantage of showing at an exhibition is the prestige and reminder effect but this in itself is never sufficient reason to justify attendance. Exhibitions are frequently unpopular with exhibitors who in many cases are only present because the competition is there. This on its own can never be a good reason for exhibiting. If the competition is there then his salesmen are not in the field and it is doubtful whether, even with the best exhibition, more than 25 per cent of the prospective buyers will attend.

This leaves the outside field more open than usual to the company not exhibiting although a fraction of the 25 per cent attending may have a gin and tonic on the competitor's stand.

In cash the cost of advertising is high. It can and it should be money returned with a handsome interest. This will only be the case if the advertiser puts his energy, thought and planning into his advertising as well as his cash. It is no good thinking that because an advertising agent is employed that it can all be left to him—the best agent in the world is only as good as his advertising brief. It may be that the agent can be extremely helpful in discussions that lead up to the brief or in initiating research which will affect the brief but it is unreasonable to expect an advertising agency to make decisions that are correctly those of senior sales management.

9

Industrial Public Relations

HARRY TRIGG

AN APPRECIATION

Many a capable public relations manager or consultant, who can be lucid about his work on behalf of his company or his clients, becomes inarticulate when asked to give a definition of public relations. Probably the main reason for this is the fact that successful public relations in industry is concerned with every area of activity from research and development to after-sales service. Consequently no short definition can project the range of action covered by the term—public relations.

Public relations is still a new element in European commercial and industrial operations. As a result there are many people who are sceptical and even suspicious of it and the men and women who practise it. In some cases this suspicion has been well founded. The dilettante, the amateur and the smart operator have done nothing to help the acceptance of public relations. In fact they have tarnished the image of PR in the eyes of many people.

Nevertheless an increasing number of people in industry have been involved in some facet of PR activity and are therefore convinced that they know what it is. To some it means a press release heavy with superlatives describing a new product; for others it represents the personal publicity they feel is needed for their own advancement and that of their company.

In too many cases it is regarded as a service which is called upon only when there is something which management wants to see appear in the press. This attitude, which stems from the belief that PR action can be switched on and off like an electric light, is often coupled with a conviction that for the rest of the time the function of PR is to ensure that the company is not bothered with questions about its operations and policies.

Effective public relations calls for continuity and an understanding of the requirements of the main communications media—press, radio and television.

One definition of the PR function in industry is—planned and positive action to create a climate of goodwill where people are receptive to a company's policy and products.

WHAT IS IT?

Public relations is in fact what it claims to be—relations with the public. In industry a company may have many 'publics'—employees, customers, shareholders, suppliers, government departments, local authorities. Sometimes PR policy and actions will be directed to reach people in all these groups, on other occasions the objective may be limited to one group, for example, shareholders.

The president of one of America's largest corporations once told his board that in his view public relations began with what they did and their attitude to what they did. It did not begin by bringing in somebody to write an epic about the company. He maintained that the man responsible for public relations should sit in at board meetings when he should think and act as a member of the public and not as an employee. His task was to sound a warning if he felt that their decisions were likely to result in bad public relations. There is little doubt that this corporation president understood how to use PR as an aid in industry.

A CRAFT

Public relations is a craft which calls for experience, knowledge, skill and a sense of timing. Although executives in industry are generally willing to listen to accountants and management consultants, many of them find it hard to accept advice from their PR manager or consultant.

They will happily use his services for press conferences and factory openings. However, his basic worth as a counsellor and a barometer of opinion on matters of policy is frequently not utilised. So often what he is offering is common sense which sometimes gets lost in the issues of company policy and personalities. It is the PR executive's role to be detached and to hold up the mirror which reflects outside reactions and opinions, frequently very different to the picture management have of the situation.

The appointment of a PR manager or consultant is often made without any real consideration of the two distinct areas of public relations, which ideally should embrace both staff services and counselling. Before embarking on a public relations programme both the firm's top management and the PR manager or consultant should have a clear understanding as to the type of service which is to be operated.

It is fair to say that a majority of PR firms and PR departments consciously or otherwise are operating most of the time in the field of staff services and only spasmodically in the area of counselling.

STAFF SERVICES

Staff services are the operations carried out to implement company policies, whether or not the PR executive participated in the shaping of such policies or approved of them.

In addition to the preparation of material for the main communications media (press, radio and television) staff services cover many activities—drafting speeches and special letters, the planning involved in opening new buildings and introducing new methods and equipment, organising visits for V.I.P.s, overseas customers and embassy officials, the production of annual reports, house journals and customer publications.

Several of these operations, in addition to some of the less obvious activities of the PR manager or consultant, are dealt with in some detail to give an indication of the wide scope of action involved in industrial public relations.

Press, radio and television

One of the first requirements in any industrial PR operation is to establish an *entente* with people in the various communications media—press, radio and television. Their goodwill and co-operation are invaluable. They must, however, be earned. Quite often industrial PR departments or consultants can be of help to them in their work by providing facilities or background information.

This type of co-operation should be given, whether or not there is any direct or immediate benefit to the company. In fact it should be welcomed by a company as it provides an opportunity for a journalist or producer to learn something about their organisation and its people.

This knowledge, however slight, can be of value to both parties in future operations. These may depend on the initiative of the PR man or in turn on the journalist or broadcaster who feels that the company—its employees or its activities—meets his requirements for an article or programme.

Here lies one of the major differences between advertising, which buys space to deliver a message, and the PR function, which by necessity must be in a position to offer these people something which is newsworthy or of interest to their public.

The aim of industrial PR should be to establish the company as an organisation willing to co-operate with the press both as a source of information and as a reliable checkpoint for questions, whether they apply to the company in particular or to industry generally. In short the press should be made to feel that this is a service they can call on when needed.

Long distance press trips are no longer a novelty. In fact, airline inauguration flights, the opening of new plants by international companies, tourism and sponsored trips by foreign governments have meant that the overseas trip is now comparatively commonplace. Industrial organisations bringing journalists from abroad should always be prepared to give their visitors the opportunity to cover at least one other story completely unconnected with the sponsor.

In 1963 daily and technical journalists from seven European countries were invited to the unique Ronquières canal project in Belgium. The sponsors—who supplied the compressed air equipment on the project—also included a visit to the Port of Rotterdam. This harbour tour was deliberately chosen as a contrast to the Belgian story. It proved to be of considerable value to the press who found that Rotterdam had become the world's number one port based on annual tonnage handled.

When King Baudouin of Belgium made a state visit to Sweden only one factory was included in his Stockholm itinerary. Realising that the press, radio and TV representatives accompanying the King would probably appreciate the chance to make a preview tour of Sweden some weeks before, the company concerned co-sponsored a reconnaissance visit, when only a few hours were spent at their plant. By providing such facilities they received outstanding coverage in Belgium, both prior to and during the royal visit.

These are both unusual cases, but the important point is the thinking behind them.

Films

In many companies the PR manager or consultant is also responsible to management for the co-ordination required in film making. In co-operation with the producer he often plays an important part in the preparation of the treatment and script. When the film is made it is his task to organise efficient distribution and to maintain the type of control which ensures that the film is used and seen by the right audiences.

Many worthwhile industrial films are not fully exploited, either at home or abroad. After the initial screenings for management and their guests, copies of the film are often left to gather dust in an agent's office overseas. Whether made for instructional, sales promotion or prestige purposes, a good film is one of the most important weapons in the PR armoury, once the right target is selected.

Exhibitions

There are many opinions as to the value of exhibitions. They range from the negative attitude based on the theory and referred to in the previous chapter—'if the competitors are there, we have to be'—to the conviction of the export manager who has found that participation in foreign fairs has meant orders and provided opportunities to establish contact with people who cannot be reached on a routine visit.

It is a PR function to exploit a company's participation in trade fairs and exhibitions. For example, the people an exhibitor wants to see on his stand should receive a personal invitation, indicating clearly where the stand can be found. This may seem obvious, but frequently the guest is expected to take his own compass bearings. The PR executive should create opportunities which can be used to attract attention to the company's exhibits. The inclusion of new or interesting equipment in TV, radio and press previews can help to arouse the interest of potential customers.

Annual reports

There are still many companies who produce an annual report which looks more like a Government White Paper than a reflection of a progressive and expanding firm. Attractive presentation with the skilful use of colour, dramatic pictures and modern layout are needed in addition to the essential figures and diagrams.

Today's shareholders expect a report which will tell them graphically something of the activities which lie behind the statistics. The content and presentation of a company report is an important part of any image building operation.

In addition to sending copies of the report to shareholders and the press many companies have found it worth while to include important customers and suppliers on their circulation lists. After all this is probably the only occasion in the year when it is practical to present all the activities of the company in a concise and effective form under one cover.

Many international groups and companies with export markets to foster also send the report overseas to their associate companies, agents and banking contacts as well as to their customers. Having found that it pays to be known, they generally include on their lists government departments which the local representatives abroad may have to approach for import licences or building permits.

Properly exploited the annual report can become a useful forerunner for sales enquiries. This applies particularly to companies with a wide range of equipment, the extent of which is often unknown at home, much less abroad.

Sponsored books

Although sponsored books have been produced for some time, it is only in recent years that industry has come to realise their goodwill potential. In these operations an established publisher co-operates with an industrial concern to produce a reference book devoted to a particular field of technology.

If the book is to be effective it must be purely objective and not a poorly disguised promotional publication for the products of the company concerned. The goal is to produce a publication which will become a standard reference for years on a subject which has not been adequately covered in recent times, if at all.

Both in Britain and on the Continent, a number of publishing houses have established special departments to promote and operate in this sector. Generally speaking, the sponsoring company underwrites the cost of the publication and takes a share of any profit.

Probably the easiest part is to decide on a subject. The difficulties lie in finding the people to write, and having done that to establish that they will have the time to prepare the contents.

In most cases the men and women needed to write such a book must be drawn from the upper echelon of a company's commercial, technical or research departments where time is invariably in short supply. If a company is to be realistic about such a venture, the authors' time must be costed in addition to the money staked in co-operation with the publisher.

A successful publication has limitless applications, both at home and abroad. It can be used equally well for customers, universities, technical colleges, public authorities, reference libraries and in many cases the armed forces. With effective promotion such a book can be an investment which pays a dividend for years in building the sort of image every company wants to project—that of the experts in their field.

Recruitment—University Contacts

The type of people needed by research and technical departments are generally in short supply. Money is not the only important factor necessary to attract a scientist to a company. The scope of activities, the facilities a company has to offer and its technical standing are important influences in this field of employment.

Obviously, highly qualified men and women are attracted to an organisation which has earned a reputation for forward thinking, where they know that the importance of their work will be acknowledged and where they know that management will pay heed to their recommendations.

It is the role of public relations to project the image of a progressive organisation which, for example, looks to research and development to produce the ideas which will help future expansion.

Lines of communication should be established with universities and technical colleges. Today's students are tomorrow's technicians. Interest in the company can be encouraged with scholarships and bursaries and where practical with regular visits by students to study various activities of the company.

Where possible members of the technical and research departments should be encouraged to give lectures at universities and technical colleges. In many cases practical instruction can be improved with the donation or loan of company equipment, for example, rock drills for mining colleges. Wall diagrams, slides, films and recorded lectures, particularly if prepared in co-operation with the teaching faculty, can make a useful contribution to their work.

In the developing countries of the world, a company which genuinely identifies itself with such efforts to assist in training people creates goodwill. It also demonstrates the intention to contribute towards the country's progress as well as prosper from it.

House style

House style calls for close co-operation between all sections of a firm. An increasing number of companies are realising the value of developing a house style which generally begins with the adoption of a standard logotype for the company name, company colours for use on all commercial vehicles and a house flag. A common house style, based on the use of a logotype, agreed type faces and layout, should be applied to all printed matter ranging from catalogues to invoices, and including letterheads and advertising. Such action provides a common recognition factor for the company and its products anywhere in the world. This is an important point in getting the maximum value for every pound invested in export promotion.

The PR department or consultant has a vital part to play in securing unity of purpose and co-ordinating the necessary operations involved in applying a house style throughout an organisation.

COUNSELLING

Counselling is probably the most important service public relations can offer the executive in industry. The basic ingredient for success in this area is mutual trust and confidence, and the creation of an atmosphere where the PR manager or consultant can offer and be called upon to give advice.

Although it is necessary for the PR executive to think as an outsider, he must be regarded as a member of the company. He must know the thinking behind management decisions and how and why certain problems have arisen. An increasing number of companies pay lip service to the idea that public relations has a part to play in formulating policy and handling problems, but when it comes to the test the necessary co-operation is often lacking. Once the issue becomes specific, involving a particular area of activity, there is a reluctance to accept advice from a man who is not traditionally regarded as a member of senior management. In America, however, it is not unusual to have a Vice-President, Public Relations, on the board; in fact public relations men now head companies.

Many times the PR executive is asked for his advice when the problem in question might well have been avoided if he had participated in the original policy discussions. No one suggests that he is infallible when it comes to decisions and policy-making in industry. However, if he carries out his true function as an adviser, whether as a member of the company's staff or a consultant, he will always try to retain the outlook and the attitude of the public the company is trying to reach. Herein lies his true worth to management.

PR MANAGER OR CONSULTANT?

There is no set answer to the query—inside department or outside consultant. Many companies have found the advantages to be gained from having both a PR manager and a consultant. With this sytem management is in a position to receive advice on problems as seen from both sides of the fence. It is also probably true that in many cases the consultant can be more detached in his approach which has obvious advantages, and his work for other clients means he generally has more frequent contact with the various communications media.

Close co-operation between a PR manager and consultant often

118 HARRY TRIGG

provides the catalyst needed to produce ideas which are so necessary to prevent PR operations lapsing into a routine.

A managing director should ask himself these questions when considering public relations aid:

Are company policy and management decisions understood by employees, agents, customers and shareholders? How does the company and its products stand in relation to competitors? Is it as well known as it should be, taking into account years of operation, sales turnover and the type of product?

Generally a consultant has accumulated experience of industrial problems and he is aware of the need to communicate ideas and decisions. So often companies take it for granted that their employees, customers or shareholders understand a certain decision or course of action, when in fact the situation is blurred and indefinite. Worse still is the board room policy which maintains that shareholders and employees should be told as little as possible. Here lies the real challenge to public relations which must be used to convince many leaders in industry that confidence and support can only grow when people feel they are informed.

There are many sound and reputable PR firms steadily proving the value of public relations in industry. Such companies, if approached, will give an honest appraisal of what they feel can be achieved on behalf of the prospective client. Contrary to popular opinion, they will also make it quite clear if they feel a company is not ready for PR or is about to employ it for the wrong reasons.

The trained consultant is always wary of the company which is in trouble and needs help quickly. He knows that it takes time to build a sound public relations programme.

When companies find themselves losing their share of the market they sometimes turn to public relations when they should first be calling for a management consultant or a marketing research specialist. The former is needed to re-organise a company and marketing research to establish what they should be making and where they should be selling it. Public relations can help to recapture a market, but management must at least reach a decision on a product line and basic objectives.

PR IN THE MANAGEMENT STRUCTURE

Once a company has decided to use public relations it is essential that the managing director should make it quite clear that the men and women responsible for the operation have his support. More often than not the PR executive is faced in the beginning with a passive resistance which can take many forms. One of the first things he will be told is that the money devoted to PR activities could be spent on increasing the sales staff.

Understandably company secretaries and finance directors find it hard to accept the introduction of a new activity which represents money going out without being able to pinpoint what this investment brings in return.

Similarly the personnel department have their own views about employee relations and the research and production departments wonder what contribution a non-technician can make to their efforts.

These are reactions the PR executive can expect to find on starting work for an industrial organisation. He should therefore devote his time to showing, rather than telling, these people how his knowledge and experience can be of use to them, particularly when it comes to opening and maintaining lines of communication within the company. Public relations 'know-how' can give support to all these various groups, very often widening their horizons.

At this stage he should emphasise that PR exists as a support for the sales department and not as a substitute. Of course, it takes time to show a sales engineer that one of the objects of public relations is to make his task a little easier in a competitive world. If PR action can make the potential buyer conscious of the company and its products before the representative reaches him it can be said to have prepared the ground.

Artillery is used to soften up the objective for the infantry; so public relations action prepares the way for the sales force—the assault troops of industry. In these days when there is often little difference between competitive products, awareness of a company and its equipment is a decided advantage in securing a meeting with the man who influences the decision as to where and what to buy.

An important by-product from PR contact is the fact that the customer will sometimes disclose minor dissatisfactions which he would not make as a direct complaint to the company. This type of contact can be useful in clearing mis-understandings which can fester into ill will between purchaser and supplier.

If a PR manager or consultant is to gain the support of the sales people, they must feel they are being consulted and informed. Copies of all articles and releases should be sent to members of the sales force at the same time as they are given to the press. Like charity, PR begins at home. Obviously it is impossible for the salesman to scan all papers and magazines. With this system he is equipped to handle any questions the customer may raise following the appearance of an article in the press.

There are no agreed areas of operation and responsibility for the PR function in industry. In some companies the PR manager or director is responsible for virtually all activities concerned with projecting the company including films, corporate advertising, press relations, exhibitions, sales and service literature, all publications and give-aways. With such a wide area of responsibility he is usually a member of senior management with various department managers answerable to him.

In common with the men responsible for sales promotion, marketing and advertising, the PR manager should be a member of any committees established to formulate policies on packaging, product names and colours.

The division of responsibilities between sales promotion, marketing, advertising and public relations must depend on many factors such as the size of the company and the range of products. The essential element is the need for co-operation and co-ordination between these activities. This applies particularly when it comes to introducing a new product or method calling for the production of sales and service literature, direct mail shots, guide advertisements, material for speeches and press releases, photos, slides and very often a film.

IDENTIFYING OBJECTIVES

Sound management insists on realistic targets for sales and production. The same yardstick must be used when it comes to public relations. One of the first tasks facing any one responsible for a PR operation in industry is to establish with management their PR objectives.

No organisation can expect at all times to be in a position to claim the finest designs, the best products, the most efficient and most economical equipment—in other words to be in a permanent state of the best with the most.

In attempting to make such claims a company would distil the poison of cynicism and doubt within its own organisation and would in the long run create mistrust in the minds of the public it was trying to reach. People are weary of constant superlatives when the currency of language is debased to such an extent that many words have lost their original value. No company produces winners all the way. In every form of industrial activity there are products and equipment which have their teething troubles and in some cases fail to come up to expectations, particularly when the company is trail blazing. Without these setbacks there would be no progress.

The PR man should regard himself as the champion of the company's reputation which must be built on the rock of facts, not the sands of fiction. It is his task to challenge exaggerated claims which, for example, may be initiated by a hard-pressed product manager thinking in terms of immediate results.

INTERNATIONAL PR

If it is to be successful, PR policy and action must be flexible. This applies particularly in international organisations where, as with advertising, the man on the spot must be allowed to interpret policy and implement it according to local customs, prejudices and politics. In some cases the social structure of a country has a distinct bearing on what can and cannot be done.

In general it is impractical to think in terms of a PR 'rule book' because the very points which may be worthy of emphasis in certain markets count for little in another. In the industrially sophisticated countries a company would want to stress the savings in manpower made possible by the use of their equipment. In the developing countries the same product would be sold stressing the ease of maintenance, even by unskilled labour.

This does not mean abandoning certain basic points of policy. If, for example, a company has a consultancy service to back its products, this theme can be applied universally.

In markets where competition is particularly intense it may be necessary to lay particular emphasis on the name of the company or product. In areas where competitors are neither so numerous nor so keen, it may be more effective in the first stages to mount an educational campaign. The objective might be to make people aware of a particular field of technology or application, for example the use of compressed air in industry as opposed to electrical power.

Local manufacture or assembly are obviously strong points in any PR campaign. On the other hand there are many areas where it is good tactics to stress the quality of the imported product based on the industrial reputation of the country of origin.

CORPORATE ADVERTISING AND IMAGES

Corporate or prestige advertising is one of the activities which can make a major contribution in the overall operation of image projection and creating a climate where people are receptive to a company's policy and products.

The fact that it is more concerned with presenting the company name and what stands behind it than promoting any specific product has seen corporate advertising adopted as a PR function in many large organisations, particularly in America. That it can be either an advertising function or PR function can be seen from the previous chapter, and in practice depends on management policy.

This type of advertising is intended to reach the many 'publics' which are of concern to any progressive organisation. 'It opens doors of the busiest offices, stimulates interest in any product bearing the company name, and plays an unseen part in the recruitment of staff. It also helps to attract capital and creates confidence among shareholders.'[1]

Corporate advertising in international publications can claim many other by-products. Given sufficient time it is an effective aid in establishing a network of competent agents. In many parts of the world good agents are scarce and *they* decide whose products they will handle. Corporate advertising in the right media can often influence their decision in favour of the company concerned.

Following large-scale adoption of corporate advertising by industry, there is a growing awareness of the concept of the multiple image. It has first to be appreciated that a company has a number of different images. The problem arises when, as often happens, these images conflict because there has been a failure to face this fact or agree on objectives for a campaign of image development.

1. Harry E. Maynard. *The Corporate Image and its Vizualisation Abroad.* Paper presented at the European Conference of Time Life International (Stockholm, 1959).

The basic images can be separated and identified.

The *current* image—how the outside world sees the particular subject.

The *mirror* image—how the company sees the particular subject.

The *wish* image—what the company wishes the particular subject image to be or to become.

The *optimum* image—the most desirable image compatible with the company's policy and long-range objectives.[1]

It requires little imagination to appreciate how the first three images can clash and prevent the development of the fourth image (*optimum*).

It is one of the major tasks of PR counselling to remind management of the attitudes and opinions of the people they are trying to reach, in other words to make them aware of the difference between the *current* and *mirror* images. When this stage is reached throughout the company's entire operations, the PR consultant or manager must be concerned with the company's progress towards the *wish* and *optimum* images.

In most companies he will have a major task in reconciling the various attitudes which are responsible for the conflict in image objectives. Robert Browning, the poet, advocated in his works that low aim, not failure, was a crime. Keeping this philosophy in mind the PR executive in all his activities must never lose sight of the ultimate goal.

PROBLEMS OF COMMUNICATION

Despite the advances in science and the increase in means of communication it has given them, people generally seem to be losing the ability to convey their thoughts and intentions. History has shown that many a battle has been lost by poor or faulty communications and it is apparent that communication in industry is one of the major areas crying out for attention and repair. There is no shortage of examples to show that poor communications between management and employees or union head-quarters and their members have often been responsible for lack of direction, misunderstandings, ill-will and the creation of conditions which can only be described as chaotic.

To a large extent public relations is the art of communicating. As industry becomes more complex and competitive, the need for effective channels of contact becomes greater and more difficult to maintain. There is little doubt that communication is a vital but still neglected study in modern industry.

Effective public relations within an organisation is invariably the by-product of good management. A company where staff and employees are well informed and aware of management policies and objectives can claim to know what public relations means, and should never experience any real

1. Aubrey Wilson, 'Researching Industrial Images', *The Manager* (London, November 1964).

difficulty in reaching its public outside. The successful use of PR within a company is so often the application of common sense coupled with a determination to establish and keep open lines of communication which must run vertically as well as horizontally.

There are still the unconverted when it comes to the use of public relations in industry, but their numbers are diminishing as they see what this aid can achieve in the hands of management who believe in it.

10

The Service Element in Added Value

DENNIS ROSE, M.A., A.F.R.Ae.S.

Contrasted with consumer goods, which are purchased for the relatively simple purposes of sustaining life, obtaining pleasure or banishing displeasure, industrial goods are required for the highly complex processes of producing profit. It is true that there are exceptions, such as those purchased and used for the destruction or saving of life itself by the military and medical professions respectively, but these will not affect the argument. The industrial buyer places little value on the mere possession of goods—indeed it is a liability to him, costed in terms of depreciation or stockholding—and most often he does not acquire any status or prestige from them. He is largely concerned with them as elements in a profit-producing system. Although during the selling process it may be necessary to appeal to the egos of certain status-hungry individuals by implying, for instance, that some of the glamour of the most up-to-date and efficient machine on the market will rub off on them, it is self-delusive in the extreme for the manufacturer to assume that it is the glamour alone which sells the product.

Viewing the goods, as the customer does, as potential sources of profit, their most outstanding characteristic is that in themselves they are useless. They cannot be integrated into the profit-producing system unless certain services are applied to them. They must, for instance, be *selected* as the right goods to fulfil a particular function and this may involve anything from obtaining a chart which shows that a $\frac{3}{16}$ in. hole needs a No. 8 drill, to a complete systems study for a computer. The goods may have to be *engineered* into the buyer's own product, as happens with special clips used in motor-car assembly, or assistance with setting-up production processes may be needed, as in the design of moulds for plastic materials. Beyond this, a purchaser may require *credit* or other *financial services*, he may need *repair and maintenance services*, *stockholding* (in the case of raw materials) and regular *supply*, for instance, of special rivets to operate with a particular machine. Many types of plant require *installation* and *commissioning*, and the supplier may also be called on to *train* the customer's operators and maintenance staff.

To the buyer, then, services of this nature are necessary to enable him to develop the full economic value of the goods, and he is generally aware of this. Most buyers of industrial goods recognise that part of the price they pay represents the value of accompanying services, even where those services are not paid for as individual items. For example, there are four or five small offset litho printing machines available on the office machinery market; technically they are very similar, but their prices vary considerably. This is due to the differences between the supporting services which the various manufacturers supply, such as maintenance, operator training and 'trouble-shooting'. In offices where no technical staff are available the quality and completeness of the service given has an obvious value, strictly commensurate with what is paid for that service as part of the total price paid for the machine.

Reckoning in terms of value for money, most buyers take account of the services offered by manufacturers of otherwise interchangeable goods, or, as frequently happens, they are influenced by the manufacturer's reputation for service. Where manufacturers do not supply the requisite services, or where from choice buyers supply them themselves, it is uncommon for the total cost of obtaining them to be calculated, and so the true profitability of using the product is unknown. This sometimes gives rise to opportunities for enterprising suppliers to investigate the true cost and show that their own products are more profitable than those of others.

As the analysis in Chapter 2 has shown, one of the major characteristics of industrial markets is their diversity. Most industrial products are sold to both large and small buyers in more than one industry, often to buyers in many industries. These buyers, purchasing and using the product in many different circumstances, require quantities and combinations of services which often vary greatly.

For instance, in the market for small vacuum pumps those purchasers who incorporate them in printing frames manufactured in quantity require only a minimal amount of service. But a technician working in a hospital laboratory who requires an identical pump may need a great deal of technical advice on how to incorporate it in his apparatus. Again, the size of the customer firm or even of a department within the firm has a great influence on the service demanded; most large electroplating shops in industry have laboratories attached to them, whereas the smaller shop generally has to rely on its supplier of plating materials for analysis of the content of the solutions in the baths.

Thus the industrial seller, who is usually not obliged to sell to the total possible market, and who certainly ought not to regard himself as compelled to do so, has before him an array of market segments, each requiring a different combination of goods and services. Even if all segments of the market must be covered in order to generate a large enough volume of sales, variations in profitability due to different requirements for service must nevertheless be recognised and allowed for in marketing strategy.

The choice of which market segments to cover will, if rationally made, depend on the allocation of resources in such a way as to maximise profit. It involves recognising what services are required to complement the product and so create its full economic value to the purchaser, deciding which of them to provide and whether to make them optional or not, costing them and deciding on a cost structure for the 'package'.

Probably the most important single aspect of this to the seller is costing. As many companies have discovered the hard way, failure to plan adequately for the cost of providing services which the customer requires—or to which he may even have a right in law—may completely erode the margin of profit. In looking at this more closely the idea of 'added value' is useful.

The concept of added value, that is to say the costs of labour, overheads and profit which, added to the costs of raw materials, fuel and bought-out parts represent the output of a manufacturer, is well known. The 'overheads' are generally taken to include all marketing costs as well as such items as rent, rates, managerial and financial costs. Although this analysis may be sufficient for overall economic purposes, it does less than justice to the services produced by manufacturers. Marketing costs are of two kinds. First there are 'inherent marketing costs' without which the product could not be sold. Among these are salesmen's salaries, discounts credited to distributors and the costs of advertising. The remaining marketing costs are those of services, and these, unlike the inherent marketing costs, can be dissociated from the physical product because the latter can be sold without them.

Thus the cost of services can be, and ought to be, clearly separated from the cost of the physical product and the services should be recognised for what they are—an integral part of the added value of the firm, but separable from the value incorporated in the physical product. Further, each of the services which the firm supplies employs labour and capital and ought therefore to be assessed, for profitability, in just the same way as the physical product itself. One set of factors which sellers must take into account in deciding what services to supply becomes apparent in this way; examining some of those services in greater detail some of the other factors affecting decisions of this kind become apparent.

SERVICES PRIOR TO PURCHASE

The first of all the services which may be associated with any product assists the customer to recognise his need for it. At its simplest, this is nothing more than the basic salesmanship of explaining to the prospect how useful the product is, but it may take highly sophisticated forms, often arising out of the findings of marketing research surveys. A manufacturer of transistors, for example, carried out a survey to locate future demand and found that portable radio offered a mass market. The next step was to persuade the radio manufacturers of the existence of the hitherto untapped potential for portable radios—and so for transistors. Manufacturers of plastic materials give this type of service extensively, their customers being frequently encouraged and assisted to produce new products from chemical and plastic materials. Perhaps a good example, and one which has already been quoted, is I.C.I. promoting 'Perspex' baths to the consumers in order to encourage plastic fabricators to buy I.C.I.'s polymethyl methacrylate, branded 'Perspex' rather than competitive materials.

This type of activity is often called 'market development' or 'back-selling'. Such descriptions can disguise its true nature as a service and render it liable to be confused with sales promotion of a more conventional kind.

Assisting the buyer in selection of the right product within a range is an activity which almost every manufacturer with more than one product to sell carries out. Yet, in spite of all the 'product selection charts', slide rules and other devices which are supplied to potential customers, product selection is not always seen as the effective marketing tool which it can be if fully exploited. Good examples of such use are, however, to be found in the mechanical handling industry, where manufacturers will carry out feasibility studies and design complete conveyor systems, laying out new production lines or even complete factories for potential customers.

When the customer is at the point where he is considering which of the seller's products to use he is beginning to be vulnerable to these techniques, which take various forms. The seller may first make a thorough study of the buyer's requirements. A paint manufacturer, for example, may make a study of the conditions under which a finished article is to be used, specifying not only the paint but also the preliminary metal treatment, spraying and stoving conditions. In many fields of engineering products, particularly those which are components of, or materials for, other products, the service of providing assistance with product selection frequently becomes the even more developed function of application engineering.

This type of service may be abused, and if it is supplied to any great extent this possibility has to be taken into account. Many prospective buyers take advantage of these services and then make their purchases elsewhere. They may even obtain similar services from several competing firms. There is, of course, nothing reprehensible in this; no moral obligation is undertaken by the acceptance of a freely offered service, and if a prospective customer who has been given 'the full treatment' subsequently goes elsewhere the resulting disappointment must not be allowed to spill over into disapproval. Rather, this should be treated as an indication that something is wrong, and the reasons should be carefully investigated.

Another, and insidious, danger of applications engineering is that it may lead the firm carrying it out to engage in an excessive number of modifications of its own products, with each sale tending to be a 'one-off' job. What frequently happens is that an unplanned, almost unnoticed, expansion of application engineering occurs and the number of special models going through the works increases, thus driving costs upwards. In such cases it is not unusual for a 'rationalisation' of this state of affairs to be offered, generally in the form of an explanation that the business of the firm depends on 'service to customers'. The business may indeed depend on giving service; if so it is all the more important to plan and control the service.

There is only one way to avoid these dangers. It is for firms to be constantly aware of what their actual role in the market is and to compare this with what their role ought to be. The planned policy may be to supply models tailored to individual requirements, or it may be to supply only a few standard models; whichever it is, the amount and quality of services to be supplied must be carefully laid down and subsequently controlled. In this way the supply of services may be put on a basis of profit so that they become a marketable part of the firm's output.

SERVICE AFTER SALES

Service after sales is of supreme importance because it is exactly what buyers think of when they consider 'service'. By this they generally mean repairs, maintenance and the supply of spares. The reputation of many a firm has been made or broken by the efficiency or otherwise of its repair and parts service. In some industries, of which process-control instruments is a good example, the choice of supplier is frequently made on the basis of this type of service even if the products are not entirely comparable. Similar situations occur in the commercial vehicle and earthmoving equipment industries.

Because of its importance to the buyer, repair and maintenance service can be a potent sales and marketing factor, though this depends ultimately on clear thinking about the place of service in the price structure of the product.

Many users of plant and equipment prefer to employ their own maintenance staff, so as to keep 'down-time' to a minimum. Others rely on the manufacturers. If there is considerable spare plant capacity, down-time presents no problem; in many other cases users cannot support the maintenance staff required or simply do not have the necessary skills available.

The demand for service thus depends very largely on the circumstances in which the product is used; the way in which that demand is met is determined largely by the seller's attitude to his product. When the product is regarded as a reliable one, then an allowance for service, not necessarily very large, is included in the price charged. This allowance should include the appropriate percentages for overhead and profit, because it is part of the added value of the product. If the product is one which clearly requires routine maintenance and is liable to need repair at fairly frequent intervals, then service of this type will not be included in the added value of the product but will become a separate series of transactions with the buyer, costed on a profitable basis.

Provided that it is profitable to the seller, the repair and maintenance service offered can be actively promoted as an attraction of the product; this may particularly be the case when maintenance is carried out under contract, a procedure which deserves more attention than it has so far received outside certain industries such as office machinery.

Associated with the question of repair and maintenance is that of provision of spares and supplies. This may be a relatively minor activity, as in the case of machine tools, or it may be the major profit-making element of a marketing operation. Examples of this occur in riveting, where special rivets are supplied to users equipped with machines for which they pay only nominal rental, and in copying machines, where one well-known manufacturer offers rental of the machines at £1 a month—maintenance included—and relies entirely on sale of the special paper used in them for the major proportion of turnover and profit.

It cannot be said that this kind of service forms part of the added value of the product, if the machine is regarded as the product, but regarding the rivets or the paper in these examples as the products, then ancillary services such as maintenance of the machines do indeed form part of the value added to the paper (for instance).

Other types of after-sales service of importance are those concerned with the installation and commissioning of plant and equipment. Although in the technical sense there is often continuity between application engineering and the installation and commissioning of plant, there is a vital distinction to be made between them, in that the latter services are frequently paid for as such by the purchasers. Properly speaking, they then cease to be part of the added value of the product; in some cases, for instance in the heavy electrical and chemical industries, installation is carried out by specialist firms.

FINANCIAL SERVICES

In comparison with engineering services, which are widely given and whose place in marketing is fairly well understood, financial services have received almost no attention. Yet as marketing tools they have potentialities of vast scope and significance. In considering the financial services, all of which are basically methods of extending credit to customers, two dichotomies need to be pointed out. These are, first, the differences of approach to consumer markets and industrial ones and, second, the varying attitudes towards credit in home and export markets.

The role of credit in consumer marketing needs no elaboration here. It is used to expand markets and—by governmental control of credit—to regulate them. In buying many types of consumer durables the customer cannot avoid being offered credit, as a glance in any TV retailer's window will confirm. In industrial markets this is very far from being the case. With one or two exceptions, they must make their own arrangements. Only a very few industrial sellers give any assistance to the buyer in obtaining credit facilities, let alone suggest that they might be appropriate.

The situation is apparently different on the export market. In exporting, the need for giving credit is plain—it is essential to offer at least as much as competitors in other countries, and in doing so exporters have available to them the services of the Export Credits Guarantee Department and those of many other institutions. This, however, cannot be said to be a positive marketing policy, but is merely to use credit as a defensive weapon in a competitive situation.

Thus, the role of credit in the British market for capital goods is a small one. Here it has to be said that this is in striking contrast with the situation in the United States.

'When Cyrus Hall McCormick perfected his first reaper, he demonstrated that it would not only reduce the toil and drudgery of farm work but also return to the user all he paid for it and more. At that time—the 1830's and 1840's—many banks and financing institutions were quite hesitant about lending money on this new type of equipment. So McCormick decided to extend credit himself to worthy farmers who wanted to buy his reaper. The venture was a sound one because the product paid for itself in use.'[1]

This was the foundation of the International Harvester Company.

As an early example of the 'marketing concept' in action this recognition of the total requirements of the buyer is striking. It was not sufficient to sell a better reaper—it was essential in addition to ensure that farmers could actually buy it.

But the full potentialities of marketing credit extend even beyond this. It is a feature of the present economic scene that even quite small variations in the level of total demand produce greatly magnified variations in the demand for capital goods such as machine tools, and there is a considerable time lag between the peaks of total demand and of those for capital goods. The producers of the latter, therefore, experience considerable expansions and contractions in their order books and in their stocks of finished goods; the buyers of capital goods find that when they wish to place orders the delivery times they are offered are far too long.

The promotion of credit facilities by the manufacturers of capital goods as a positive marketing policy can go a long way towards offsetting this situation. In times when demand is slack they can generate fresh orders by offering speedy delivery to customers. The customers can defer payment or, at least, spread the payment over a period when the machines are in production and thus yielding profit—during a phase of the business cycle which is favourable to them (but not necessarily to the capital goods suppliers). The stabilising effect of this policy on manufacturers of capital goods and on their users, and so on employment and demand as a whole, could be considerable.

One of the most important of the ways in which purchasers of industrial equipment can obtain credit is by leasing. A number of financial houses are now offering leasing terms under which transactions ranging from £500 to

1. Herman Ebsen, quoted in 'Top Management Forum', *Industrial Marketing* (Chicago, June 1963).

£2 million have been known. In a typical transaction the customer advises the lessor of the type and cost of equipment required and the appropriate obligatory leasing period is agreed. The equipment is ordered by the customer, since he knows the specifications, but his order is confirmed by the leasing company, which is subsequently invoiced by the manufacturer.

Such arrangements have many advantages for the customer; however, the use which the *seller* can make of this type of facility is a marketing area which has been almost entirely overlooked. There is, however, one example of the use of leasing in marketing which is worth describing.

The British Aluminium Company, in conjunction with the Mercantile Leasing Company, have sponsored and promoted a plan which enables industry to lease virtually any type of aluminium container. In this, not only the British Aluminium Company but also many of the fabricators of aluminium boxes, trolleys, bins, skips, casks, drums—in fact any container which can be made in aluminium—take part. The lease is simple in operation. The future lessee specifies and agrees with the fabricator of his choice exactly what is required, a lease is entered into with the Mercantile Leasing Company, the appropriate order is placed and delivery is made. Thus the user does not need to tie up his own capital in containers. Further, under the Container Leasing Plan, the British Aluminium Company agree to repurchase containers which the lessee no longer requires from the leasing company—whose property they are until this happens.

There is no reason why similar types of arrangement should not be used in other industries, under the sponsorship of the producers and sellers of goods just as much as under that of leasing companies.

In the day-by-day business of marketing capital goods such a policy represents a new dimension in salesmanship. It is no longer sufficient for the salesman to know what the customer wants and to try to sell the products of his firm against those of the competition. He must be fully acquainted with the current and the developing financial position of the customer and must be ready to realise that while the production manager, for instance, may be fully convinced of the need for new plant, the financial director may not be. The salesman must, therefore, be ready with a credit plan to place in the hands of the production manager, who may use it to convince the financial director of the practicality and advantages of placing an order at the time rather than postponing it.

This requires a considerable change in outlook on the part of the manufacturers of capital goods. Whereas their main concern is at present to sell against competition from other suppliers, they must now in addition sell in such a way as to overcome the effects of the business cycle, both on themselves and on their customers.

CUSTOMER TRAINING

Customer training is regarded by some companies as one of the most important of their services. It is carried out both in the operation of plant and equipment and its servicing, and is generally offered free of charge to the customer. In contrast, many firms producing even highly complex equipment offer no training facilities beyond instructional handbooks, and these do not always receive the attention they deserve.

The reasons for this wide variation in attitudes to training are fairly clear. A firm well established in its market may rightly take the view that customer training creates long term product preference and prestige, firstly by impressing its facilities in the minds of a captive audience of trainees, and secondly by helping to ensure a high standard of operation and maintenance of its products, wherever they are seen.

However, training services are very expensive to provide, they yield no immediate and little medium term sales, and it is often argued that money spent on them would be more usefully employed in other forms of promotion. This is more likely to be the attitude of firms other than the market leader in any particular field.

Whatever the nature of the customer training facilities operated, they should be carefully reviewed at reasonably frequent intervals. The more highly organised a training school is and the higher the standards achieved the more it develops an inner logic of self-justification and the greater the danger of its absorbing resources which might be better used elsewhere. The dangerous period probably begins when the school comes to be regarded as a 'prestige' symbol rather than as a service of positive value to purchasers of the firm's products.

PRODUCTS, SERVICES AND MARKETING STRATEGY

Theodore Levitt in Chapter 18 states that 'A truly marketing minded firm tries to create value-satisfying goods and services that customers will want to buy. What it offers for sale not only includes the generic product or service but also how it is made available to the customer, in what form, when, under what conditions and at what terms of trade. Most important, *what it offers for sale is determined not by the seller but by the buyer.* The seller takes his cues from the buyer in such a way that the product becomes consequence of the marketing effort, not vice versa.' The italics are mine, however, because although this is a fair expression of the marketing concept as applied to markets of a homogeneous nature, it does not necessarily form an adequate basis of a strategy for all industrial markets.

Industrial markets exhibit such wide variations in the nature and quality of demand that any firm which is at the mercy of its customers to the extent that they determine what it offers for sale deserves sympathy— but very little else. Rather, it is for the firm to analyse the market, discover the varying requirements of different sectors of it and satisfy those particular types of demand which it is best able to meet with its own particular blend of skills and resources.

Almost any industrial demand, as has been seen, contains components of demand for physical products and for closely associated services. Without the latter, the product is of no value to the buyer. These services, even when associated with the same physical product, are required in greatly varying degrees by large and small users of the product and by those in different industries, and this adds many dimensions to the range of choice open to sellers in what they sell and to whom they offer it.

The total product, that is, the combination of physical product and services, is what the buyer obtains for his money, and it is enlightening to regard it as raw material to which value has been added by the manufacturer. The added value comprises various elements of physical product and of service, each of which requires for its production the employment of labour, capital and others of the manufacturer's resources. These resources are always limited, but they can be allocated to the production and distribution of physical goods and of services in many varying combinations, each of which yields a certain profitability. It is just because industrial markets offer a range of choice to the seller in what combination of goods and services he supplies that opportunities arise to employ the available resources in various ways and consequently to maximise profit.

Looking once more at a case previously mentioned, would it be more profitable for a vacuum pump manufacturer to employ highly qualified staff to sell to laboratories, or should these personnel be employed in the development of pumps for larger scale use? This kind of question can only be answered by considering the full impact on resources, productive, technical and financial, as well as any changes in the amount and composition of turnover which would be involved.

Thus any industrial marketing strategy which takes into account both the physical product and service elements of added value must depend on matching the available productive resources to the demands of those sectors of the market in which they can most profitably be employed. The human, financial and technical resources must be allocated to products and services in relation to the importance placed upon them, and it is in correctly assessing the buyer's judgement of their value that the seller achieves his success.

11

Physical Distribution

D. JOHN AYLOTT, M.A.

DEFINITION

'Physical distribution' is commonly confused with 'the choice of marketing channel' and as a marketing function in its own right, it is largely unrecognised.

Physical distribution in industrial marketing may be defined as the process of interpretation of an order to effect the movement of industrial goods from the point of manufacture or storage to the customer in accordance with marketing policy.

The breadth of the definition of industrial marketing is such that it is not possible to discuss physical distribution as a series of specific examples but neither is it necessary to resort to vague generalities for throughout industry there is a common pattern of events commencing with the taking of an order and culminating in the payment for goods received. The execution of this aspect of business is the direct concern of marketing and will work for or against the success of the marketing operation depending upon the efficiency with which it is carried out. The yardstick against which this efficiency is measured should be defined in the marketing policy of the company.

Large sums of money are spent on sales representation and advertising and tremendous marketing effort is made to secure a customer with a view to obtaining business in the form of orders. This establishes the initial contact and in very many instances the customer has little or no further contact with the supplier until the goods are advised, delivered, invoiced and statemented. The accuracy and method by which this series of events is carried out will either endorse the previous sales effort or alternatively jeopardise any goodwill which may have been built up.

PHYSICAL DISTRIBUTION—A MARKETING FUNCTION

The warehousing and movement of industrial goods is the day-to-day business of specialists, the works manager, warehouse manager, transport manager and indeed, the handling of orders may be delegated to a contracts department or order office, but the activity of all these departments is directed, in one way or another, by the marketing policies of the company.

In considering the activities which begin with the receipt of an order and encompass all those activities directly concerned with the interpretation of an order and the movement of goods to a customer, it is convenient to consider the total activity in three parts.

Although not all the policy matters discussed are equally relevant in different industries, it is suggested that they are all matters on which a decision should be consciously made if only to discount it as irrelevant.

Systems, rules and decisions governing the interpretation of an order, the creation of internal orders, advice notes, invoices, statements, movement sheets and proof of delivery notes.

Availability of goods to the correct specification, in the correct location at the correct time.

Transportation of goods to the correct destination, by the correct method to give effect to the marketing policy with regard to time, reliability, service and cost.

MARKETING POLICIES: PHYSICAL DISTRIBUTION SYSTEMS

The length of time available between the receipt of an order and the receipt of goods by a customer—normally referred to as the 'lead time'—will determine not only the method of processing orders and the production of despatch instructions, but also the relevance of each of the other policies to be discussed. Clearly, if the lead time is unimportant, specific marketing decisions can be made relative to each order, but if it is limited then these decisions must be taken in anticipation of orders in the form of rules based on marketing policy. In any event, the apportionment of such time as is available between order processing, production and transportation is a matter of the utmost importance. It may be far more economical to increase the speed of order processing than to adopt a faster means of transportation or decentralised warehousing.

It is important to define who can authorise urgent orders to have preferential treatment. In one industrial undertaking, 30 per cent of all orders were marked 'urgent' until the general manager intervened and personally authorised each one. The level fell to less than 1 per cent. A laxity on this control can make nonsense of any policy or system.

The order initiates the chain of events leading to the delivery of goods and the effectiveness of physical distribution cannot be better than the order that gives rise to it. This leads to a requirement for a marketing policy with regard to the form in which an order is received, the means of communication of that order and the responsibility for ensuring its accuracy.

In the event of an order being received from a new customer, a procedure for obtaining a credit reference may be necessary. This again is the subject of a marketing policy and requires definition.

A customer who will not pay, or who is dilatory in this matter, may soon become a liability and a policy regarding the acceptance or refusal of an order in these circumstances is most essential. This not only protects the company from incurring bad debts but also protects the customer from the non-delivery of goods or an untimely demand for payment where the company has agreed to a credit facility. The volume of orders being handled may make it necessary to adopt an unvarying policy but the more usual procedure is to filter out orders for those customers subject to credit restrictions. These can then be dealt with individually.

Constant delays can occur in preparing orders for invoicing if a company operates a complicated discount structure or gives special terms to specific customers. Here again the problem is particularly serious in companies handling a high volume of orders in a minimum time. In some businesses, there is the further complication of purchase tax and representatives' incentives. Some, or all of these, are necessary and need not interfere with the smooth operation of order handling provided the rules are made known and adhered to by all concerned.

Where goods are manufactured and despatched specifically to a customer's order, the importance of this problem is reduced in that there is more time available for invoicing and each invoice has to be prepared individually.

WAREHOUSING AND MARKETING POLICIES

One of the two reasons for adopting a policy of decentralised warehousing is to give increased service to customers by reducing the time taken for delivery. Hence the marketing policy, with regard to the service to be offered to the customer, may determine the warehousing policy but as there are many other factors weighing against decentralisation, it may be that a reduction in the time taken by the administration of physical distribution will be the correct solution.

Finally, the marketing policy will determine the number of stock lines which are being carried for general sale and for specific customers and clearly this will have a very distinct influence on the method and cost of warehousing. A policy to keep everything which has ever been made 'because it may come in useful' will result in a large proportion of slow moving or obsolescent stocks. This is not only expensive—estimated at 15–25 per cent of the cost of the goods per annum—but hinders the day-to-day operation of the profitable lines. Stocks of spare parts present a particular problem in this respect but this makes it all the more important to have a live marketing policy, properly costed, to determine the correct method of operation.

In addition to reducing the slow moving lines, value analysis and variety reduction enable the profitable lines within a company to yield their full contribution instead of carrying a large number of less profitable ones. This is the direct responsibility of marketing management, but in practice it is marketing management who resist this action.

In a business devoted to customer built goods, warehousing becomes simply a link in the chain between production and the customer. Production control whose function it is to give effect to the policies of the company in respect of the production of goods in line with orders received, becomes responsible for ensuring that the goods are available for despatch in the right place at the right time. In this case it is justifiable to think of production control as an integral part of the distribution function.

TRANSPORTATION

In reviewing the methods of transport available to industry it will be seen that the costs increase as the time to cover a given distance is reduced. It is a marketing decision, having due regard to all the associated factors involved to determine the service level required and hence ultimately the method of transport to be adopted. The advice of specialists will need to be sought but the method chosen directly affects the cost of the product and the service provided.

Once the method has been determined in relation to service, remaining problems can be left to the specialists in materials handling. There is, however, one further aspect of distribution directly affected by the marketing policy, and this concerns proof of delivery, particularly where distribution is effected through subcontractors. Unfortunately the importance of the 'goods inwards' function in industry is grossly underestimated and this leads to considerable wasted effort in administration departments in questioning the whereabouts of goods, sometimes already received. In these circumstances, proof of delivery becomes important not only to the customer but also to the intermediate carriers. Provided proper provision is made, a question relating to the whereabouts of goods in transit can be answered not only by the fact of despatch but also as to their last recorded location. This is a service which an industrial customer has a right to expect as it may seriously affect his operation.

The cost and complication of this service is considerable but it is an area in which good service does much to reinforce the goodwill between companies. In fact it is the reverse which causes so much ill will. Goods despatched but untraceable put a customer in a difficult and embarrassing position.

TECHNICAL ASPECTS

It is no more possible to define technical methods for the handling of the administration of goods than it is to define specific marketing policies. It is, however, practicable to analyse the various functions which may be required to be carried out in effecting physical distribution. Once again not all of these will be directly relevant or carry equal weight in any particular industry but the pattern of events is similar and each aspect should be carefully considered even if the result is to reject it.

The chain of events linking the receipt of an order with the receipt of the goods by a customer is shown below:

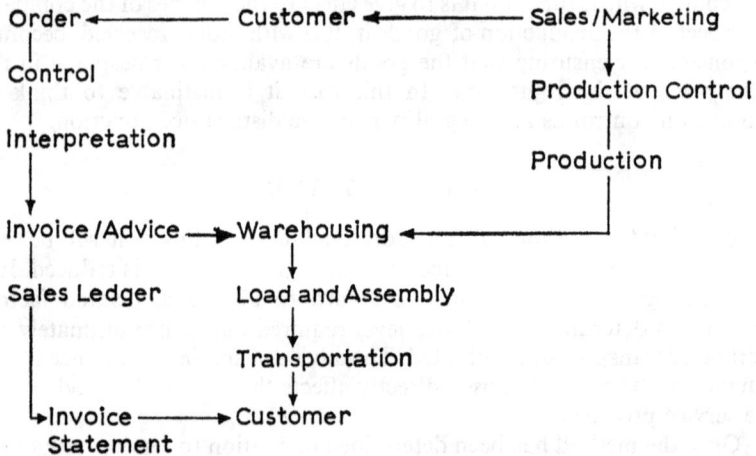

```
Order ◄──────── Customer ◄──────── Sales/Marketing
  │                                        │
Control                              Production Control
  │                                        │
Interpretation                        Production
  │                                        │
  ▼                                        │
Invoice/Advice ──►Warehousing ◄────────────┘
  │                    │
Sales Ledger      Load and Assembly
  │                    │
  │                    ▼
  │               Transportation
  │                    │
  ▼                    ▼
└►Invoice ──────► Customer
  Statement
```

There are two broad variations on this pattern of events. First, if the business is making to customer order, the interpretation may be carried out in the contracts, design or drawing office and fed via production control to production and the warehouse. Secondly, where the business is manufacturing stock and a system of pre-invoicing is used, the invoice and advice note will be raised before the despatch instructions are released to the warehouse. A feedback from the warehouse is then used to release the invoice.

Physical distribution commences with the receipt of an order from a customer. The means by which the order is to be communicated and the address to which it is to be sent must be made known to the customer either through advertising media, catalogues, order forms or representatives. This is particularly important where orders are handled at a number of centres or where the system is such that it can only process orders received by one means of communication.

The form of the order will vary not only with each customer but with each industry, ranging from a brief telephone call to a lengthy legal document stemming from an enquiry and tender. Whatever the form, the point at which the order is acceptable should be defined and an adequate check made to ensure that it is the intention of the customer to enter into a legally binding agreement and that all the necessary information is available. This must include; customer's name and address for delivery of goods; customer's name and address for invoicing purposes; customer's order number; a clear and accurate description of the goods or services required by quantity and type; price; date on which delivery is to be effected; any special instructions.

The order should not be accepted unless all the relevant detail is available as it may lead to subsequent delay and to dissatisfaction.

Customers' orders are handled by the sales or contracts office and the purpose of this is to ensure that the correct order information is available, that the order is acceptable, and to raise an internal order to give effect to the production or despatch of goods. An order may not be acceptable for any of a number of reasons. The order may be outside the normal activities of the business; the order is too small or too large; the customer may not be known and references may be required; the customer may be subject to credit restrictions; a condition imposed by the customer may be unacceptable or impossible to meet.

The function of interpretation from customer's order to internal order initiates a series of events which commit the selling company to expenditure and at the same time determines what the customer will receive.

The internal order will require to be coded and referenced for internal use but quick access to the customer's order is essential if a good standard of service is to be achieved.

The price quoted by the customer and any representative's remuneration must be checked together with any special terms or discounts which may apply. The internal order will normally become the source document from which an invoice is prepared, and in pre-invoicing systems wrong information will also delay the preparation of the despatch documentation.

PROCESSING

Once the customer's order has been interpreted, the information has to be processed to give rise to the despatch of goods, invoice and statement to the customer. This may occur in one of three ways depending upon the type of business. First, in a business manufacturing to customer's order, the internal order itself will initiate the design and manufacture of the goods and despatch is normally initiated in the despatch department as goods become available. The advice note will be raised in that department and a copy used to initiate the raising of an invoice. Second, in a business supplying ex-stock or effectively ex-stock with only final assembly work to be carried out, the internal order may be used immediately to initiate despatch and, following despatch, a copy of the advice note is used to create an invoice (post invoicing) or, thirdly, the internal order may be used to create a complete set of paper work, including the advice note, proof of delivery note, and invoice subsequent to which the relevant paperwork is passed to despatch for action (pre-invoicing). The advantages and disadvantages for adopting pre or post invoicing are:

	Advantages	Disadvantages
Pre Invoicing:	All paperwork created simultaneously leads to reduced administration costs.	Delays despatch of goods while paperwork being created.
	All paperwork is identical, usually carbon copy, which reduces chance of random errors.	Special arrangements have to be made to overcome stock shortages.
	Suitable data processing techniques in high volume business.	
	Invoice available immediately despatch effected.	
Post Invoicing:	Enables minimum of paperwork to be created before despatch giving good service level.	High administration cost in processing information twice.
		Greater possibility of error between advice and invoice.
		Greater delay in posting invoice after goods have been despatched.
	Enables custom made goods to be despatched as available before completion of order.	Greater likelihood of goods being despatched and not invoiced.
		More paperwork spread over greater period unavoidable.

While each business must determine the correct method to adopt, pre-invoicing is advantageous administratively provided goods are despatched ex-stock, stock shortages are kept to a minimum and the service level to customer allows sufficient lead time to create the entire paperwork before despatch.

Whichever method is adopted, the outcome will be the creation of an advice note and invoice and, as both of these are sent to the customer, it is important that they are legible and presentable documents. They must also be useful to the customer and bear his order number and reference and describe the goods in a way he can understand. Data processing systems often limit the number of letters available for description with the result that 'Sheets of Bright Stainless Steel' may become 'Shts Br St St'. The advice should arrive with or before the goods and the invoice after the goods. It must state the quantity of goods actually despatched and whether this is a part or complete order. The invoice must identify the advice or advices to which it refers and both advice and invoice should be printed on suitable paper designed and travel tested to stand up to the normal handling encountered. Finally the advice must give some indication, not only of the contents of a package, but also of its outer appearance for identification purposes.

The arrival of an advice note, with or without the goods, the arrival of the goods and subsequently the invoice represent a large proportion of customer contact with the supplier and it is true to say that throughout industry this important aspect of marketing is not only overlooked, but very badly handled.

SERVICE LEVELS AND ADMINISTRATION

The object of including an analysis of the systems as part of the physical distribution is to put the whole operation in perspective. So often despatch is thought of as a function commencing in the despatch office when in fact the series of events starts hours, days, weeks or months beforehand. Moreover, in many companies, the administration costs of distribution are completely divorced from the cost of the warehouse and transportation. An appreciation of the cost and nature of the administration is particularly important in arriving at the correct service level and method of operation.

With the three distinct features of administration, warehousing and transportation in mind, an improvement in service level can be achieved by an improvement in any one or more of these areas and it may be far cheaper to streamline the systems than to adopt decentralised warehousing or a different method of transportation.

THE PURPOSE OF WAREHOUSING

Much time and energy has been devoted to discussing the desirability of centralised and decentralised warehousing with the regrettable result that those companies operating a centralised system want to decentralise, and those operating a decentralised system want to centralise. In some instances, the history of a company even shows this process to occur within its own organisation. In order to resolve this, it is necessary to examine the purpose of a warehouse and then subsequently to examine what determines its location.

Warehouses are to hold a stock of finished goods ready for despatch and hence in some industries, warehouses are unknown. The electricity supply industry where the product cannot be stored and heavy engineering or shipbuilding where the product is made entirely to customer's order and hence, on completion, it is 'distributed' immediately, are examples of these industries. In such cases the production capacity and sales have to be matched as well as possible to meet the sales requirement.

In other industries which do sell ex-warehouse, the ideal situation would exist where the sales' offtake is absolutely regular, matched with the supply rate, and always following the predicted product mix. Such a situation never prevails and hence a 'buffer' is introduced in the form of warehouse stock to 'uncouple' supply and demand, that is to allow supply and demand to operate independently within certain defined limits.[1] This can be the *only* reason for having a warehouse but it is not the only solution to meeting varying demand. By the nature of its product, the electricity supply

1. Albert Battersby, *A Guide to Stock Control*, Pitman (London, 1962).

industry cannot warehouse its final product and it has therefore to accommodate the variation in demand by equipping to meet maximum demand at any time. This can be achieved in other industries but it is very expensive. The coal industry on the other hand establishes large reserves over the summer months to meet the heavy demand in the winter. Warehousing is therefore just one method of buffering supply and demand and it should be thought of in this way.

WAREHOUSE OPERATION

The reason for wanting to buffer supply and demand can be restated by saying that the demand is required to be independent of the supply in order to achieve speed and flexibility in the distribution operation. This can only be achieved if the supplies to the warehouse are properly controlled to maintain the 'buffer' and if the warehousing operation itself is carried out efficiently.

Goods must be carefully examined on receipt for quantity, type and quality and they should be located accurately. Goods wrongly located or subject to inaccurate records are effectively lost. A study is desirable to ensure that the goods are received wherever possible in a condition suitable for reshipment with a minimum number of extra operations, that they are clearly identifiable and in the correct unit quantity in line with the normal pattern of offtake.

The appropriate storage facilities and handling methods should be installed to ensure that the stock does not deteriorate, that it can be used in rotation and that it is readily accessible when required. This requires proper financial investment in buildings and equipment and a proper management appreciation of the cost of the operations involved to achieve the control and service required.

On receipt of despatch instructions in the form of an advice note, invoice, delivery instructions or internal order, the despatch manager is responsible for grouping these in such a way that the correct goods are sent by the correct method of transport to the correct address at the correct time and with the maximum utilisation of available transport. In order to achieve this the following information needs to be provided for each despatch instruction at the point of despatch:—

The number and description of items to be transported, the customer's order number, weight/volume of the shipment, destination of the goods, special restrictions on delivery time, place or method, any unusual urgency, advice information, shipping marks and transport type if outside the normal method.

This information should be specified to the despatch office before the operation commences. It should not be necessary for further information to be sought at this stage. A common method of operation is then to sort the orders into time of delivery, area for delivery, type of transport and loading sequence if relevant.

By analysis of the weight or volume involved, the amount of transport required of each type and the route to be followed by each to give the maximum number of deliveries in the shortest time and distance can be determined. There are so many variables in this operation that it repays close study and the employment of experienced traffic clerks. This operation leads to the preparation of shipping documentation in the form of movement sheets to authorise the movement of goods by the carrier, whatever form of transport is used, and to feed back to the sales administration department the fact that certain goods have been shipped.

Computer techniques are now being developed but due again to the number of variables and the need to define rules connecting them progress at the present time is slow.

The selection of the correct goods for a customer will only present difficulty if the goods are not accurately and completely described on the advice note/order/copy invoice or if the goods cannot themselves be recognised. The choice of a suitable coding or internal order numbering system, together with a continual awareness throughout of the importance of clear identification and accurate paperwork, will enable the despatch operation to proceed unhindered.

The means of handling goods within any warehouse will naturally depend upon the type of goods being handled but once again the correct choice of method and the allocation of proper assembly areas for goods prior to despatch is vital to the smooth running of the organisation. The choice of the particular handling method to be used falls outside the subject matter of this chapter, but in principle it must be compatible with handling of goods received, with the movement of goods in the warehouse and again for despatch.

A warehouse is not simply an area in which goods are kept but is the centre of a highly complex activity involving many aspects of a company's business. Its primary purpose, it has been shown, is to buffer supply against fluctuation in demand. Against this background the reasons underlying the adoption of decentralised warehousing can be considered. There are two and two only.

CENTRALISED AND DECENTRALISED WAREHOUSING

The use of decentralised warehousing can only be justified either by the requirement of a service level which allows insufficient lead time for the transportation of goods from a central depot or by a reduction in transport charges brought about by the use of bulk transport between depots. However, there are many disadvantages in adopting a policy of decentralised warehouses and every other means of increasing service levels or reducing costs should be considered first. A high service level is clearly dictated by marketing policy, but in order to achieve this attention should first be given to the streamlining of systems and to improving warehousing methods to give improved service often at reduced cost. Furthermore faster transport may be considerably cheaper and more flexible than a series of satellite warehouses, all of which have to be staffed, equipped, administered and stocked.

Unless the order handling and paperwork systems are also decentralised, the advantages may be lost or nullified due to the extended communications between the order offices and the outlying warehouses, leading in turn to greater likelihood of error and poorer control. A central stock recording system also becomes necessary so that orders may be routed to the warehouse carrying the requisite stock and situated nearest to the customer.

If the system is decentralised, all basic data regarding the address to which customers should route their orders, stock availability, order interpretation, credit status and credit references must be communicated to the satellite warehouses. Thus, not only are the lines of communication extended but much of the administration is duplicated or even multiplied by the number of satellites.

The adoption of faster transport will certainly increase the cost of the operation, as demonstrated later in this chapter, and more frequent deliveries may require some part loads to be shipped but in conjunction with streamlined systems and good warehousing, this may prove to be far more economical and satisfactory than setting up satellite warehouses.

If the service level is still unsatisfactory after considering all these possibilities, then decentralisation may become necessary. In this event, the warehouses must be located as close to the centre of demand as possible to reduce transport time to a minimum, and the administration and order handling procedures must be reviewed and adapted to that method of working.

Unless the method of transport used for the bulk movement of material costs substantially less than the method required for local distribution, it is unlikely that decentralised warehousing can be justified on these grounds. The saving on transport may be nullified by the extra cost of decentralised warehousing, administration and control. For this reason, it is normally only bulk raw materials which can justify this approach and examples are coal moved in bulk by rail or oil moved in bulk by pipeline and further distributed by road transport. In these cases, order handling and administration is also decentralised and the 'warehouses' are located close to centres of demand but clearly and more importantly near to a point conveniently supplied by the bulk transport method, for example, a rail head or the docks where ships are the bulk carriers.

Even in these circumstances, some form of centralised control becomes necessary in the event of a shortage in order to make the best use of available stocks irrespective of location.

It cannot be emphasised too often that a policy of decentralised warehousing can only be justified by the requirement of a high service level or reduction in cost by the use of bulk transport but even then it should not be adopted until every other method of improvement or cost reduction has been considered.

TRANSPORTATION OF GOODS

Emphasis has already been placed on the need for the use of correct systems in physical distribution and the real test of the effectiveness of these comes at the point of despatch with load assembly and transportation. This operation calls for the physical association of goods with the relevant paperwork into unit loads for movement, and conditions should be such that a minimum of errors occur at this stage for they will lead not only to customer dissatisfaction and loss of goodwill, but also to high transport and administration charges in putting the matter right.

In order to achieve smooth operation of this function the paperwork giving rise to movement has to be comprehensive and in standard form. Broad rules must be established with regard to the selection of transport to be used and the general service level expected from this part of the operation. Materials handling and identification must be studied to ensure ease of movement on to the transport and the ready identification of goods.

In order to give effect to the marketing policy of the company, it is essential to define certain broad rules to guide the despatch office in their choice of transport. Experience shows that lack of liaison with regard to urgency and choice of transport type can lead to endless friction when, for example, an urgent consignment is delayed on the railways when it should have been delivered air freight.

There are five main methods of moving goods in common use; post, air freight, rail—passenger and goods—road—own transport and carriers—sea and inland waterways.

Other methods include overhead or underground cables for electricity, aerial ropeway, conveyors and pipelines which are now used for transporting gases, liquids and solids.

It is not possible to generalise on the best method to be used, but there are a number of factors to be considered in making the choice.

The measure of service—or speed of delivery—must be taken from the point of collection to the point of delivery. Long delays at airports may negate any advantage to be gained by air freight over short distances, or inefficiency at a railway station can defeat the purpose of passenger goods by rail.

The measure of cost for comparing one method of transport with another should be carefully studied, especially with regard to transport operated by the supplying company. It is easy enough to establish the cost of goods per ton using hauliers as this is settled either by negotiation or tariffs, usually on a contract basis. The cost of 'home fleet' operation in most companies is very much more difficult to assess due to the flexibility in allocating overheads and the need or otherwise of the transport operation to make a 'profit'. For comparative purposes, the approximate relative costs of different types of transport are given at the end of this chapter.

Linked with this is the question of whether a company should rightly be involved in the transport business. The approach should be for a company to have to justify being in the business rather than to justify using contractors. For the most part, hauliers are specialists and have the advantage of being able to utilise their transport far more fully than most manufacturing or distributing industries and the service they provide, while far from perfect, is for the most part not unsatisfactory.

The use of specialised transport is on the increase as evidenced in particular by the extensive increase in the use of tankers for handling bulk liquids and powders. There is, however, very much more work to be done in this field and a large proportion of companies would benefit from a critical review of their transportation methods.

As there is this wide variety of method and difference in price, it is important for a policy to be laid down within a company with the agreement of the marketing management, in order to give effect to the marketing policy within an agreed price structure. This, however, should not be allowed to restrain the freedom of the despatch manager in the execution of his function for many situations can arise which call for immediate action. He should then be answerable for these deviations from the company policy.

CONCLUSION

Physical distribution, as distinct from the choice of marketing channel, is a tool in industrial marketing which is insufficiently recognised. The role and importance of physical distribution within the total marketing activity is neither understood nor given the study its importance demands. Too often the scientific and engineering expertise combined with a high level of marketing ability lead to a significant reduction in production costs. These are immediately dissipated by inadequate and antiquated physical distribution methods which have failed to keep pace with the advances in production methods and other marketing activities of the business.

The result of closer and more consistent study of physical distribution by firms would pay a reward commensurately far higher than the efforts required for its study.

Because physical distribution is a significant point of contact between the customer and supplier, efficiently carried out it can be used not only to supplement the previous sales effort, but to demonstrate the efficiency of the supplying company and open the way to increased business.

AIR 300 (London to Edinburgh)

POST 240 - 270

PASSENGER TRAIN 100 (negotiable with British Rail)

GOODS TRAIN 44

CARRIERS 16

SEA 15-20

OWN FLEET OPERATION 10 (High density distribution on short journeys)

Comparison of costs of different transport media in and around the British Isles.
The table gives an approximate comparison of the cost of moving a ton of goods over
a significant distance in the British Isles based on an index of Passenger Train = 100.

12

Pricing in Industrial Marketing

LEON A. SMULIAN, B.Sc., M.I.E.R.E.

Every product has, to both buyer and seller, a price, cost and value. To the manufacturer or supplier of industrial goods and services the price set is intended to recover total costs plus a return commensurate with the effort and risk involved on the capital invested. It is the extent of this return that is the manufacturer's major interest in his product and can be quantified at any point in time. This value is an objective quantity since it can be compared directly with the profitability of some other product or investment.

To the buyer of these products or services, however, it represents what it is worth to him in the light of his knowledge at that time. In other words, value to the customer is a subjective quantity and depends upon circumstance. To a shipwrecked sailor on a raft a golden jug is of no value, but a wooden jug full of drinking water is of infinite value. The buyer of industrial goods and services, fortunately, or unfortunately, is not faced with such a clear cut situation, but is able to quantify their value in terms of savings, innovation and productivity.

The real value of a product can be shown to include many associated and often intangible assets: for example, the value of a product which is accompanied by a comprehensive applications engineering service will be higher than one that is not. Similarly the value of materials or components which are believed by the public to possess some desirable qualities can be greater to the manufacturer of consumer goods than other unknown but equivalent materials or components. Prompt deliveries, consistent quality and quantity discounts, are among the other factors which affect value at any given time.

As will be seen from Chapter 2 the same product can be used for different purposes by different customers and the value is likely to vary with the application. The applications themselves are constantly changing with time and the product value to any given customer will change with them.

In predetermining the price that a product will bring, it is necessary to examine all these factors with an attitude that is not only quantitative and objective but is also qualitative and subjective, and then translate the values deduced into currency.

The vendor of consumer goods must also examine the social and other influences that motivate the mass market since it is on an assessment of these factors that he relies to a considerable degree when estimating the size of the market and the volume of his production.

The suppliers of industrial products which are incorporated in consumer goods rely on a similar assessment of volume—known as a derived demand—when establishing their prices. With very rare exceptions, the cost of all products is closely tied to the quantities and rate at which they are produced.

The techniques by which *demand* and *competition* in industrial markets can be measured and stimulated are discussed in detail in other chapters of this book as are also the other two factors which have a major effect on pricing, namely *cost* and *company objectives*. The ability to examine these four factors and to draw the correct conclusions is essential to the success of any industrial enterprise, and it is proposed, therefore, to examine them in order to assess their particular influence.

DEMAND

Having evaluated the total market for a product and then broken it down in terms of customer groups, each having different uses for the same product, an analysis may well indicate that the product has different values to each one of them. This is the first step towards establishing a price in relation to the value and volume of a particular sector of the market and enables the possibility of price variations to different groups to be considered. Price differentials can be achieved, for example, by discounts to the large quantity user group, or by selective quality or specification to another, with the theoretical aim of maximising profits in each sector of the market.

'A customer classification scheme helps to answer two important questions relevant to pricing: what sales volume is likely to be generated at different price levels? Also, what opportunities might there be of charging different prices for the product to different customer groups, and what are the competitive advantages of doing so?'[1] In practice this situation is extremely difficult to obtain. Selling prices to any group will usually move towards the lowest offered. However, it is important that the reasons for different user values continue to be recognised, and that the low value sector of the market does not, by absorbing too great a proportion of the product output, reduce the total revenue to a figure which is less than the total cost.

The relationship between quantity and the cost of production and distribution is one of the most significant factors affecting the price at which a

1. E. Raymond Corey *Cases and Concepts*, Prentice Hall (Englewood Cliffs, New Jersey, U.S.A., 1951), page 216.

product can be sold. Every product requires a learning period during which productive efficiency is raised and product failings are eradicated.

Unless it is possible to gauge with reasonable accuracy the sales volume which can be expected at a given price, the basic assumptions on which the costs are estimated will be fallacious and the viability of the project in real danger. It is customary to refer to this relationship, that is the rate at which sales volume is estimated to vary with price, as the demand curve, and describes the 'price elasticity' of a product.

It must be emphasised that price elasticity as the function of a demand curve is a conceptual approach and not closely related to facts that have been established in practice. It should be considered as an analytical tool to be used in the initial price setting exercise and subsequently during the life of the project to forecast total market reactions to price changes from any source.

Having prepared a system of customer classification it is possible to use this concept to forecast what quantity of a new product will be sold at what price levels, and to represent this in the form of a demand curve. The curve is constructed by listing the existing competing products in each customer group. For each competing product it will be possible to set a price which will be either competitive with or possibly replace the existing product and the sum of the price against volume estimates, in each group, will yield a composite demand curve.

Quite apart from the obvious effect of demand on price and vice versa, there are other influences on price that are often overlooked. A derived demand for industrial goods has already been mentioned and here it is possible for the customer to negotiate price reductions on the assumption that this will enable him to reduce the price of his own products and thereby increase his own sales where these have been lagging. In the event that the customer has made an incorrect analysis and his sales volume does not increase, the supplier of the industrial goods concerned may well find himself selling a smaller quantity at a lower price in what is now an unsuccessful attempt to boost a falling market.

The buyer's sensitivity to price will also be affected by the supplier's reputation, level of advertising, technical service and other marketing activities. In the innovating stages of a new type of product these factors may also be as significant to the demand as the price. Subsequent development, however, brings competitors into the field, and, on acceptance by the buyer of the fact that satisfactory equivalents can be purchased, his sensitivity to price will now be the most significant factor affecting his buying decisions.

To sum up: demand is not only affected by price but also by other considerations of value offered, and these considerations are usually powerful enough to prevent a change in price bringing about an equivalent change in demand.

COST

Manufacturing costs are defined as material plus labour plus the associated overheads and expenses. It has been seen that these, at any given volume and rate of production, inevitably set the lower limit to the price at which goods can be sold at other than a loss. Any increase in selling price above this figure represents a profit and it is often assumed that cost plus pricing is the rock upon which successful operation must be based. It is the extent of the 'plus', however, that enables a business to innovate and weather the storms of changing demand and the unexpected disappointment. The desire to maximise profits, therefore, is not pure greed and it is important to the manufacturer that he recognises the extent of the total activity required to recover his fixed overheads and expenses, since any extra activity can be considered as incremental to profit. A business that is operating in these over-recovery conditions is able to adopt a 'marginal approach' to pricing which by assuming the recovery of full costs over all activities enables extra profits to be earned on incremental costs, that is direct manufacturing costs, that would not exist unless a certain order was undertaken, where this is desired.[1]

In his study of *Product Policies of Nonintegrated New England Paper Companies*, Stuart A. Rich describes a 'marginal approach' to pricing which can be usefully applied to other industries:

'Costs tend to set the lower limits of product prices, and since they vary with volume they also influence the amount produced. The costs referred to here are those directly attributable to the product in question, that is, those which would be avoided if the product were dropped. It is these costs, rather than full costs including overhead allocations, which set the floor on prices, at least in the short run. In the long run, taking the product line as a whole, full costs must be recovered and a profit earned in order for the firm to stay in business. This means that the price structure for the entire product line should be set so as to maximise the difference between total revenue and total cost. Let us see how this might be done by using the marginal approach to pricing.

'In using the marginal approach to pricing, a company tries to secure from each product the greatest possible marginal contribution to common overhead and profit. As noted above, the 'marginal contribution' of a member of the product line can be defined as the difference between the price received and the cost directly attributable to the product in question. This approach may require some rethinking about what the significant costs are in setting individual prices. Many business men in the paper industry as elsewhere try to adhere to full cost pricing. This means that they estimate the total costs of a product, including overhead allocations, and add a margin of some kind for profit. This method tends to ignore the realities of demand and competition as well as the arbitrary nature of many

---

1. A fuller discussion of this concept will be found in Wilfred Brown and Elliot Jaques *Product Analysis Pricing*, Heinemann (London, 1964).

allocated costs. A better approach would be to price each product according to the demand and competitive situation in the market where it is sold.

'As an aid to maximising the revenue secured from the total product line, it may be useful to classify its various members according to their contribution as follows:

1. Products which contribute more than their *pro rata* share toward overheads after direct costs are covered.

2. Products which just cover their *pro rata* share.

3. Products which contribute more than incremental costs but do not cover their *pro rata* share.

4. Products which fail to cover the costs saveable by their elimination.

'With such a classification in mind, management would then be in a better position to study ways of strengthening the performance of its total product line. Pricing decisions on individual products in the four categories listed above would be made in the light of demand and competitive conditions facing each grade category. This means that some products, such as new specialty grades, may be priced to yield a very high margin of profit, while others, such as certain highly competitive standard lines, may have to show an actual loss. By retaining these marginal grades to "keep the machines running" and to help absorb fixed overhead costs, management may be able to maximise the total profits from all its lines. A few items which make no contribution may have to be kept to round out the line offered.'[1]

The successful implementation of a product pricing policy of this nature, clearly requires extremely accurate information to be made available concerning sales forecast and current production costs, since all the decisions taken must be based upon the financial situation in the business at that point in time. The attitude in Britain towards cost accounting tends to be rather more historical than in America, with the result that the more subtle reasons for cost variance tend to be forgotten. However, it is these subtleties which are all important if the true costs of the product are to be understood, since without this knowledge it is not really possible to establish prices which bear the true relation to the total activity of the business.

COMPETITION

Competition is to the highest price what cost is to the lowest, and consists of many tangible and intangible features. There is no doubt that its true evaluation, that is—the ability to compare like with like and to present the products to customers in this way, is the guiding light to industrial pricing if profits are to be made and a stable enterprise maintained. The value of appreciating every aspect of competition is that the supplier is obtaining,

1. Stuart A. Rich: *Product Policies of Nonintegrated New England Paper Companies.* D.B.A. thesis, Harvard University, Graduate School of Business Administration (Cambridge, Mass., June 1960).

indirectly, the benefits of his competitors' thinking and efforts and an intelligent technical and commercial appraisal of competitors' products has the beneficial effect of pooling accumulated experience from many sources. There are special circumstances in which the product under consideration has such a high degree of innovation that it will enable its purchaser either to build products, which for technical reasons were not hitherto possible, or alternatively, to produce products which were hitherto possible but can now be produced at a much lower price. The price at which this product can be sold can be established almost entirely on its innovatory value or, alternatively, on the savings made by replacing the product already established. Provided that the innovator has satisfied himself on the demand and cost, the maximum price will be established as that which the market will bear. Even under these exceptional circumstances, however, in which a monopoly position through patents or other special advantages prevails, careful balance has to be maintained between an exorbitant and a reasonable price if immediate competition by other companies, even at the risk of infringement, is to be avoided.

One of the common causes of loss is the inability of an innovatory product to recover its cost and show a profit in a given time. Often the time lost is sufficient to render the whole project permanently unprofitable as a result of the rapid technical changes which are continuously bringing new products on to the market.

Where a product is in direct competition with other similar devices, varying only in small features and quality for example, the information required to establish a price which is both competitive and profitable is very much more complex. Its acquisition and analysis requires an approach which is essentially scientific since, however keen and however convinced the salesman may be of the product's reception, the margin for error is considerable.

Quite apart from influencing prices for new products, competitors' reactions to the newcomer in the market have to be predicted. The new supplier may have decided to 'buy his way in'. This is done by offering prices which are very much better value for money than a competitor who may well, if the product represents a large enough part of his existing business or forward thinking, drastically reduce his own price in order to squeeze out the new competition.

Price changes for established products also produce competitor reactions and the extent of these reactions will depend upon the competitors' costs. It has already been shown that cost and volume are closely associated, the need to estimate a competitor's costs is therefore as important as establishing the value of his product and his share of the market.

A reduction in price by a high volume producer is likely to be followed by other high volume producers offering an equal product value. The low volume producer will either have to show that he is offering superior value and maintain his price, increase his volume by intensifying his selling activity or, in the extreme case, to cease production.

Price increases, however, are almost always associated with increased costs and usually explained by recent wage awards. They are usually initiated by high volume producers who believe that neither the total market nor their share of it will be affected and their lead is usually followed in some degree by their competitors.

COMPANY OBJECTIVES

The objective of a business is to supply the goods and services required by the society in which it exists and, in so doing, to obtain sympathetic and appreciative recognition. Goodwill in fact is that attribute of a business which promotes its forward stability and which helps to overcome the set-backs from which every enterprise suffers from time to time.

The objective of pricing is to maximise the profits of the business while, at the same time, continuing to increase the goodwill of customers in particular and society in general.

Pricing decisions are required to meet these two, sometimes opposing, objectives and since they rely on estimates and forecasts contain a considerable amount of uncertainty and hence opinion.

Even after careful consideration of all the factors examined, the personality and business attitude, bold or timid, of the person responsible for the final decision will play a large part in deciding whether to establish prices that are aggressive and experimental or cautiously cost-plus.

Irrespective of the price set, however, the fact is that the price is actually determined in the market and it is only by understanding the product in relation to the market and vice versa that the pricing decisions which meet all objectives can be quantified in terms of value and hence currency.

PRICING STRATEGY

It has been suggested that the lack of conceptual tools and empirical evidence have contributed to the 'faith, hope and 50 per cent' philosophy which underlies so much industrial pricing practice. But it is easier to discard theories underlying pricing practices than to develop new workable theories. An examination of the factors which create imperfect markets and in particular price insensitivity has led to the conclusion that a more liberal view towards price changes is justified in many cases, that price-demand relationships are more continuous in nature than commonly thought and that each pricing situation requires exploration in its own right.

'Price insensitivity arises from the existence of any desensitising, local, unique, point of sales differentials. The degree of price insensitivity is a matter of (i) the number and kind of such desensitising factors which operate in a given market and (ii) the amount of "spread" in the distribution of the desensitising differentials.'[1]

1. Richard T. T. Sampson. 'Sense and Sensitivity in Pricing'. *Harvard Business Review* (Cambridge, Mass., U.S.A., Nov./Dec. 1964).

If this argument is accepted then it follows that any pricing strategy based upon cost plus fixed selling prices or marginal analysis will only be correct for a moment in time. Manufacturers of industrial goods seek to obtain a price which will yield them the greatest net return. Unfortunately once this price is found it will not remain the optimum price for very long.

The most acceptable solutions to the majority of problems which are not purely emotional are usually established by breaking them down into a series of appropriate events or circumstances. Apart from those subjective qualities which require experience and a feel for the product and market, there is no reason why pricing should be an exception to this rule and a particularly good example of this attitude has been suggested by Alfred Oxenfeldt which, while not fitting every circumstance, offers a useful starting point in perhaps the most difficult of all marketing decisions—establishing an optimum price for a product or service.[1] Its basis is the development of a policy-orientated approach to pricing which reduces the range of prices considered in specific situations and consequently improves the decisions which result. The approach calls for price decisions to be made in six successive steps, each one narrowing the alternatives to be considered at the next step. The six stages are: selecting market targets, choosing an 'image' for the firm and product (the 'multiple image' concept is discussed in Chapter 9), composing a marketing mix, selecting a policy, determining a pricing strategy and finally arriving at a specific price.

This approach might be regarded as a process of selective search where the number of factors deserving close consideration is reduced drastically by making the decision in successive stages. A summary of Oxenfeldt's work more than justifies a place in any description of pricing processes and in attempts to develop a more scientific approach to pricing.

Market targets. The preceding discussion on 'demand' has already set out the function and importance of establishing market targets. By virtue of fixed commitments a firm is limited to several market segments which it can reasonably hope to capture. It has customer connections on which it can capitalise and it has a variety of strengths or weaknesses that limit its choice among potential submarkets for intensive cultivation. One important criterion in the selection of market targets is the customer's awareness of, and sensitivity to, price.

Image. Once the markets to be developed are defined it is necessary to select the methods which will achieve the goals set. The development of a favourable image is an important method since among the non-price factors affecting demand, and particularly in an age in which product differentials are increasingly more illusory than real, the image can offset price disadvantages. The type of image a firm can create for itself or its products

1. Alfred R. Oxenfeldt. 'Multi-Stage Approach to Pricing'. *Harvard Business Review* (Cambridge, Mass., U.S.A., July/August 1960).

depends to a considerable degree on its fixed commitments and resources. With its physical and personnel resources there is a limit to what it can do to alter the prevailing opinion—because this reflects all that the company was and did in the past. In that sense, the basic commitments limit the type of image a firm can establish, how much time it will require to establish it and the cost. Just as an image is an effective weapon in cultivating particular markets, price helps to create the image. It is for this reason that the selection of the correct image which is consistent with the firm's market targets implies particular forms of price behaviour.

Marketing mix. The third stage in multi-stage pricing calls for the selection of a combination of sales promotional devices that will create and reinforce the desired company and product image and achieve the maximum rate of sales for the planned level of output. At this stage, a role must be assigned to price. The role in which price is cast should be selected only after assessment is made as to the relative effectiveness and appropriateness of each sales promotion device that might be employed. The need to conform to the prior decisions about the image greatly limits the number of alternatives that a price setter can reasonably consider. Without setting specific budgetary limits at this stage, some answers are required to the questions of how heavily to advertise, sales force expenditure, product development and improvement costs, range depths, stock levels, delivery times and the degree of emphasis to be given to price appeal.

Oxenfeldt in his carefully reasoned argument admits that the composition of the marketing mix is a very difficult and highly subjective task but points out that these decisions are facilitated when answers are subjected to the test of conforming to the desired company and product image and to the firm's fixed commitments.

Determining policy. In determining policy, answers are required to a further series of questions. How should price compare with the 'average' price in the industry? How quickly can price reductions or increases by competitors be met? How frequently is it advisable to vary price? To what extent is stability of price advantageous? Should the firm make use of price fixing arrangements if legally permissible? What is the role of 'price promotions'? Once again by virtue of having made evaluations and decisions called for in the preceding stages the number of choices on these points is limited. Further, each company must take account of the 'added value element in service', which is dealt with in great detail in Chapter 10, as well as the user segments the firm is most anxious to penetrate and valuation of the rival products. On the basis of such considerations plus its target market segments and marketing mix, the firm can decide whether it can afford to charge much more or less than its rivals.

Pricing strategy. It is difficult to draw a sharp line between policy and strategy but it is possible and useful to make some sort of differentiation between them. Oxenfeldt distinguishes them in that policy is formulated to deal with anticipated and foreseeable situations of a recurrent type; strategy is required to guide management in setting price during the time that a special situation exists. Markets are frequently dominated by special situations that the basic policy was not designed to meet and these situations often require price adjustments to be made.

Yet again, the alternative strategies available to a firm which has gone through the sequential approach set out, will be limited. Explicit recognition of these earlier stages of the pricing decisions should prevent hasty short-run actions that occur so often and that can be so destructive.

Specific price. The final step—the selection of the specific price—circumscribed as the pricer must now be, is usually still one in which a decision has to be made from a number of alternatives. To the extent that he is able, he should be guided by the arithmetic of pricing—that is by a comparison of costs and revenues of the alternative prices within the zone delineated by the prior stages of the pricing decisions. Having taken into account market targets, image, marketing mix, pricing policy and strategy he can afford to ignore everything but the calculations of costs and revenues. The first five stages of decision are designed to take account of business considerations which may be ignored if price is selected solely on the basis of prevailing costs and revenue conditions.

The multistage approach which has been summarised from Oxenfeldt's work differs from the usual approaches to pricing in two major respects. First, it demands a long-range view of price by emphasising the enduring effects of most price actions on company and product image. It might be said this approach constructs a policy frame work for the price decision. Second, it allows the price decision to be made in stages, rather than requiring a simultaneous solution of the entire problem.

CONCLUSION

Physical distribution and pricing seem to share the dubious honour of being the activities within the control of marketing management about which least is known and where empiricism continues to hold sway. Yet both these activities contain within them the most obvious danger areas which can threaten not only the life of a product but the very existence of a firm.

There is every indication that the conditions of market leadership in the future may be established more by a scientific approach to pricing than by the inspirational qualities which underly so many pricing decisions today.

It is remarkable therefore that so little study has been devoted to either of these activities as compared with, for example, industrial advertising and marketing research.

In the consumer goods field, price has for long been acknowledged as a most powerful weapon in the hands of the marketing managers. In industrial marketing it is rarely understood and still less consciously used as a marketing tool. In the world of tomorrow, increasing competition may decrease the range of price discretion in pricing, but the opportunities for error will still remain.

13

International Marketing

FRED DAVIES, M.A.(Oxon)

A company which enters the international sphere of operations is immediately faced with an unfamiliar set of problems. Some of these, taxation, industrial relations, legal and government regulations will be new and may demand the attention of experts. Others, such as market attractiveness, competitive structure and cost-price profitability structure are problems which are already familiar in the domestic market but now appear in a new environment. These are also the problems of the local manufacturer with whom the company is now going to compete. Both have to solve the same problems so that it is not unreal for a company to regard international marketing as the sum total of marketing operations carried on in a number of domestic markets in various countries of the world at the same time.

This is not an oversimplification, neither does it imply that overseas marketing is identical with home marketing. But it may serve to bring the present subject into proper perspective. Therefore all that has been said about marketing in general applies whatever the product or the market. The important factor is that the marketing mix[1] which was devised for the marketing of a product at home will need to be re-examined and undoubtedly altered when the time comes to enter overseas markets.

This is extremely important. International marketing by widening the size and scope of the market offers opportunities for practising a variety of marketing techniques: it also demands some changes. In the home market a machine tool may ride very successfully into the market behind a reputation established over half a century until it has become synonymous with the product. Overseas the company may still have to establish such a reputation and acceptance and the 'marketing mix' will need to be revised to do this.

1. Originally conceived by Professor Neil H. Borden, of the Harvard Business School, this is a convenient framework for understanding the problems of any marketing situation at home or abroad, preparatory to decision making. By definition, the success of a business man 'as a marketer depends largely on his understanding of the forces of the market that bear upon any product or product line and his skill in devising a "mix" of marketing methods that conform and adjust to these forces in ways to produce a satisfactory net profit figure'.

A second general point which emerges from the concept of international marketing as the sum of a series of domestic operations conducted overseas is that it is essential from the beginning to have a clear cut plan of overall strategy. Many management decisions cannot be taken in isolation but only after considering their implications for other markets. Such decisions will cover advertising, product design and planning, company image and market share objectives, and involve consideration of a number of factors.

ASSESSMENT OF MARKET POSITION

Without a very clear idea of the importance of a foreign market to the company, a number of operating decisions will become purely haphazard. Involvement may be deeper than the company realises and this can affect decisions.

A manufacturer of business machines with a European subsidiary company did not realise that within two years of opening up operations he had taken one-third of the market and had become the price leader for a particular quality machine. Yet he continued to treat the German market as marginal, to enter a price cutting war on less sophisticated machines and so imperil the established position which he had built up.

Once embarked upon a particular course of action, it may not be easy to change ideas and strategy and it is, therefore, important to have an explicit objective at the onset of operations. A not so perfect plan resolutely carried through may well be preferable to operating without a plan at all.

FLEXIBILITY

Consideration of flexibility will also affect management decisions in the international field in a significant manner. Flexibility may be considerably limited by the market itself—the business machine manufacturer already referred to was, in fact, limited in just such a fashion as a result of his product policy. The question in his case may well have been the broader one of getting out of an inflexible situation by broadening his whole line in the market.

Consider, however, how the opposite situation may work. An American manufacturer of automotive products who is a price leader at home could not cut his prices without endangering the market. In a European country, however, where he enjoys only four per cent of the market and has a price advantage he could well afford to offer reduced prices as an alternative to a costly advertising campaign (which may have been the correct thing to do at home) as a means of expanding his market share.

Flexibility in international operations may be restricted by competition and many companies which move into the international field do so without considering either the magnitude or the scope of foreign competition. A foreign competitor may well choose a third market as the scene for a show of strength which is critical to the whole operations of your own company.

It needs careful analysis of the situation to appreciate that what may appear to be a local struggle is in fact an international one. Such an analysis could not be made unless international operations are conducted according to some planned strategy and once appreciated may limit flexibility of operations in an overseas market.

Indeed flexibility overseas may be restricted by the nature of domestic operations. This can be illustrated in a case where a quality image has been developed and would be seriously damaged by the marketing of an inferior product in an overseas market—highly desirable though that may be in the isolated circumstances.

This brief analysis of the environment in which international decisions are taken demonstrates that this is a function in which co-ordination is absolutely essential. This is true in respect of all products, probably more so in the case of industrial goods the marketing of which is becoming more and more a team effort rather than an individual performance, For example, overseas pricing can become a policy matter which may far exceed the competence, training and above all, the time of the man on the spot and cannot be settled in isolation.

If a company is to market its products successfully overseas it should at the outset appoint a senior executive with responsibility for 'international operations'. In making this appointment the title 'international director or manager' is preferable to 'export director' as showing appreciation immediately of the environment within which this man will operate.

The international scene is probably the easiest area in business in which to be fooled—and to fool the others. The international director needs to exercise all of his critical faculties to the full to get his facts right and to analyse all situations in depth and, above all, never to count on being unique.

The decisions which an international director will have to take fall into four simple headings. These headings frequently overlap and the decisions need to be taken in the environment outlined. These decisions are basically: whether to go overseas; choice of markets; when to enter and the form of the overseas operation.

Investigation of these questions can be carried a long way by making use of sources of information already available at home, although it cannot be urged too strongly that a personal visit to an overseas market is essential to conducting successful operations there. However, in using sources of information and in a personal visit it is essential to be able to ask the right questions, and then to make the maximum use of the answers when these are obtained.

Sources of information in the United Kingdom are multitudinous and enquiries at the regional offices of the Board of Trade; foreign departments of the major joint stock banks; Chambers of Commerce and national trade organisations or the embassies and consulates of the foreign countries involved will usually start the enquirer off in the right direction.

Although Chapter 6 on industrial marketing research is concerned with home markets the techniques described, with adjustments to meet the particular circumstances of each country, can be applied to collect vital information for international marketing decisions to be made.

ENTERING INTERNATIONAL MARKETS

This should be a decision of top management and one which can only be taken after a careful analysis of the conditions. It is a major policy decision which has to be taken once in the life of every overseas trading company and one which needs to be taken equally carefully as new products are introduced during the life of the company.

It must be realised at once that certain companies do not belong in the overseas business at all, not all products manufactured for the domestic market are acceptable overseas and not all companies are suited to the overseas environment. So, the first requirement before reaching this crucial decision is to carry out a review of existing facilities.

First, the company itself. What resources has it for entering upon an overseas operation? This review needs to take into account not only the production resources to determine how much of production is available to feed overseas markets with basic requirements, repeat orders and replacement parts but also the corporate organisation itself. The company which enters the international sphere needs adequate resources of finance, man power and entrepreneurial ability to be able to see the project through to a profitable conclusion. This may mean that certain resources will have to be redirected from other fields of activity and the cost of such redirection accurately assessed.

Indeed, at this stage the company will need to identify and review the major factors influencing the profitability of its existing operations in order to decide what effect a decision to go overseas might have upon that profitability—both in the short term and in the long term situations. It will need to go further and review its general objectives such as market share, rate of growth and return upon investment which will all be affected.

These decisions cannot, of course, be taken without also considering external factors. Predominant among these will be the competitive conditions of the industry and the activities of competitors. The decision to enter international operations may be dictated by the action of a competitor in taking that step himself. Alternatively, a decision to move overseas ahead of your competitor may be worth considering if it reduces his flexibility of operations. The present struggle for world markets in the computer field may be viewed in this context.

Then there are the factors surrounding the product. Performance in the home market will be some guide to the export potential of what you are making provided it is realised that domestic experience is not always comparable with international conditions. However, a product which is performing well at home will be a better starter than one which still has its teething problems. The home market situation will also be a guide as to the possible demand overseas by identifying users and the industrial development of which it is a part.

However, these decisions cannot be taken in isolation but only in relation to the product development programme of the company and the programme for new product introduction. Here the question of timing which will come in at every stage will be important.

At this point the company should be giving thought to the support which may be necessary for its product in overseas markets. A piece of sophisticated machinery sold in a highly industrialised home market may have adequate distribution and servicing outlets already at its disposal. These may not be available and may therefore, have to be established in less developed territories. Indeed, even in highly developed territories, a prerequisite of going overseas must be the provision of adequate after sales service if this is necessary.

This brief analysis of the basic question of whether to go abroad demonstrates how important it is that the company should approach this with the right attitude. A determination to see the policy through to its ultimate objective is essential as is the setting of these ultimate objectives right from the beginning.

CHOICE OF MARKETS

Having taken the basic decision to move into the international sphere, and before deciding upon which of the various methods to adopt, consideration must be given to a choice of markets.

In deciding whether to go overseas at all, the question of availability of capacity will have been examined and this must be a deciding factor in the selection of markets and in deciding how many to tackle. The importance of having adequate stocks of the product to meet anticipated demand and the provision of replacement parts can never be stressed too frequently.

Nevertheless, it is clearly desirable to maintain a good spread between overseas markets, especially in a world where import controls of one type or another can be imposed speedily and without warning.

Certain factors are obvious in the selection or elimination of possible markets. The appropriate government rules and regulations affecting the product both in the overseas country and at home should be examined. Prohibition upon the export of strategic goods and materials to certain countries will eliminate some markets while import quotas, high rates of duty, anti-dumping regulations and severe valuation procedures may close the door to others. In this category also, the international manager should investigate the existence of local standards regulations or underwriters' requirements and calculate the cost of modifications to the product which may be necessary in order to comply with these.

A further basic requirement for the successful entry into a foreign country may be that the economy should have reached a stage in its development adequate to support the product in its ancilliary aspects. The standard of education and training is one factor and so is the ability to provide installation and after sales servicing from within its own resources and labour force. Moving overseas may involve the provision of these services and additional ones of finance and credit if the market for the product is to be established. Communications, transport facilities both between the domestic market and the overseas country and within the overseas market are also vitally important at this stage.

However, care must be exercised not to allow this to become a static analysis. What is being assessed in the international field, as in every marketing situation at home, is the market which can be created for the product rather than the market which exists. The interest is in growth factors and market potentials.

The size of the market must, therefore, be of prime interest. This means the statistics of production, consumption, and imports must be examined, but forecasts must also be made to determine trends. It is probably rare for any business venture to be started without some attempt at forward planning or forecasting but, because the operation is in an environment which is foreign the proper use of statistics may be more critical in the overseas field.

This is a subject in itself which can only be touched upon briefly. The importance of selecting the correct facts and the overriding importance of timing is emphasised. It is so easy to look at the current size of a market and then immediately jump to a conclusion as to what the future size will be—without relating the statistics to the stage of development of each separate market for different products.

A sophisticated analysis of potential market size for industrial equipment will not confuse the consumption figure with the ownership figure; nor the geographic size of the country with the economic size; the import figures with the import potential, including the danger of a policy of import substitution, and whether the market is supplied locally or through exports. In a growing market there is the ever present problem and danger of excess production, as the European market for electrical appliances has shown. The international manager who is forecasting future events needs to be quite clear what factors have been used and what assumptions made to forecast future growth; what impact they have and how long they will last. Similarly, in a rapidly growing market, competition is likely to be keener and profit opportunities reduced.

The choice of markets, if it is made carefully, is not an easy matter because not only is the market potential being assessed but also future profit opportunity. An analysis of the plus and minus factors in each of the markets under consideration will help in this decision. To this end the following factors are some of those which need to be carefully examined in the context of the product in question.

Income—the point at which the product or industrial service to be sold is coming within the range of more buyers able to afford it.

Degree of development—interesting comparisons can be drawn from other countries which have already gone through the same stage of development.

Saturation—in particular the possibility of excess capacity.

Replacement—it is easy to underestimate the potential demand by making a calculation of future market requirements based only upon ordinary wear and tear and without taking into account the possible upgrading of the product by the user and the extent to which it may replace other products. This substitution factor may be one of prime importance in developing markets as the standard of living rises and as sophisticated equipment comes into a more general use.

Technological change—it is difficult to assess the impact of this especially as it may involve an acceleration principle in the use of intermediate products and raw materials. The sales of packaging materials to end users, of synthetic rubber products to the automobile industry or of various plastic products to the textile industry will illustrate this point; although the end user is a growth industry the intermediate supplier may be growing more rapidly. It is important to identify the industries in foreign countries to which you relate your own and then to analyse their stage of technological development.

Timing—in all of these decisions, is always important. It affects the decision whether to go overseas when this is considered as part of the overall international marketing strategy; to enter an overseas market which is experiencing a shortage of a product even though it means rationing the home market; to restrict the flexibility of operations of international competitors.

It affects the decision which markets to go for, since with different countries in varying stages of development the right time to enter one market does not necessarily coincide with the right point in time in another country.

If the decision is whether to move overseas in the manufacture of some basic raw material, for example, chemicals, then timing is extremely important and an early and large-scale entry is essential. The industry is capital intensive with high fixed costs but operating costs decline rapidly with increased production and the economies of scale. This situation favours the early entrant who is able to establish price leadership and discourages the late entrant who will find little flexibility left to him.

However, as you move away from the bulk raw materials towards more differentiated products the position changes. For one thing, marketing, which in the case of bulk raw materials is more in the nature of long term diplomacy, becomes more important. There is more scope to play with the factors in the marketing mix as a product is further differentiated and acquires features which can be exploited. Price which is an important factor in the one case may not now be so important as source loyalty or after sales service. Large-scale production with high fixed costs may not be the dominant feature of the industry which may be characterised by smaller units, sub-contracting the manufacture of complex components but utilising skilled craftsmanship. The manufacturer of motor cars, instruments or electric motors may therefore find that he has greater flexibility in the timing of his overseas entry than a chemical manufacturer or aluminium producer.

ORGANISATION FOR INTERNATIONAL MARKETING

Finally, the nature of the overseas operation or 'how to operate' is considered. There are several ways in which this particular problem may be tackled and no general rules can be laid down. Circumstances will dictate the organisation and these circumstances will include the nature of the company's structure and capacity, the product and the marketing structure of the overseas country.

From a separate foreign company to the employment of a variety of types of intermediaries there are many forms the organisation can take. A foreign company either wholly owned or completely autonomous; a joint venture; a licensing arrangement or some form of direct export from home. The foreign company may be a sales company only or it may also manufacture. It may be a completely new creation or it may be acquired by purchase which may involve the buying of management ability as well as physical assets.

Clearly, industrial goods, which often rely to a large extent upon team selling and which must often be 'pushed' through the channels of distribution by personal selling or the sales forces of distributors, will call for a greater involvement of the parent company in the overseas operation and will be less adequately handled by the agency type of arrangement.

To assist in a decision as to the form the operation should take, certain aspects only can be suggested for consideration.

First, the question of production itself and the possibility and economic advantages of assembly overseas or full manufacture. Manufacture at home or overseas in a subsidiary company offers control over production and the joint venture or license arrangement with a foreign partner offers opportunities for broadening the product line by association with the products of other manufacturers in an overall range.

From the point of view of marketing, it is necessary to go back to the original plan with its ideas of market share and the means of obtaining this to see how the various forms of operating will contribute towards this.

On the financial aspect, a licensing arrangement may produce a low return and a joint venture means shared profits. The overseas subsidiary company will involve overseas investment with possible long term financial rewards whereas direct export may bring more immediate results.

Research and development may be assisted by a licensing arrangement or a joint venture which could lead to a return flow of information and improved product development. Against this, however, must be set the possibility that an arrangement with another autonomous company may lead to conflicts of management.

Government regulations especially tariffs and direct controls can often be circumvented by some form of overseas participation either in licensing or a joint venture.

The form of organisation will ultimately need to be established according to the general corporate objectives of the company. This is a management decision which cannot be taken in isolation but only in relation to the company's position in the home market and in other foreign markets, and to the company's long-range plans for an international product specialisation.

Where direct export is involved there is often a tendency to think ahead only to that point where the goods land overseas. However, once a product enters a foreign country certain changes are taking place and these changes involve the product, its channels of distribution and the methods of selling. Clearly, if a company cannot for any reason employ its own sales operation abroad there is more need for personal visits from home to follow the goods through to the ultimate user. The choice of an overseas organisation and its operation should be taken not only as part of the plan to look further than just getting the goods overseas but also to identify who makes the purchasing decisions and then understanding their requirements.

ANALYSING FOREIGN OPPORTUNITIES

To assess the practicability of entering a foreign market, a manufacturer needs to go beyond judgements of market growth—he needs to know in some detail the competitive strength of the domestic manufacturer and the amount of flexibility which this position will allow him to have.

A useful analytical tool in determining answers to these basic questions has been developed—operating marginal analysis.[1] The 'operating margin' is the difference between the sales price and the cost of materials purchased. It is within this difference that a manufacturer has to conduct his operations of manufacturing, selling, research and development and all the other corporate activities involved in getting the goods from the factory to the user—and show a profit.

There is nothing new in this—it is a concept which has already been referred to in Chapter 10 as 'added value'; what is new is the use which the authors of the article suggest may be made of it in analysing overseas marketing situations.

But first it is necessary to examine the concept and see how it may be arrived at. Within the operating margin, costs may be divided into two categories.

1. Raphael W. Hodgson and Hugo E. R. Uyterhoeven. 'Analysing Foreign Opportunities', *Harvard Business Review* (Cambridge, Mass., March/April 1962).

Involuntary expenses consist mainly of minimum manufacturing costs and vary with the scale of production. They are incurred by anyone in the industry and an engineer skilled in the product line and manufacturing process can calculate these and develop a relationship between these costs and varying levels of output and different manufacturing methods.

Discretionary expenses are a different item and not so easily calculated by the outside enquirer. They are dictated by corporate strategies; by decisions, for example, whether to show large profits or whether to invest in a stronger marketing position by improving service to customers or by establishing distribution outlets. However, a careful analysis of this element of the operating margin is necessary if low profits in growth industries are to be interpreted correctly. A picture of this side of competitive companies' activities can be built up from talking to people in the trade and discovering the size of the sales force, the volume and nature of sales promotion, the nature of the distribution arrangements and the extent of technical services. Analysis of competitive companies' published accounts, if available, or a mercantile report and other financial statements will throw light on the discretionary expenses which must, of course, include profits.

The lower limit of the operating margin, the cost of materials, can be determined objectively whilst the selling price can usually be equally well established.

By merging these factors together, a fairly exact figure can be arrived at which will assist corporate planning and help to establish the conditions for entry into a market. Above all, they enable a company to estimate the extent to which the price leaders can dictate price policy and whether these conditions will leave it an operating margin sufficiently wide to permit growth.

The position of the company seeking to enter an international sphere in competition with other manufacturers already established or contemplating a similar entry now becomes clearer. It must be able to live within the operating margin as dictated by the price policy of its competitors and this must be sufficiently wide to allow a growth achievement.

Certain rules can be established which may not have been obvious on a more superficial analysis. The most important condition of entry is that the company's initial marketing objectives allow discretionary margins which are large enough to enable it to survive and to sustain its growth objectives. This underlines the importance of what has already been said about establishing an overall plan from the beginning of the overseas operation—deciding upon market share objectives and deciding what production and sales efforts are necessary to achieve these.

A second rule is to analyse in depth the company's position relative to the industry leaders and to estimate, by consideration of their involuntary cost and discretionary expenses structure, their ability to lower prices and its ability to survive under the most adverse eventuality.

Generally, the wider the operating margin, the better the opportunity for entering a foreign market.

Turning to the question of which markets to enter, the same analysis can be used to advantage. By comparing operating margins of companies in different countries and using domestic operating margins it is possible to evaluate opportunities in several markets overseas, provided that due allowance is made for the possible adjustments to products, and the provision of distribution facilities.

So also on timing and on the form of overseas participation it can be seen how this analytical framework can be utilised in a decision whether to export from home or set up local manufacturing facilities and when to time an entry. The flexibility of the new entrant will be greater if it can be established that existing industry leaders are intent upon holding their line on prices or if price reductions can be predicted by analysing the leader's involuntary costs.

CONCLUSION

Whilst international marketing involves domestic marketing on a wide front it has distinctive features of its own. The degree of risk is often wider and the decisions cannot be taken in isolation but only as part of the general corporate marketing plan. However, the area of risk can be considerably reduced by careful analysis of the whole situation, by evolving a strategy and by pursuing this with determination.

The lessons which are learned in the highly competitive atmosphere of overseas trading can usually be applied to advantage in the home market and the constant exposure to the activities of foreign manufacturers frequently produces new ideas in product development and use. Indeed, the foreign field frequently offers increased scope for the marketing man to develop his activities in an interesting and unconventional way not always possible on the home market.

14

Marketing Managers and their Development

E. A. LEVER, B.Sc., B.Com.

'A business organisation is a combination of men, money and machines so co-ordinated that they can fulfil an economic objective.'[1] Organisation planning is concerned with achieving the appropriate co-ordination which includes the selection, training and development of both executive and operational personnel.

The marketing of industrial goods comprises all the activities dealing with the movement of goods and services to meet customer needs and wants in industrial, institutional and commercial markets. Marketing is not synonymous with selling; selling—getting orders—is an important part of marketing, but marketing also includes the planning and co-ordination of all the activities of the company aimed at producing the right goods, at the right time, at the right price, presented and distributed in the right way and promoting their movement to customers, using—in addition to the sales force—the other marketing forces such as advertising, sales promotion, service and public relations. All these activities should be planned and co-ordinated to achieve the proposed economic objectives of the organisation with the greatest possible efficiency. Marketing management is the term applied to this aspect of an organisation's activities.

The achievement of the economic objective of the company depends upon marketing defined in this way. The chief marketing executive is a participant in top-management decision-making, and represents the interests of marketing in the major policy formulations which constitute the framework of co-ordination of the organisation's various activities. How is he to be found and developed?

Before giving consideration to the desired skills and characteristics of a chief marketing executive, it is important to set out the essential conditions under which marketing management can best accomplish its work. These have been summarised by A. P. Felton[2] and are:

1. H. Stieglitz, *Organisation Planning*, National Industrial Conference Board (New York, 1962), page 2.
2. A. P. Felton, 'Conditions of Marketing Leadership', *Harvard Business Review* (Cambridge, Mass., U.S.A., March/April 1956).

'(i) Top management should recognise that the nature of the marketing problem is fundamentally different from the nature of the production problem. This has vital implications for (a) executive selection, (b) marketing strategy, and (c) sales organisation. Failure to take these differences into account is a frequent source of friction and inefficiency.

'(ii) Management should recognise the dynamic quality of the marketing problem; that changes are continually taking place, not only in the market but also in channels to the market. The change is so continuous and so widespread that it renders every sales plan subject to a high degree of obsolescence. Failure to grasp this point has led many companies to formulate policies and plans that are too rigid to permit their adaptation to new market situations and altered environmental conditions.

'(iii) Marketing management today needs a very much greater degree of conceptual skill—the ability to see the enterprise as a whole and to understand how the various functions of the company and its sales organisation depend on one another.'

The 'marketing concept' was developed to achieve an awareness of the interdependence of management function by focussing the attention of decision-makers on a common factor—the customer. It is worth stating, therefore, within the context of this chapter that one definition of the marketing concept in relation to management is 'a way of managing a business so that each critical business decision, whether made by marketing people, engineering people, manufacturing people, financial people or people in any other activity of the business is made with a full prior knowledge of the impact of that decision on the customer'.[1]

The marketing executive may wish to make changes of marketing policy, but if the meaning of the marketing concept is appreciated fully, he will never do so without considering not only the effects on customers, but also the effects internally in the company, on his colleagues in Production, Finance and Research.

CHIEF MARKETING EXECUTIVES

It has been said that 'if you could find a man who has made a distinct success in sales management, who has done well as an advertising manager, who has a distinguished record in research, who has made good as a credit man, who understands a cost-accounting system, has a fine reputation for his knowledge of styles and a splendid ability to detect trends, who has been a successful banker and financier, and who, added to that record, has the ability to co-ordinate and work with the production end of the business —you would have a made-to-order chief marketing executive.'[2]

Few, if any, men like that could be found. So the first step in developing

1. C. E. St. Thomas, 'A Basic Guide to Marketing for the Smaller Company', *Industrial Marketing* (Chicago, June 1959).
2. Lee H. Bristol, quoted in H. C. Barksdale *Marketing in Progress*, Holt Rinehart and Winston (New York, 1964), page 131.

a marketing manager is to set down a job description. This should be precise but at the same time flexible enough to avoid rigidity and to permit a good man to develop. The importance of job write-ups is emphasised by its impact on the total corporate complex which is considered in detail in Chapter 17.

A practical job description of a chief marketing executive can now be considered, since the problem of developing marketing managers can hardly be solved without a development objective, however ideal this may appear to be.

General responsibility

The marketing manager is responsible for developing and recommending objectives, policies and programmes for sales, sales service and marketing activities; for co-ordinating, developing and maintaining favourable relations with customers and the trade; for recommending all marketing budgets; and for seeing that the marketing aspects of all policies and activities are considered and provided for to achieve the purposes of the company.

Organisational relationships

The marketing manager will generally be positioned in a direct line relationship to the general manager, who is his immediate superior.

The marketing manager normally has direct (line) authority over personnel in the sales service and advertising departments and has as his immediate subordinates, the sales, advertising, service, marketing research sales training and sales promotion managers.[1]

Functions

The marketing manager is responsible for the formulation of marketing policies and programmes. He should develop a secure board approval for such policies and regularly undertake to evaluate and report on the organisation's marketing programmes.

He should co-ordinate all sales operations, including the selection, training, development and evaluations of the sales force.

The marketing manager should direct and supervise the advertising and sales promotion activities of the organisation. He should approve the selection of advertising agencies and sources.

1. There may be a case, in some organisations, for positioning one or other of these sub-units adjacent but not subordinate to the marketing manager. Marketing research, for instance, may be called upon to prepare critical or evaluating data upon some part of the marketing policies or operations of the organisations. In such a situation, the position of marketing research personnel within the marketing department may give rise to undue internal frictions. Thus, to avoid the pressure to which such a unit may be subjected and to facilitate the necessary conditions of objectivity and impartiality for research work, the marketing research unit may, more appropriately, report directly to the general manager or to the board. This is more fully discussed in relation to marketing research in Chapter 5, but the situation can also apply to other functions.

The marketing manager should supervise and co-ordinate sales service activities, ensuring that favourable relations are developed and maintained with customers. It is ultimately his responsibility to establish satisfactory services for customers and to this end he should ensure that adequate records and procedures are maintained of, for example, customers' complaints.

The marketing manager should supervise and authorise marketing research projects for his organisation. It is his responsibility to interpret and where necessary to implement, results of such projects and to ensure that other units of the organisation are informed of findings relevant to their interests.

He initiates, approves and recommends such changes—in product line, packaging, advertising, pricing—as will maintain or enhance saleability of the company's products. He should also review customer reactions to product and major modifications.

The marketing manager should maintain contact with trade and industry groups and supervise participation in trade activities.

He will direct the administration of any branch operations, providing warehousing and distribution facilities where those are necessary.

The marketing manager should initiate pricing and merchandise control and work out acceptable solutions to problems arising. He should recommend policies and programme as a basis for handling such problems in the future.

He should maintain his awareness of developments and trends in markets, products, competition, and related matters and should communicate this special knowledge to others within the company.

The marketing manager should review budgets for the sales, advertising and related marketing activities and recommend them for board approval.

He should review existing incentive pay systems in the marketing department and recommend changes in them to the general manager for his approval. He should attempt to develop and maintain a high standard of morale and efficiency among the staff.

Authority

The marketing manager should define clearly and in writing the responsibilities of personnel over whom he has direct authority; delegate adequate authority to them in writing and provide them with adequate facilities to fulfil their responsibilities. He should adhere to and support the approved basic line-and-staff company organisation, passing as much authority as possible to the departmental heads immediately beneath him. He should see that appropriate written limitations are imposed on his immediate subordinates in respect to contractual commitments, expenditures, and action affecting personnel.

The marketing manager will serve as chairman of the marketing committee, if this is provided for in the organisation.

Within the limits of company policy and sound business judgement, the marketing manager is empowered to take any necessary action to carry out the responsibilities with which he has been charged.[1]

SELECTION

A 'man specification' for the marketing manager should be outlined on paper for discussion to decide the sort of person who, if found, could be expected to carry out successfully the job as defined. It is unlikely that anyone will measure up fully to all the points and eventually top management judgement has to be exercised to decide on the man to be taken—or promoted to this position. The judgement will often be made after interviewing prospects and here a warning should be given about interviewing procedure, particularly if a 'man specification' is not strictly adhered to. There is a volume of evidence which shows that the unplanned interview by an untrained interviewer is a very poor means indeed of choosing staff.

An often quoted case[2] illustrates this point. Twelve sales managers interviewed fifty-seven candidates for salesmen's vacancies independently. Each manager was asked to rank each candidate from first to fifty-seventh and, in fact, each candidate received widely divergent rankings from top to bottom of the list. Although all the managers were experienced at their own job, their method of selection was no more reliable than if they had picked out the successful candidate with a pin.

'The reasons why interviews can be so unreliable are not difficult to find. If the interviewer has not been trained in the skills of conducting an interview, he is almost bound to make subjective judgements based on his own background, prejudices and preferences. He may frame his questions in such a way to learn nothing at all about the candidate, or he may discover many facts which are irrelevant to the job for which the candidate has applied. In other words, an unskilled interviewer would not know what he was looking for in an interview, would allow it to develop in an unplanned and uninformative way, and would have his assessment of it coloured by his own predetermined ideas or by the 'halo' effect of one of the candidate's characteristics. On the other hand, there seems to be no doubt that the interview can have a high degree of success if it is properly planned and conducted.'[3]

Having discussed the characteristics of the ideal marketing manager, his role, responsibilities and authority, it is relevant to turn to the career paths of future marketing managers, or developing marketing managers.

1. I have drawn on the work of H. Lazo and A. Corbin, *Management in Marketing* McGraw-Hill (New York, 1961), and E. F. L. Brech, *Organisation*, Longmans Green (London, 1957), for help in formulating this job description. It should, however, be noted when referring to these books that, while the first adopts the complete marketing concept, the latter conceives the marketing manager as being responsible to the general sales manager. The difference in the dates of publication may be significant.

2. H. R. Hollingsworth, *Vocational Psychology and Character Analysis*, Appleton (New York, 1929).

3. *Survey of selection methods in British industry* Information Summary 108, British Institute of Management (London, 1963).

A young man does not normally become a marketing manager at an early age, any more than a sales manager or an advertising manager. He will get experience initially as a functional specialist in, say, the sales department, the drawing office or the advertising department. He should be periodically appraised for management potential, continuously trained in his particular specialist function and shown its relationship to other functions in the firm. If he is judged to be a potential marketing manager he should be shown the whole of the business, and not just his own corner.

Peter Drucker puts this well. 'Organisation structure must make possible the training and testing of tomorrow's top managers. It must give people actual management responsibility in an autonomous position while they are still young enough to acquire new experience.

'Work as a lieutenant or assistant does not adequately prepare a man for the pressures of making his own decisions. On the contrary, nothing is more common than the trusted and effective lieutenant who collapses when he is put on his own. Men must also be put into positions where they at least see the whole of a business, even if they do not carry direct responsibility for its performance and results. Though experience as a functional specialist is necessary, certainly at the start of a man's career in management if exposed to it too long, a man will be narrowed by it. He will come to mistake his own corner for the whole building.

'Training is not enough. A man must also be tested in his capacity to manage a whole business responsibility. He must be tested long before he gets to the top. And he should be young enough so that failure on his part does not finish him for good, but still allows the company to use his services as a specialist, or a lieutenant. The job, while independent, should be small enough so that failure in it does not endanger the prosperity or survival of the business. And in the large enterprise there should be several such jobs in succession for a man so that future top managers can be selected by the only rational principle of selection and tested by the only adequate test: that of actual business performance on their own. The job must also be junior enough so that a man who fails can easily be removed.'[1]

More industrial firms could, with advantage, adopt the product (or brand) manager organisation structure, successful in many consumer goods manufacturing organisations. A manufacturer, for instance, in the grocery field may have product managers respectively for soups, instant coffee and baby foods. Such product managers are usually responsible to the chief marketing executive but, in a limited product field, are held responsible for market research, development, selling (through the sales force) advertising, sales promotions, budgeting—in fact for the profitability of their product. A fuller exposition is contained in Chapters 16 and 17. Experience as a product manager fits in well with the responsibility principle so wisely stated by Dr. Drucker.

1. Peter F. Drucker *Practice of Management*, Heinemann (London, 1963), page 178.

TRAINING

On the subject of training before appointment to marketing management, a British Institute of Managements Survey[1] showed that of all the marketing, product and brand managers (in eighteen companies) covered in the survey one company had sent product managers to the Administrative Staff College, Henley, in five other companies there had been training respectively with an advertising agency, management accountancy, in the field as salesmen, on sales courses or acting as deputies, whereas all the other companies reported no specific training.

For further training, two companies had training centres, four companies reported that they sent men to attend suitable external courses, while three said that training was received 'on the job'. Another company reported 'in-company training of an informal nature', while another said 'we consider all executives to be under continual training. Assistant brand managers receive more formalised training, but are fully functional and operational on some assignment from their first day. Three-monthly training reports are issued.'

Training in the field as a salesman is usually the most valuable part of bringing on a future marketing executive in the industrial goods field because of the great importance attaching to service, in the widest sense, to customers and the technical aspects in the personal selling. In fact one might reasonably say that it is from among the sales force of an industrial manufacturer that future marketing executives can most often best be found.

Nevertheless, the all-important requirement in marketing management of being able to co-ordinate the work of others must not be overlooked. Effective co-ordination depends on conceptual skill, on what has been called the sensing of the organisation as a whole.[2] Unless guided carefully a salesman may become too much of an individualist, perhaps even a lone wolf, in his dealings with his company. The salesman is often out of close contact with his head, or regional, office and in industrial selling sometimes becomes frustrated by the apparent lack of awareness of 'the office', which seems unable to appreciate his customers' requirements, and which he continually has to try to persuade to redesign products. And so, just as the best salesman may not make good as a sales manager, or leader of a sales team, because he has not been trained to distinguish between doing and managing, too long a spell in the field, unless carefully supervised, could inhibit the development of ability to do the co-ordinating work of a marketing executive, to plan for the future, to control the present, to try to ensure achievement of the objectives and to evaluate what has happened.

Thus a good sales manager is not necessarily a good marketing director.

1. *The functions of marketing, brand and product managers.* Information Summary 93, British Institute of Management (London, 1961).
2. Chester Barnard, *Function of the executive*, Harvard University Press (Cambridge Mass., U.S.A., 1938).

But here we may run into semantic difficulties. 'Marketing' is not yet widely used in this country as a description of an important function in a company, although many sales managers—often implicitly—undertake many of the responsibilities pertaining to marketing. The fact is, however, that the job description of a top marketing executive means that he must be motivated by the objective of company profit rather than just of turnover, have considerable ability to think things through and plan accordingly, define problems for investigation and, above all, have the ability to get the best out of product development, sales, advertising, sales promotion and service executives, and to present all marketing aspects of this business to his board of directors. Many sales directors and managers are doing such things well—and so are taking a top marketing executive role.

Increasingly in the United Kingdom, marketing courses of a general and a specialist kind are being developed. Such courses, which may range from one day to three years in length, are provided by Universities, Colleges of Advanced Technology, Technical Colleges, trade and professional associations, independent training establishments or management consultancy firms. The endowment of Chairs of Marketing at the Business Schools to be established at London and Manchester[1] and at Lancaster University will be an acknowledgement that marketing has attained full academic status in Britain at last.

The longer courses normally incorporate a substantial number of related peripheral subjects in addition to the central core of marketing. Such subjects as economics, psychology, sociology, law, quantitative techniques, accounting, economic history and geography, mathematics and languages are all extremely relevant to the education of marketing personnel. Quite apart from the educational value of such work for potential marketing managers, there are two additional benefits to be derived from formal education relating to marketing. First, the aspiring executive, while he may be practising in a very narrow functional capacity in his company work, through the medium of education, can maintain and develop his overall view of the field of marketing and its relation to other functions and the economy at large. Thus, such an educational programme may help to offset the narrowing influence of specialisation in the early career stages. Second, by means of regular exposure to educational situations, executives and trainees alike should continue to learn and develop their analytical abilities. In so far as this occurs, personnel may be encouraged to develop their own initiative and originality, rather than settling into routine patterns of thought which can be a potential danger in an organisation by inhibiting the manager or his staff from recognising changing conditions and adapting themselves and their activities to them.

In addition to educational courses, business games, a recent development in management training are of considerable interest. Those dealing with marketing are usually simulation exercises in which a model of a

1. Lord Franks, *British Business Schools*, British Institute of Management (London, 1964).

business and the market structure are described and a small group—or several competitive groups—is set a marketing problem. Decisions made by a group, such as on production quantities, stock levels, pricing, research and development and advertising expenditures, allocation of salesmen's time to customers (all of which are more or less interacting), are scored quantitatively, in accordance with rules explained at the beginning of the exercise, and usually lead up to income statements, from which the groups can see the financial consequences of their decisions. Business games which have been aptly termed 'living case studies', are valuable additions to training for marketing management.

But the fact remains that the most important asset of a potential marketing executive is his personality, his ability to get willing team work by a group of specialists towards a known and accepted goal. It has been said that business *is* personality and that the higher a man gets in the management structure the less he needs the technical qualifications he required when he was climbing the structure. He has to learn to delegate, and not to be inclined to interfere in the work he used to do when he was a junior. In short, he has to manage, and not to continue to do many non-managing activities. Marketing management—like all managing—is planning, directing and controlling.

The marketing concept requires a marketing manager to be a business-man, responsible for achieving the budgeted profit goals of the company, and an adequate return on the company's capital. He should be judged in terms of his success in achieving these aims. He cannot hope to succeed unless he has something of the personality features mentioned earlier and has been able to develop them under forward-looking top management guidance.

Financial Control of the Marketing Function

DAVID BURNS, B.Sc. (Eng.), A.M.I.Mech.E.

NEED FOR ACTION

The evolution of management concepts and techniques, brought about by the need for increasingly efficient company operation, has not paradoxically resulted in the same degree of specialisation in the industrial marketing function as is present in other areas of business management.

The responsibility, authority and accountability of the modern marketing manager have indeed widened to the extent that he is no longer concerned only with the narrow confines of field sales and sales promotion. Increasing competition, rising costs and narrowing profit margins have made it necessary for the marketing manager to extend his operational responsibilities to include marketing research, advertising, sales planning, physical distribution and thus financial control of the overall marketing function.

An essential prerequisite for the present day marketing manager is that he thinks and acts as a business man. The success of his company will depend not only upon possession of the conventional attributes associated with his position, but also upon his knowledge of his company's products, its design and development capabilities, the market place and the effect on this of forward economic and political trends, and particularly upon his understanding of his company's financial structure and ability to finance sales profitably.

The growing awareness amongst all businesses that the success or failure of its activities is largely and sometimes entirely governed by the effectiveness of the marketing function, has led many to the conclusion that the chief executive should be marketing oriented. This trend will inevitably increase the vertical promotional prospects of many marketing managers. Already in the U.S.A. 20 per cent of company presidents are men who have risen through its sales division.

PROFIT RESPONSIBILITY AND PROFIT AWARENESS

No matter how high the abilities of a marketing manager in other directions, if he is lacking in an understanding of financial concepts, he will be unable to foresee effectively the end results of his planning and the actions he has to take to bring these about. The marketing manager should, for example, be able to interpret his own and other companies' balance sheets, be familiar with management and profit and loss accounts, have the ability to analyse the real value of a customer account in terms of its net profitability now and in the future, and ensure that all accounts are creditworthy, pay promptly and tie up the minimum amount of capital in inventory.

In each aspect of industrial marketing there is a need for the planned allocation and integration of company resources in terms of men, materials and time. Each involves the use of money invested in the company and from which investment a return is expected, either as a dividend, or as a capital appreciation, often both. Either way, a company is required by its investors to operate in any trading year at a profit and to increase this profit in each succeeding year by the use of accumulated profit reserves.

The importance of the profit motive in defining the responsibilities, authority and accountability of a marketing manager may be seen from the job description in the previous chapter.

INFLUENCE OF THE PROFIT OBJECTIVE ON STRATEGY

The correct marketing strategy, properly planned and applied, will achieve the profit objectives of a company, provided that the criteria upon which the planning has been based remain valid throughout and that some emphasis has been placed upon financial considerations. However, for maximum effectiveness and flexibility of operation to meet and control unforeseeable changes in operating conditions, or circumstances whose precise degree of variation cannot be predetermined, marketing functions must be related to their cost and to the desired or maximum achievable level of profitability of company operations overall.

This is the role of financial control, which, in its application to the marketing function, differs in no way from financial control of any other aspect of company operations in the use of management accounting techniques. However, it must be appreciated at the outset that the marketing function cannot be considered in isolation. Certainly it has its own special problems, but the function is related to, and must be integrated with, company operations as a whole.

Financial control solely of marketing, whilst possible, would not enable the marketing effort to be fully co-ordinated with the total aspirations of the company, which are, quite simply, to make a profit. There is a trend of thought which states that the primary business of a company is to be of service to its customers to the benefit of the community and to the economy, profit being the means whereby such services continue to be rendered.

Service to customer, community and the economy are proper objectives of a business, but they are the effect of the causative profit motive. It is perfectly possible to provide a high degree of service and incur a loss in so doing, a state of affairs which, if continued, would normally result in the liquidation of the company and the withdrawal of the services which it provided. Such a condition would render a positive disservice, particularly to shareholders and creditors of the company. The marked difference in quality of service from those industries and nationalised bodies who are strongly profit-motivated and those who are not, are too abundant in everyday life to need detailing.

PROFIT MOTIVE

In the same way that public opinion is becoming sufficiently educated not to regard the occupation of selling as disreputable, so it is hoped that company chairmen and boards of directors will come to regard the making of a profit as a respectable and praiseworthy objective and not merely the side result of more altruistic endeavours.

It is because profit is an end result that it is regrettably often lost sight of until production of year end accounts. This motive should be the starting point of our thinking. Past and present history abounds with the sorry stories of companies who, though profit motivated, were unaware of how to make this motive work for them. Can one really feel sympathy for the chief executives of companies who fail to resolve the problem that faces us individually, corporately and nationally at some time or other—a shortage of ready money, either in terms of hard cash or credit availability? These chief executives commit the cardinal sin of allowing their companies to run out of money and thereby place them in the hands of the liquidators. Why do they run out of money? Simply because they do not plan their activities in such a way that sales are related to the availability of financial resources to support such sales. They overtrade and commit expenditure in excess of income, and their accounts systems function so slowly that the warning signals do not sound until it is too late.

Profit, therefore, although the primary motivation from which every other activity derives its momentum and direction, can only be achieved with safety if it is pre-planned, with financial control as the means and management accounting as the tool.

ROLE OF MANAGEMENT ACCOUNTING

Management accounting entails forecasting and preplanning in detail the company operations as a whole for a year ahead, with a breakdown, month by month, of the sales shipments that it is anticipated will be made and the profit or loss which will result. The calculations involved are comparatively simple, but the information on which these are based stems from every phase of activity of a business, activities which must be co-ordinated on the basis of intelligent appreciation of past history, present facts and anticipated future events.

This forecast of operations establishes marketing objectives which must be achieved and budgets of expenditure within the limits of which costs must be maintained, in order to attain a predetermined desirable level of profitability. Management accounting sets up the means whereby information on company activities may be obtained, collected together, processed and finally presented in such a form that actual results may be compared to those previously established by the budgets.

This, in fact, is what is meant by control. To control a function, a standard must first be set. Next, actual events must be measured as they occur and be compared to the standard. The variation or difference between the actual measurement and the standard set indicates the degree of control that has to be applied to bring the function back to the standard. The kind of control action to be taken must be related to the importance of the function and its interrelation and effect on other functions.

The management of a business is a complex matter and in many respects is still more an art than an exact science. The functions of a business do not obey exact laws but are subject to the irrationalities of human behaviour. A forecast of operations, therefore, whilst based on the structured interrelation of the functions present in any given business, and the required behaviour of each function, is subject to influences whose precise cause and effect are not always known, or have not been sufficiently studied to reduce the margin of error. It is extremely important to realise and to accept that error will always be present and that no forecast of any future event will be precise. However, continuous measurement of events and comparisons with forecasts will enable the degree and cause of errors to be determined, so that corrective factors can be applied to reduce progressively future errors to the minimum possible.

In financial control the more frequently that differences in actual results from those forecast can be examined, the finer the degree of control obtained. The determining factor is the length of time which it takes to collect, process and present information to an acceptable standard of accuracy, and here the cost of these functions in relation to the use made of the data presented, cannot be neglected. Generally, manual entry, analysis and computation of information is slow and subject to human error, and final presentation of processed data may be too late and contain inherent inaccuracies for proper control action to be taken.

For this reason, mechanical accounting and of recent years data processing, analysis and storage by computer has become necessary, particularly where a large volume of data has to be handled. A computer is also of particular value in analysing the manner in which any function in a business behaves under alternative sets of conditions, and the effect of such behaviour on interrelated functions. It will be appreciated that the determination of the probable variation in a forecast of operations under different circumstances will involve much trial and error, and if this is carried out manually the task becomes laborious and assumptions are

Table 1
TYPICAL FORECAST OF OPERATIONS
(Units are in value)

	Year Total	%	Month 1	%	Month 2	%	Month 12	%
Forecast of shipments	10,000,000	100	750,000	100	600,000	100	1,000,000	100
Materials	3,000,000	30	262,000	35	240,000	40	280,000	28
Labour	900,000	9	75,000	10	78,000	13	50,000	8
Overhead (233%)	2,100,000	21	176,000	23	180,000	30	190,000	19
Total Product Costs	6,000,000	60	513,000	68	498,000	83	550,000	55
GROSS PROFIT	4,000,000	40	237,000	32	102,000	17	450,000	45
Engineering	500,000	5	30,000	4	30,000	5·0	40,000	4
Service	100,000	1	7,500	1	8,000	1·3	5,000	0·5
Selling	400,000	4	37,500	5	40,000	6·7	50,000	5
Administration	600,000	6	30,000	4	32,000	5·4	40,000	4
Interest	200,000	2	11,250	1·5	15,600	2·6	15,000	1·5
Licence/Service Fees	200,000	2	15,000	2	12,000	2·0	20,000	2
Total Indirect Costs	2,000,000	20	131,250	17·5	137,600	23·0	170,000	17
NET PROFIT BEFORE TAX	2,000,000	20	105,750	14·5	(35,600)	(6)	280,000	28

Note: Figures in brackets denote *loss*

often made in order to simplify this work. Such calculations can, however, be carried out quickly and with reasonable accuracy by the use of a computer.

FORECAST OF OPERATIONS

A typical forecast of operations is made up of the elements denoted in Table 1, and those applicable to financial control of the marketing function will be dealt with in detail.

The forecast of operations is broken down into monthly divisions. This enables a comparison to be made on a monthly and cumulative basis of forecast and actual results, as presented by the profit and loss statement and detailed expense budgets.

Forecast of shipments

The starting point of the forecast of operations is always the forecast of shipments. Shipments, as used in the context of this chapter, denotes the value of goods despatched, or services rendered, and for which an invoice has been submitted in the period in question.

As everything else stems from the forecast of shipments, it is essential that it is as accurate as possible and certainly within plus or minus 10 per cent. Even a variation of this order can affect the final net profit before tax by 1 per cent either way.

For a company with many years of past history behind it and the foresight to record and analyse accurately previous shipments by units and value for each kind of product sold, consumption trends and seasonal variations can readily be established. This information, together with good market intelligence, should enable such a company to forecast for a year ahead to a high degree of accuracy on existing products, barring unforeseeable changes in the political and economic climates, which are always difficult to guard against.

For a new company, or one that is diversifying or introducing one or more new products, the problem becomes more acute and the inaccuracy of the forecast is likely to be higher. Good market intelligence is the key—it is essential to know in depth every aspect of the market into which a company is selling and to make use of market surveys in areas where there are unknown factors or where cross-validation is necessary.

Necessity for accurate forecasting

This aspect of financial control of marketing cannot be too strongly emphasised. Only too often, those responsible for providing the information on which a sales forecast is based regard the task as a drudge and an unnecessary evil, distracting them from what they consider to be their proper function in life, namely obtaining orders. In fact, confusion very often exists in the minds of salesmen between orders and shipments, simply because they regard their task as finished once an order has been obtained from a customer. To them it is someone else's worry whether the order will be met on time, delivered in the required volume and subsequently paid for by the customer within an acceptable period. Figures are consequently thrown out almost wildly, just to be rid of the chore, and in order not to be proven wrong these are mentally adjusted to err on the ultra-conservative side, so that credit can later be given for having exceeded the forecast. Alternatively, super optimism prevails and hurried expansion plans, later proved to be unnecessary and costly, are put into effect.

These are not wild exaggerations. Regrettably, both of the conditions described are common in industry to this day. Overcautious shipment forecasts have resulted in an inability to meet the real market demand from production and this condition has been only partly alleviated by costly overtime, sub-contracting of work outside, and hurried plant expansions. Inevitably, order cancellations result, competitors are encouraged in business and the distribution of market shares settles down to match the real productive capacities of the supplying manufacturers. The salesmen in the field, who may have been partly responsible for the overcautious shipments forecast, feel the full brunt of customer complaints of overdue deliveries and fall in product quality. This latter is the result of a shift in emphasis from planned production and quality control to maximum output and 'let's hope the quality gets by'.

Equally, overestimation of shipments forecasts, particularly with a new product, can result in excessive plant capacity and a high level of slow or non-moving inventory, both extremely costly to support financially. The salesmen in the field again feel the full brunt of these circumstances, only this time from within their own organisation, which harries them to 'get out there and sell, damn you'.

STATISTICAL ANALYSIS

The most satisfactory solution is to maintain within the sales organisation an internal statistics section, often integrated within a marketing research division. This is for the specific purpose of collecting data on shipments and analysing this continuously to determine consumption trends, applying weighting factors based on continuous and intermittent market intelligence, the latter obtained from field visit reports, market surveys and information published in trade, technical and financial journals and press. The statistics section can then at discrete intervals submit a preliminary shipments' forecast, based on an assimilation of the data it has collected, to the marketing manager, who can refine this forecast by direct discussion with his sales managers and the field sales force.

The shipments' forecast itself should be made up from a detailed analysis by each product sold and each account to whom it is sold, both by quantity and value, the latter from actual or anticipated selling price. Normally, the breakdown is made monthly and summarised by product groups for each month and quarter. A typical analysis sheet and summary are shown on Tables 2 and 3.

FORECAST OF SHIPMENTS—ANALYSIS SHEET—PAGE OF

Year: _____ Date: _____

Product Group: _____ Device No.: _____ Price: _____

CUSTOMER A/C	JAN		FEB		MAR		APR		MAY		JUN		JUL		AUG		SEP		OCT		NOV		DEC		YEAR	
	QTY	VAL	QTY	VAL	QTY	VAL	QTY	VAL	QTY	VAL	QTY	VAL	QTY	VAL	QTY	VAL	QTY	VAL	QTY	VAL	QTY	VAL	QTY	VAL	QTY	VAL
EXISTING A/C																										
NEW A/C																										
TOTAL																										

Table 2

FORECAST OF SHIPMENTS (BY VALUE)

Year:
Date:

PRODUCT GROUP	JAN	FEB	MAR	1st QTR	APR	MAY	JUN	2nd QTR	JUL	AUG	SEP	3rd QTR	OCT	NOV	DEC	4th QTR	YEAR TOTAL
MONTHLY TOTAL																	
LAST YEAR																	
% DIFFERENCE																	
CUMULATIVE																	

Table 3

SALES ORDER TARGETS

The forecast of shipments, once agreed, enables the volume of sales orders which will have to be taken in the year in question to be derived from an estimate of the desirable level of balance of orders in hand at year end.

The shipments' forecast will normally be made during the last quarter of a year and the level of orders in hand at the end of the current year can thus be estimated with reasonable accuracy. Assuming this to be say £250,000, then in line with increasing turnover in the subsequent year the desirable level of orders in hand may be permitted to rise to say £400,000. If the shipments' forecast is £1,000,000, then sales will be committed to obtain new orders during the year in question to the total value of £1,150,000, thus:

Table 4

Opening order balance	£ 250,000
New orders in year	£1,150,000
Total	£1,400,000
Less forecast of shipments	£1,000,000
Closing order balance	£ 400,000

This then sets the sales order target, which should be broken down into product groups and monthly sales targets.

ORDERS IN HAND

A word of caution should be introduced here concerning orders in hand. The content of these should be reviewed from time to time, particularly if the market is narrowly based on a relatively few large volume accounts. This places a company in a particularly vulnerable position, if actual call offs do not come up to those anticipated, as some large volume orders may have been placed by a customer merely to get the best possible price. If, during the course of a year, such contracts show no sign of materialising in totality, then a price adjustment should be made and the unrealistic portion removed from orders in hand. Orders which will not be met in a year by call offs can only distort the picture of orders in hand.

It is for this reason that some companies ignore the value of total orders outstanding on the books and take account only of the value of goods released against forward shipment dates. This is what can be factually counted on at any time for forward shipment, barring unforeseen subsequent cancellations or with-holding. In some industries, sales orders are completely committed to forward firm delivery dates, when the value of releases and orders outstanding are one and the same.

INVENTORY CONTROL

The point concerning orders in hand has perhaps been laboured, but it is important to realise that one primary factor influences the ability of a company to be of service to its customers (by this is meant its capability to produce the right goods at the right time) and this is the level of inventory which is carried.

Inventory requires capital to finance it, and not only must the inventory level be kept as low as possible, consistent with the desired degree of customer service, but it must also be turned over as many times as possible.

Inventory level is determined by a number of factors, the primary being the sales forecast and order releases, the influence of each being dependent upon their relative weights. Although it is widely held that the marketing activity does not determine inventory level, this is in fact not correct—inventory is laid in only because of sales planning or as a result of sales action.

In this regard the marketing staff carry a heavy responsibility, as the cost of carrying excessive inventory can be as high as 20 per cent per annum of the laid in value of the excess stock. Wrong guesses can be very expensive and means must be taken to remove the guesswork.

COMPUTERS IN FORECASTING

Computers assist immeasurably in sales forecasting and inventory control, but in the main the digital type of computer is too expensive and costly to run for most companies. They have the alternative, however, of buying time on a digital computer or of purchasing a relatively inexpensive purpose built analogue type.

One of the latter, now available to marketing managers, is based on the simple concept that no forecast can be expected to be perfect. Nevertheless acceptance of this concept lies at the heart of operational research (O.R.).

O.R. measures and constantly monitors the size of errors in a forecast, so that management can reach the optimum decision, with due regard to the assessment of these errors.

The simplest form of statistical forecasting is the arithmetic average over a certain number of past periods. The average gives the same weight to every past period. In the forecasting system known as exponential smoothing, the weight given to past periods can be varied to suit different conditions.

For example, sometimes more accurate forecasts can be achieved by paying little attention to the demand which existed several periods ago, whereas in other instances the reverse is true and little notice should be taken of, say, a more recent sudden upsurge in demand, because experience shows that it is unlikely to continue or re-occur.

With the analogue computer referred to, the relative emphasis given to recent and past figures of demand can be chosen to suit the particular turnover characteristics of each item. If there are upward or downward trends in demand, the computer makes suitable allowances in its forecasts.

If forecasts of more than one period ahead are of interest, these can be made either specifically for a certain period or cumulatively over the periods between the present and some given date in the future.

In addition to these simple forecasts, the analogue computer can also make others of the maximum or minimum expected demand, with varying levels of confidence as required. For example, it can calculate the maximum and minimum expected demand on a basis which ensures a 95 per cent confidence that the actual demand will, in fact, lie between the two figures.

The principle upon which the particular computer referred to operates is to prepare a forecast, measure how far out the previous forecast was and correct the new forecast accordingly. In this way, the reliability of the forecast can be predicted exactly and it is possible to achieve the lowest levels of stock compatible with a desired level of customer service.

A statistical forecast is made by projecting forward in time, information obtained from historical data and, when appropriate, making allowance for trend. The equations which can be built into an analogue computer allow this to be carried out giving any desired importance to most recent data compared with the oldest data by varying the value of what is known as a 'smoothing constant'.

It has already been pointed out that it is important to realise that forecasts are rarely 100 per cent accurate, but it is of equal importance to measure the accuracy of the forecast previously made. This error is averaged or 'smoothed' by the computer to produce a figure called 'mean absolute deviation', which is related to the 'standard deviation of forecast errors'.

In Figure A the graph shows the number of forecasts made, plotted vertically, against the error in the forecast plotted horizontally. If the forecasting system is a good one, then most of the forecasts will have a small error. As the error becomes greater, the number of forecasts will be less. It can be shown that if one standard deviation of error is added to and subtracted from the zero error forecast, then there will be a 68 per cent chance that the actual figure that occurs will be within these maximum and minimum forecasts. By adding and subtracting a number of standard deviations, forecasts can be made for any desired degree of probability and the actual figures will lie between the maximum and minimum figures. The analogue computer uses 'mean absolute deviations' for this purpose, as it is computationally more convenient.

Figure B shows graphically an illustration of a forecast made of sales in the 'Lth' period ahead. The present average and trend are combined to make a forecast one period ahead and then this is projected forward in time to forecast the likely sales in the Lth period (L can be up to twelve periods). By measuring the average forecast error and multiplying this by a constant K_1, a forecast of maximum and minimum sales in the Lth period can be made with any desired degree of confidence set by the value given to K_1.

In an exactly similar manner, a forecast can be made of the cumulative sales over L periods ahead (up to twelve), together with maximum and

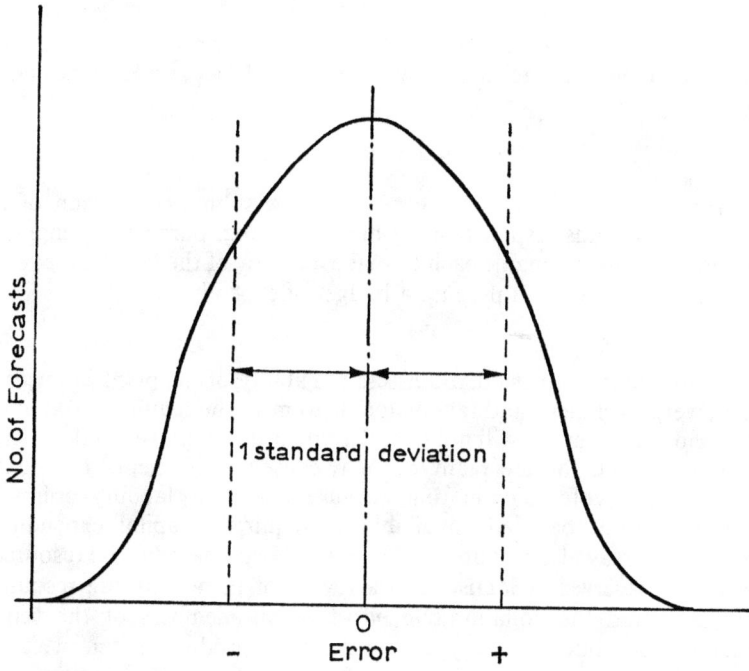

Fig. A

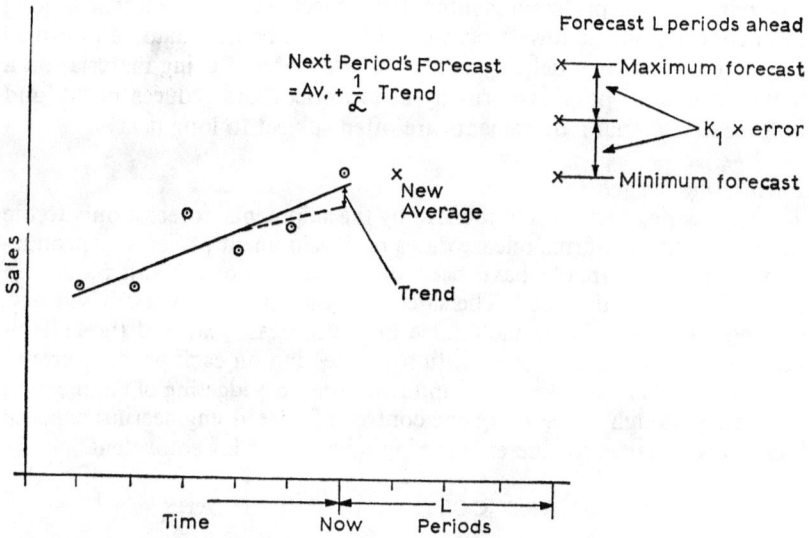

Next Period's Forecast
$= \text{Av.} + \frac{1}{L} \text{ Trend}$

Forecast L periods ahead

Maximum forecast

$K_1 \times$ error

Minimum forecast

New Average

Trend

Time   Now   Periods   L

Fig. B

minimum forecasts determined by the average error and a constant K_2. Controls on the computer will allow the value of L, K_1 and K_2 to be chosen and varied at will.

BUDGETS OF EXPENDITURE

The preliminary shipments' forecasts are now submitted to each of the departmental heads responsible for manufacturing, purchasing, engineering and accounts, to enable each to make a review of the facilities required to meet the forecast and prepare a budget of expenditure.

Manufacturing budget

The manufacturing division will assess the ability of the plant in terms of manpower, machinery and raw materials to meet the required production rates, and such a review will not only determine additional capital expenditure requirements for new plant, but may cause the shipments' forecast to be modified in volume or in time because new plant, labour, tooling or materials cannot be made available as required. Capital expenditure requirements may also be outside the limits of available financial resources, either from reserves or loans. Such a review of manufacturing resources takes time and the collaborative effort of all members of the senior executive team, but ultimately a forecast which production can meet will be agreed and manufacturing expense budgets and material procurement schedules finalised.

Purchasing budget

The purchasing department is intimately concerned with the latter, as long term contracts at the lowest possible prices can be negotiated and orders for materials on long delivery placed in good time. Buying material on a 'hand to mouth' basis is normally at top prices and reduces profit, and unforecast material requirements are often subject to long delays.

Engineering budget

The engineering section is influenced by the shipments' forecast only to the extent that this confirms release dates of development projects to production. These will already have been discussed previously with Sales and Manufacturing and agreed. The sales division will also have advised new projects likely to arise in the course of the forecast year and the level of activity to be expected in application engineering on each product group. Nevertheless, sales exert a major influence on the budgeting of engineering expense, although the subsequent control of agreed engineering expense budgets is a matter for the engineering manager or his equivalent.

STANDARD COSTS AND OVERHEADS

The accounts department, on presentation of a preliminary shipments forecast, will normally review not only the administration requirements of the organisation and prepare from this a budget of administration expense, but will also review with Sales and Manufacturing the actual and standard manufacturing costs of all products and product groups. Manufacturing cost is here taken to comprise the elements shown in Table 1, that is the build up from material cost, direct labour used, and overhead, the latter usually being expressed as a percentage of the direct labour.

The overhead percentage is a direct reflection of the cost of supporting services to manufacturing, and includes the depreciation on all capital equipment and the cost of providing facilities for inspection, storage, maintenance, repair, transport, and tooling, light power and heat, consumable supplies, packing and all ancillary services of production planning, engineering and control. A high overhead rate does not necessarily reflect inefficiency—the greater use of automatic production equipment and power tools will increase overhead but reduce direct labour, and a rising volume of production will produce a stage at which new and possibly costly tooling will be paid for by a reduction in overall production costs.

For example:

Table 5

	Year 1	Year 2	Year 3	
Material Content	30	30	30	
Labour used	15	10	5	
Overhead	15(100%)	15(150%)	15(300%)	
Total Production Cost	60	55	50	
		Saving 8·35% on Year 1	Saving 9·1% on Year 2	Overall Saving on Year 1— 16·7%

This emphasises the importance of accurate shipments forecasting, as an increase in level of shipments, if realised, will enable the full benefit to be obtained from more efficient production methods.

PRODUCT MIX AND EFFECT ON PROFITS

The review of manufacturing costs between Accounts, Manufacturing and Sales will usually show that there is for any product group an average manufacturing cost which can be expressed as a percentage of the average selling price for individual products within the group. Selling price is here taken to be the net return to the company with any discounts to wholesalers and distributors deducted.

The overall manufacturing cost for all products sold will reflect the mix of individual product groups and will determine the final gross profit margin. As this has to be as high as possible, the most profitable mix should, under normal circumstances, be chosen when making the shipments' forecast, unless it is policy to do otherwise in order to break into a market and discount the present for the future.

Where the detailed review of actual costs reveals products which are making a loss or showing a gross profit margin below standard, either the prices of such products will need to be increased, or the products redesigned, re-engineered or re-tooled to reduce manufacturing cost.

VALUE ANALYSIS

Value analysis, that is a method of determining the intrinsic worth of each component part of a product relative to the function which it has to perform, can usefully be carried out on those products which are in the loss or low profit area. In the last resort, a product may have to be withdrawn entirely from the range, unless it is one which supports other high profit bearing items.

PROFIT DILUTION

However, it must always be borne in mind that it is often possible to make a better year end profit with less effort, selling a small number of high profit bearing items than a large number of low profit bearing items. Every product sold carrying a profit below standard, merely dilutes the profit from sales of other products. It is therefore necessary when reviewing the profitability of individual products and product groups in particular, to take a long hard look not only at gross profit margins, but also at costs below the line; that is, selling and administration costs. If these can be held static and sales volume increased to the point where advantage can be taken of more efficient production methods, then a loss product can be turned into a profitable one. The profitability of an operation cannot be judged from mere turnover alone, as this can be a false criterion.

BUILD UP OF FORECAST OF OPERATIONS FROM COST CENTRES

The presentation of the preliminary shipments' forecast to Manufacturing, Engineering, Purchasing and Accounts, as previously described, should ultimately result in an intermediate forecast of shipments which is acceptable and realisable through the integrated and co-ordinated effort of all concerned, and the review of manufacturing costs will have determined the gross profits achievable.

It will be seen from Table 1, that in order to arrive at the probable net profit before tax, estimated expenditure on such other costs as are incurred in the day-to-day running of the business must be established. Engineering expenditure, including that for research and development, has already been mentioned, as this is sometimes included in the build up of manufacturing costs.

The costs of selling, administration, service, interest on borrowed capital, licence or service fees, and any other fixed or variable expenses which the company may have to bear as a cost centre must also be determined to arrive at the total of indirect costs, which, when deducted from gross profit, establish the net profit before tax.

Initially, expenditure in the current year for each of the cost centres mentioned in the previous paragraph will be examined and analysed by Accounts and allowances made against each detailed item for an increase or decrease in activity, as shown by the intermediate forecast of shipments. This will produce preliminary budgets for the forecast year in question, expenditure having been scaled at a level which will result in a predetermined year end profit. Most companies will be satisfied with 15/20 per cent before tax, some with less. Whatever the target profit, it will dictate the budget allowances for the various cost centres and these may have to be trimmed to achieve the desired results, or the whole forecast of shipments reviewed once more to achieve a more profitable mix. This is a process of gradual refinement, until, on paper at least, the possibility of making the profit desired is shown.

Marketing cost centre

A budget of proposed expenditure for each cost centre has now been established and this will be presented to each department concerned for detailed examination and comment. Here we are concerned only with that applicable to Marketing and a typical budget expense sheet is shown on Table 6.

Salary cost centre

The items under indirect labour, account codes 121/124, should be self-explanatory. A decision has nevertheless to be taken in drawing up the budget for the forecast year, whether existing staff will be sufficient to meet the requirements of the forecast of shipments and the related sales order target. It is also opportune to consider whether the field sales force and internal sales administration staff are sufficiently effective. A question of paramount importance is whether or not improvements in efficiency can be made.

For the field sales force, the total cost of each salesman employed should be related as a percentage to the net sales he achieves. This will determine the spread of percentage sales costs between salesmen and enable the overall average percentage cost to be found.

Each industry will have its own standard as indicative of effectiveness in the field, and the author's experience has shown that this can vary from less than 1 per cent for a small, highly technical sales force selling low cost products in high volume to a limited number of outlets, to nearly 15 per cent for a large, semi-technical sales force selling low cost products in relatively small volume to a large number of outlets.

An analysis of percentage sales costs can be extremely revealing, not only in terms of the effectiveness of individual salesmen, but also in relation to product gross profit margins. Excessive field sales costs can be caused by poor planning of sales calls, inadequate knowledge on the part of salesmen, lack of sales ability, poor territorial distribution, focus upon the wrong market sector and a host of other related factors, not the least of which may be the lack of effective incentives.

EXPENSES—MARKETING

Month: _____

A/C CODE	HEADING	BUDGET FOR MONTH	EXPENSE CURRENT MONTH	DIFF.	BUDGET YEAR TO DATE	EXPENSE YEAR TO DATE	DIFF.
	Indirect Labour						
121	Executive Salaries						
122	Salesmen's Salaries						
123	Admin. Salaries						
124	Clerical Salaries						
	TOTAL						
	Expenses relating to Labour						
221	N.H.I. Contributions						
222	Graduated Pensions						
223	Pensions—other						
224	Commission/bonuses						
	TOTAL						
	Operating Expenses						
301	Employee Procurement						
302	Operating Supplies						
303	Office Supplies						
304	Market Research						
305	Advertising—Press						
306	Public Relations						
307	Exhibitions						
308	Literature						
309	Other Advertising Expenses						
310	Car Expenses						
311	Travelling—other						
312	Entertaining						
313	Dues and Subscriptions						
314	Maintenance—office machines						
315	Gas, electricity, water, oil						
316	Postage, telephone, telegrams						
317	Rent and Buildings						
318	Insurance—other						
319	Insurance—officers life						
320	Rates—Property						
321	Depreciation—land—buildings—office—machinery—cars						
322	Misc. operating expenses						
	TOTAL						

Table 6

Field sales force—performance, standards and incentives

In general, the percentage cost of a salesman, related to his sales order volume, is relatively constant for quite a wide spread of industry, and will be between 2 per cent and 4 per cent. This means that a salesman who will cost his company say £3,000 per annum in total, including salary, commission, car expenses, entertaining, hotel and meal expenses, should be achieving an average annual sales order volume of £100,000. This is considered to be a reasonably accurate guide in estimating the number of salesmen required to achieve a given sales order volume.

In budgeting the cost of indirect labour expenses for marketing, provision must also be made for any salary increases which may be made throughout the year, and under account codes 221/224 the forecast cost of National Insurance, company pension contributions, commissions or bonuses. Direct and indirect expenses are sometimes amalgamated to give an applied cost which can be anywhere from 10 per cent to 15 per cent up on basic salaries.

On the subject of incentives for field salesmen, there are a number of methods, all of which have some merit under certain circumstances: earnings based entirely on commission; a low basic salary plus high commission rates on all sales; an average basic salary plus commission on sales above a platform level, the rate of commission *increasing* at discrete intervals; a high basic salary plus commission on sales above a platform level, the rate of commission *reducing* at discrete intervals; a high basic salary plus bonus at management discretion.

Additional incentives, often obtained only through competition with other salesmen can be in the form of free holidays, 'star' awards or gifts to wives, to name a few typical types.

In the author's view, all of these methods ultimately rationalise into a total remuneration for a given performance, calculable both by employee as well as by employer, and it is total remuneration that is the final incentive for the employee. Given an adequate rate of pay, sufficient fringe benefits and security based on continuing effective performance, with annual salary increments for above average results, a higher overall performance can be better obtained than by any other method. This prevents wasted time, both by salesmen and accounts, in calculating and agreeing commissions earned, and prevents the salesmen from concentrating on the easy to sell low profit bearing items or even 'loss leaders'.

Under the heading of operating expenses there are a number of items whose meaning is self-evident, and detailed mention will be made only of those where expenditure can be appreciable in relation to the total budget.

Employee recruitment cost centre

Code 301, employee recruitment, is frequently overlooked and consequently a cause of expenditure over budget. Turnover, under conditions of low unemployment, can be fairly brisk, particularly on clerical grades of staff and even with senior salesmen and executives, where demand exceeds supply from competing companies. Salary increases can sometimes be cheaper than maintaining old salary scales and indulging in the expense of employee recruitment to replace lost staff, particularly when the replacements enjoy at commencement the higher salary that would have prevented the loss in the first place.

Advertising cost centres

Advertising, codes 304/309, is a generic title under whose umbrella all forms of sales promotion are generally herded together, and a budget allowance made of about 1 per cent to $1\frac{1}{2}$ per cent of forecast sales shipments. This can of course be higher for some industries and when a new product is being launched.

The figure of $1\frac{1}{2}$ per cent mentioned should be taken only as a guide, as it is initially only of academic interest, since it is necessary for budgeting purposes to estimate as accurately as possible the breakdown of proposed expenditure under the various headings outlined above.

Codes 304/309 divide advertising between its various constituent parts, namely trade and national press advertising, public relations work, exhibitions, sales literature and 'other', the latter comprising the cost of sales display material, Christmas gifts and calendars.

Unfortunately it is not possible to assess accurately the return from advertising, particularly in the industrial field. Replies to direct mail shots and reader enquiry cards from trade news journals in which advertising or editorial matter has been placed enable some measure to be obtained, but unless accurate records are kept of the conversion rate of such enquiries into orders, even this measure can be misleading.

It is essential to keep the company's products and image before potential and existing buyers, as a means of breaking into new markets, expanding existing markets, and as a conditioning agent for back-up of the field sales force. But, to control one must be able to measure, and this is particularly difficult in the area of advertising. Experience, based on trial and error, is the only reliable guide so far developed.

Transport cost centre

The cost of providing transport for salesmen, code 310, is not often appreciated until a detailed analysis is made. Cost here includes the annual depreciation allowance for the vehicle, and this should normally give write off in three years. Also included is tax, insurance, repairs and replacements, service, petrol and oil, the latter based on estimated annual mileage. Company ownership of vehicles is economic only if a large number is involved and advantage can be taken of fleet discounts and a company owned transport service department, otherwise comprehensive rental is probably cheaper. Some companies permit a salesman to provide his own car and pay him either an annual allowance or a mileage rate, the latter on a decreasing scale with increase in total mileage. Whichever method is currently employed, it is worthwhile investigating all other alternatives, and as a general guide a budget of £500 per annum per car, inclusive of petrol for 20,000 miles is considered reasonable.

Travel and entertainment cost centre
Under the heading of travelling, code 311, is included journeys by means other than company car, for example by aeroplane, ship, train and hire car for special occasions. The budget should make allowance for envisaged visits overseas to customers, agents, exhibitions, or intercompany if units are established overseas.

A budget for entertaining expenses can be particularly difficult to establish unless some fairly rigid rules are laid down as to what can, and cannot, be allowed, with an indication of the amount that is considered reasonable. This may, of course, vary with the level of salesman concerned and the status of the people upon whom he calls. Some companies leave the question of the cost of entertaining and whom they will entertain to the discretion and integrity of the salesman, but whilst this is fine in principle it can lead to abuse and is difficult to control without resorting to embarrassing inquests. More important, such a policy makes budgeting difficult and if past costs are used as a guide, they may well have been too high. It is thus felt that either a daily allowance should be given or a firm ruling made as to the maximum expenditure that will be considered under various conditions.

Miscellaneous costs
Postage, telephone and telegrams, though included in the example budget for marketing expenses, are often items which are very difficult to split up between sales, administration and production, usually because a common switchboard and mail room are maintained, and the cost of logging every call, cable and postage stamp can be prohibitive, to say nothing of the cost of subsequent analysis and segregation. However, occasional analysis of costs in these areas can be very revealing and will show where economies can be made, for example by the installation of Telex, or formal authorisation for long distance and overseas telephone calls and cables.

MANAGEMENT BY EXCEPTION

Once the preliminary budget for the various headings has been established and totalled, this can be compared to the allowance made initially in the forecast of operations, and adjustments can be made, if necessary, until a final budget is approved. Subsequently, the expense sheet will be presented by Accounts at the end of each month of the year in question, and a comparison will be given between actual and budgeted expenditure, both for the month and cumulatively for the year to date. Differences can then be analysed in greater detail to ascertain precisely where and how they have occurred, and appropriate corrective action taken.

It is usual, in the operation of management accounting, to review the forecast of operations at quarterly intervals for a forward period of six months. This does not necessarily mean that the budgets have to be altered. However, if the overall situation has changed materially from that originally forecast, then drastic action may have to be taken and the budgets revised.

Again, in operating management accounting, it is usual for budgets to be accompanied by a monthly profit and loss statement. If this reveals that the forecast profit has been reached or exceeded, then the detailed budgets need not be examined too closely, but if the profit target has not been achieved or a loss made, then a full scale inquest must inevitably result.

CAPITAL EXPENDITURE BUDGETS

It is also necessary to prepare annual budgets for capital items of expenditure, such as office extensions, new or replacement furniture and equipment and cars. It is normal for the capital budget in any one year to bear a relationship to the total depreciation allowance for the previous year, and a factor of 1·5 is often used.

MEDIUM AND LONG TERM FORECASTING

The procedure previously outlined for short term forecasting of operations is often carried out also on a medium to long term basis—that is for a period of either five, seven or ten years ahead. Obviously the further ahead in time a forecast of shipments is made, the greater the inherent errors. A five year forecast, if carried out in sufficient detail, can be accurate to within 20 per cent and enable short range planning to be put into effect in terms of forward manpower, plant and financial requirements. A ten year forecast can reveal areas of market saturation and the need for new products to support continued growth.

PROJECT ASSESSMENT

A subject which cannot go unmentioned in the context of financial control of marketing concerns the profit assessment of new projects. This is dealt with in Chapter 4 under the heading of 'product justification', where the detailed analytical steps which should be taken for a full and comprehensive appraisal are outlined.

As a preliminary to such a study in depth, it is often helpful, however, to carry out what is in effect a dry run on a somewhat more sketchy basis, using estimates of probable costings in order to determine whether or not it will be profitable to proceed beyond the market research or design study stages.

Only too often companies go blindly into the development and launching of a new product, basing their justification for the expenditure involved

PROJECT ASSESSMENT						

PRODUCT NAME: *DIGITAL EXTRICATOR* **DATE:** *APRIL 1 1984*

DESCRIPTION: *EFFICIENCY GENERATOR* PREPARED *by S.N.AFU*

TARGET SELLING PRICE: *£ 5. 4.0*

COMPETITION: *NONE*

MARKETS: *ALL*		Year				
		1	2	3	4	5
	Market potential quantity Volume × *1000*	*20*	*40*	*60*	*80*	*100*

BUDGET COSTS
Initial

	£	
Market survey:	*1500*	amortised over 3 years'
Design study:	*900*	production = *£ 0.02* /unit
Development:	*4000*	
Qty *10* of Prototypes:	*1000*	amortised over 3 years'
Qty *100* of Pre-production:	*1000*	production = *£ 0.05* /unit
TOTAL	*8400*	

Production

	£	*Special*	£
Material cost each:	*1.75*	Tooling estimate:	*2500*
Labour cost each:	*0.25*	Jigs & Fixtures:	*1500*
Overhead at *200* %	*0.50*	Machinery:	*5000*
		Test Fixtures:	*1000*
PRODUCTION TOTAL EACH:	*2.50*	TOOLING TOTAL:	*10,000*
Tooling amortisation:	*0.03*	amortised over 5 years'
Market survey amortisation:	*0.02*	production = *£0.03* each unit
Development amortisation:	*0.05*		
TOTAL COST EACH:	*2.60*	TOTAL CAPITAL INVESTED	
Selling Price:	*5.20*	Initial costs:	*8400*
GROSS PROFIT:	*2.6 = 50* %	Special:	*10,000*
Selling/Admin. costs:	*0.78 = 15* %	Working capital:	*50,000*
Licence Fees:	*0.52 = 10* %	TOTAL:	*68,400*
NET PROFIT:	*1.30 = 25* %	Average interest on capital invested @ *6%* over 3 years = *£4000.* Include in admin. costs	

BREAK EVEN TABLE

	Cumulative Recovery	Cumulative Costs	Profit/Loss
	£	£	£
YEAR 1	*104,000*	*94,400*	*9,600*
YEAR 2	*312,000*	*246,400*	*65,600*
YEAR 3	*624,000*	*474,400*	*149,600*
YEAR 4	*1,040,000*	*778,400*	*261,600*
YEAR 5	*1,560,000*	*1,158,400*	*401,600*

Break even point after: *end 1st* years

Return on capital invested: *590%*

Table 7

on either faith, hope or a hunch. However, it is only common sense that any new marketing venture should be backed by a reasonable assurance of success before anything is spent on research, development or the production of prototypes.

The project assessment sheet shown as an example in Table 7 enables the probable return and breakeven point to be established from preliminary estimates, and if these show the project to be a financially acceptable proposition, then the design study and development stages can be entered into with somewhat more confidence than otherwise.

Break even would normally be expected after 2/3 years and as in practice costs will always be higher than estimates, a considerable margin of error should be allowed in the latter.

Generally, it is not possible to make even a preliminary project assessment without first taking the initial step of a marketing survey. Also, as the various stages of marketing survey, design study, development and production of prototypes are completed, costs can be examined at the completion of each and the assessment as a whole refined in line with Chapter 4. If at any stage it becomes apparent that total costs will exceed initial estimates to the extent that the whole project will no longer be profitable, then this is the point at which to call a halt.

CASH FLOW CONCEPT

Mention should also be made of a concept that is frequently used to give a continued assessment of the financial strength or weakness of a company—this is known as the cash flow concept. This is an attempt to estimate for several months ahead the flow of cash both into the company in terms of payment for goods sold and going out of the company to meet expenses.

Usually the forecast of operation, and budgets stemming therefrom, are arranged so that a higher rate of cash is coming in than is going out, and liquid resources are thereby continually built up to 'self finance' further expansion. However, if outgoings are greater than incomings, the difference has to be met from liquid resources or by borrowings, and if the latter is necessary, it is as well to know in advance, so that negotiations can be concluded in proper time and the monies available when needed.

Usually, in order to support an operation financially, it is necessary at any one time to cater for: outstanding debtor accounts, that is monies receivable, to the extent of their cost, which may amount to two to three months of the manufacturing costs of past shipments; the laid down value of inventory and work in progress, which may amount to two to three months of the manufacturing cost of forward shipments; depreciation for one to two months; general running expenses for one to two months; the net assets of the company.

The total of these amounts must be balanced by the issued capital of the company, plus reserves of retained profits, plus borrowings.

If this total leaves a balance sufficient to support forward cash flow requirements, then all is well, otherwise more capital must be acquired or debtor accounts, inventory or general running expenses reduced.

CONCLUSIONS

It has only been possible to give an outline of the present-day financial responsibilities of a marketing manager. Moreover, the concepts themselves are in the process of evolving into even more refined techniques. For example, network analysis, which has previously only been applied to large-scale capital projects, is now finding considerable application in the planning of marketing strategy. As this is a specialised subject in its own right, its omission in the context of this chapter is deliberate.

There is a need, therefore, for the marketing manager both to put into practice as applicable to his company the financial controls previously outlined, and to familiarise himself with every new financial technique that has an application to marketing. This will require careful reading of management journals and attendance at seminars and conferences which are held from time to time on such subjects and above all an open mind towards new methods. The time spent will be well repaid.

In a dynamic society the marketing manager who remains static will soon find himself and his firm left far behind.

Integrating the Marketing Functions

A. FRANKLIN COLBORN, B.Litt., M.A. (Oxon.)

The integration of the marketing function means welding a group of persons into a team which will exert its total effort on foreseeing and supplying profitably the needs of the users. The measure of its success will be how much of production is sold profitably and how far its efforts ensure continuity of the profitable sale of maximum production.

The object of any examination involving a marketing team is not generally to set up a new marketing organisation. Most are already in being. The question is how ought marketing organisations to develop and on what broad lines? The marketing teams and the industrial users with whom the team is in contact are all individuals and this involvement with human relationships and situations makes it impossible to propose and elaborate scientific principles which would enable an ideal organisation to be set up. The objective, therefore, of this examination is, if possible, to draw out good guide lines and broad tests of the quality of the work the team is doing.

It is the responsibility of the board of a company to determine what it can afford to hand over to its marketing manager and what it must keep in its own hand, but there is no doubt that the responsibility for the co-ordination of the marketing operation must be quite emphatically that of the chief marketing executive.

The team which the chief marketing executive is called upon to build is extremely diverse in the training, experience and talents of the people who make it up. They have to be brought together from the single positions they occupy throughout the organisation. Because their day-to-day special occupations are different, it is not possible to instruct the team on precise objectives and methods as, for example, a team engaged in accounting or stock-control.

They must be united around an idea which at one and the same time contains a statement of the aims and purposes of their total effort and which provides them with a single rallying point within their own organisation. This idea must be the principle behind all marketing: *the sovereignty of the user*. 'The user is the source of business welfare and destiny. He is what your business is all about. It is the customers who decide the fate of every business.'[1]

A useful test for day-to-day decisions which is easily accessible to every member of the marketing team is that of the marketing approach already quoted in Chapter 14; a way of managing a business so that each critical business decision, whether made by marketing people, engineering people, manufacturing people, financial people or people in any other activity of the business, is made with the full, prior knowledge of the impact that decision will have on the customer.[2]

The advantages of this definition are that it provides the marketing team with its own terms of reference and simultaneously gives it a concise statement of principles and beliefs which the marketing team has an obligation to extend to every other branch of the business. This test, applied individually or collectively, provides more answers on which the team can reach constructive agreement than most other abstract exhortations on user-sovereignty.

ORGANISATION

However well worn and diagrammatic a chart of organisational structure may be, it provides a useful and rapidly assimilated picture of groupings and responsibilities. The basic aim is to gather together similar tasks or activities under a single control, and at the same time provide definite assignment of authority and responsibility.

Figure A shows a normal form of market relationships which is useful to apply when considering the formation of a team. It is useful again after the team has been formed to demonstrate the position of members within the organisation. It is concerned primarily with the definition and demonstration of authority and responsibilities. It suffers by its form when it appears to show parts of the marketing organisation further from the centre and therefore apparently more isolated and, erroneously, less important than others.

Figure B, on the other hand, is a considerably more ambitious and lively description of the meaning and work of the marketing department, It was devised by R. Craig-Wood and shows the organisation of the marketing activities of a large manufacturing company. The company draws its vitality and inspiration from its user-customer, who is elevated by a deliberate and symbolic act to the position generally occupied on such charts by the managing director.

The circular form of the chart is also deliberate and symbolises the strong, smooth working of a balanced, closely knit, centrally directed team.

The sequence of the departments round the chart is deliberate too. It demonstrates the flow of information, thought, decision and action. It begins with the user and ends with the user.

1. J. P. Matthews, R. B. Buzzell, T. Levitt, R. E. Frank. *Marketing*, op. cit., page 11.
2. 'A Basic Guide to Marketing for the Smaller Company', op. cit.

MANAGING DIRECTOR

MARKETING DIRECTOR

MARKETING RESEARCH MANAGER	SERVICE MANAGER	DEVELOPMENT MANAGER	PROMOTION MANAGER	GENERAL SALES MANAGER	DISTRIBUTION MANAGER
Statistics Economics User Research Sales Forecasting Data etc.	Maintenance Repair Installation etc.	Product planning	Advertising Exhibitions Catalogues Technical literature PR, etc.	Field sales force management Selection and training Product scheduling etc.	Stock control Warehousing Transport, etc.

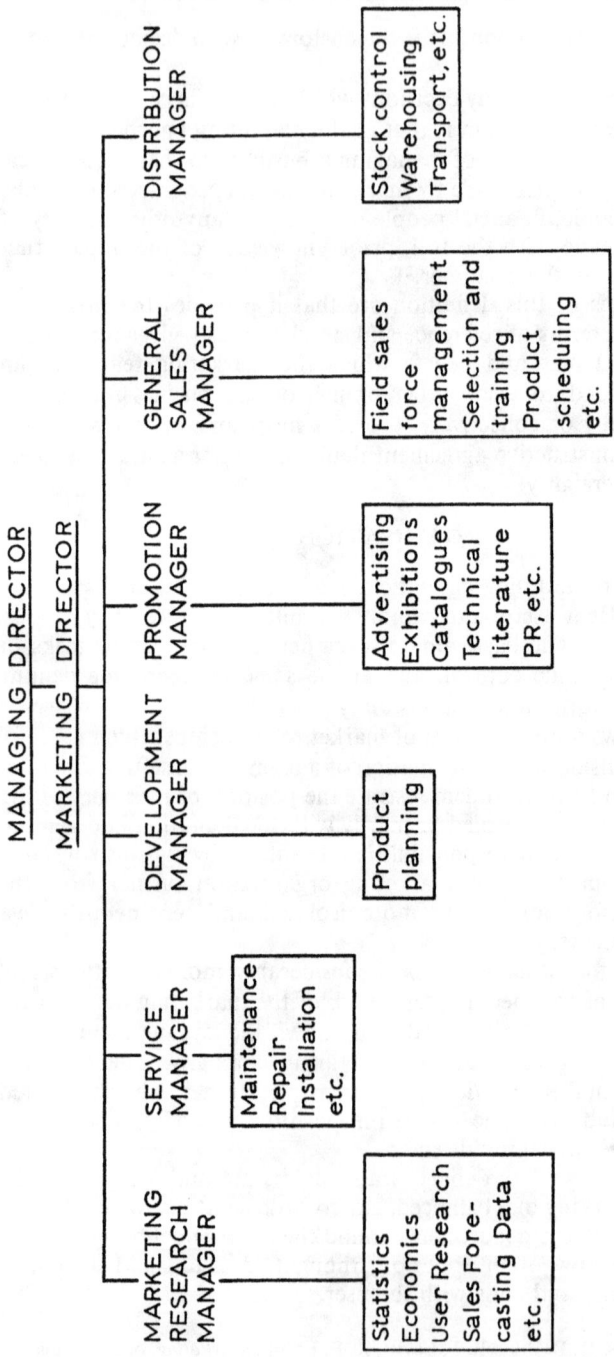

This is a normal organisation chart concerned with the illustration of the responsibilities and authority of the marketing director for co-ordination and of the managers for executive action

Fig. A

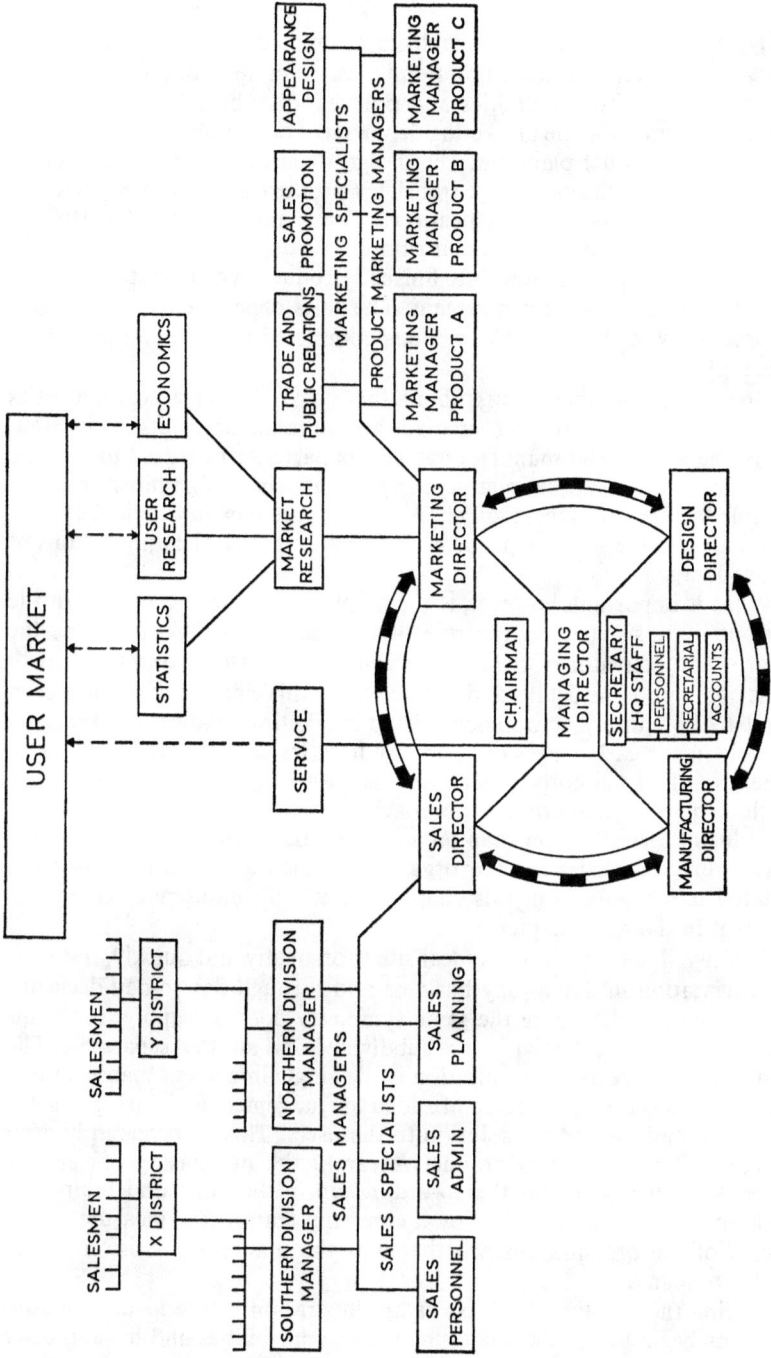

Fig. B

By means of marketing research, facts are fed into the organisation about the market, size, structure, trends, users' preferences, activities and attitudes, competitors' activities and policies, distributors' activities and attitudes. From these the marketing department creates marketing strategy and initiates product planning. The design department, working in close double-harness with marketing, translates product plans into engineering realities, blue-prints and specifications. The manufacturing department, which here of course has been contributing throughout the design operations, translates specifications into finished products which are then in turn handed over to the sales department. The sales department finally places the product with the user. The circle is completed and the company is in business.[1]

One of the notable points about this chart is that a separate sales director in this company has been made accountable for profitable distribution of the goods after manufacture. This is partly to be traced to the size of the operation. Another characteristic is that the design director is responsible for new product research. Neither of these is inevitable, but both are worth consideration dependent on size and technical complications of the product.

What is important, however, is the emphasis on the sovereignty of the user and its insistence on the role of the marketing department as the initiator and activator of the life, the continued existence and the growth of the company. The details and symbolism of this circular chart have been found to be entirely comprehensible to marketing teams and especially valuable in the early stages of team building. Its validity within the wider context of the total corporate activity is shown in the following chapter which also gives an alternative approach by breaking down the groupings by 'industry served' rather than on a product basis. In actual practice it is perhaps unlikely that a circular organisation plan can be wholly product-oriented like Figure B in this chapter, or wholly industry oriented like Figure B in the next chapter.

The two diagrams show an ideal situation neatly and quickly, but their implementation in day-to-day business and through day-to-day decisions is severely strained. There the same symmetry does not apply. Problems inevitably arise when activities are subdivided and allotted separately. The most perfect marketing organisation is the single intelligent man who had an original idea for a product, and added the judgement and daring to solve a problem and present the solution to the users. This man was in himself the controller of the new product research, the purchasing officer, the pricer, the seller. How far the co-ordination in the mind and brain of a single man can be approached by a company team is the measure of the success of the organisation, whether it is the marketing division or the whole company.

Taking the one-man business as an illustration of the ideal situation, problems begin as soon as the founder's responsibilities and his authority

1. *Marketing*, The British Productivity Council (London, 1963).

are divided among individuals. At the moment of division loyalties are split.

DIVISION OF FUNCTIONS

It may be useful to examine first the various categories of division under which a marketing organisation can in theory be classified, and then to consider the maintenance of relationships between the members which will ensure total and simultaneous effort. Generally speaking, when re-examination of an existing organisation is planned, it is looked at from the combination of four broad types of business arrangement. These, singly, are: by function, that is the assignment of duties to men who are specialists in one kind of business activity such as research or advertising or trade relationships; by product; by geographical areas; by customers and customer requirements. These divisions constitute a neat basis of examination but none mutually excludes any other, and a combination of all four is frequently, indeed generally, found inside an organisation.

The circular diagram of a large manufacturing company which has just been considered illustrates a *functional* classification of the marketing specialists, the *product* classification of the marketing managers, the *geographical* classification of the divisional managers, and the *customer* classification of the salesmen. The chief value of these formal classifications is to provide a number of convenient alternatives which can be applied in turn as patterns for a new or for an existing organisation, and the advantages of each, or all in combination, assessed.

For example, Remington-Rand in the United Kingdom changed their marketing from a geographical pattern to a product pattern. The original organisation was horizontal with seven regional managers handling four quite different product ranges. They were in effect expected to act as regional managing directors. In broad principle, the decision was made to reorganise vertically. A new managing director with strong marketing experience and philosophy set up four new marketing divisions, three for industrial and one for consumer products. The objective of each was to concentrate on marketing its respective product and concern itself as little as possible with administration, which was taken over centrally. The executives to manage the new product divisions were chosen for their belief in user-marketing and their previous success as managers. Each new divisional manager was given the support of a product manager. One new senior marketing 'technician' was brought in at headquarters (to work immediately under the managing director) with responsibility for product development and for commissioning marketing research on behalf of the marketing division.

Remington-Rand reported that the effect on marketing efficiency of these structural changes began to show within a few months. Communication became easier and quicker. Better feedback and the exchange of ideas leading to speedier product development and improvement was obtained. New vitality was evident throughout the organisation, and the new divisions began to show volume-sales increases of 15 to 25 per cent in the first year.

An example of re-grouping by function and geographical area combined is provided by the U.S. Steel Corporation which set up eleven marketing units to look after the eleven geographical areas where most sales were expected to be. These units assumed full responsibility for creating the best possible selling climate for the central line-sales organisation by providing specialist staff to convey the fullest information about new products and new uses for steel. The eleven marketing units call on other U.S. Steel departments for help and advice on, for example, engineering, applications research and most effective publicity outlets. The underlying thought is certainly to provide the closest connection between the user and the centre. In a sense the marketing unit is the representative of the user at company headquarters.

SETTING GOALS

Success, however, is not entirely traceable to replanning structure and categories of responsibility. It is due in high degree to the compulsory re-thinking of the objectives which re-organisation involves and the new vitality which comes from restatement of a single planned goal which seems capable of attainment by easily understood and convincing steps.

One of the most useful functions of the marketing manager is to re-state to the organisation the business objectives of the company which, when programmed and timed, constitute the marketing plan. The marketing plan in this sense should be re-stated and formalised in writing at least once a year. This does not imply that the plan is calculated to cover only one calendar year ahead but ensures the frequency with which it is reviewed. It will contain: a reiteration of the user orientation of the company; the foreshadowing of any major decisions which are contemplated as a result of changes due to outside events, whether due to technological, economic or customer changes; the setting of standards for the immediate and middle-term future; any changes in organisational structure involving new authority or shifts in responsibility.

CONFLICTS WITHIN THE MARKETING STRUCTURE

It cannot too often be emphasised that whatever the formal structures adopted, the quality of the decisions made depends on the quality of the employees and the central preoccupation of the whole marketing team with the problems of the user. Although a team may have accepted entirely the principle of user-polarity as that with which the effectiveness of its own work is judged, there are inherent conflicts within the team by reason of the nature and the authority and duties of various members. Such conflicts are, for example, those between sales and credit control, advertising and design, service department and distribution, area managers and head-quarters.

The question arising here is: are these exacerbations the result of the structure and organisation of the marketing team or are they the result of the personalities involved? If personalities are in question, there are no rules, but if a deficiency in the organisation is diagnosed it is generally a deficiency which has to do with communication. The opportunity can be given to the conflicting elements of the organisation to meet and discuss their problems.

Meetings by working parties to discuss a defined disagreement with a time limit are far more effective than committees with vague terms of reference where responsibility is shared among so many as to be non-existent. It is in fact only on the basic assumption of the intelligence of the team and the ability of its members to meet each other on equal terms as specialists that any industrial marketing business can function profitably and with continuity. To bring conflicting parties together requires totally unbiased leadership, and the relationships between the marketing executive and his team are critical for success. The executive has to make the decision himself as to the pattern his relationships shall follow, formal or informal.

Generally speaking, industrial in contradistinction to consumer marketing will depend far more on informal relationships between the members of the team since over a very wide range of products industrial purchasing is generally less repetitive and the pattern of business less regular. Initiative in every branch is to be cultivated.

The top man exercises control by setting up objectives, approving the plan for achieving them, verifying the results and taking corrective action. For the rest, if his confidence in his staff is firm, he may well reduce his day-to-day intervention by making his principles known to the people he controls:

> Test your action by reference to the marketing concept of the solution of user-problems.
> Use your discretion and judgement up to the point where you feel your immediate superior would disapprove.
> Do not hesitate to ask your superior for advice.

COMMUNICATIONS

One of the main reasons for failing to apply total effort inside the company simultaneously, and indeed one of the main reasons why the need for co-ordination arises at all, is the physical separation of various parts of the marketing organisation. The most isolated individual is generally the salesman. Probably the most difficult of all the tasks in communication is to keep the salesman who is facing the customer fully informed of the company's progress and intentions. If the company is small he can obviously be brought back to headquarters for prearranged meetings between all parts of the organisation. If the organisation is large, an area manager can be made the key to the co-ordination and motivation of every salesman under his supervision.

A change is coming over the duties of the area or district sales manager. Previously a large part of his time was spent in communicating statistical and marketing and selling intelligence to headquarters, but the communications between area managers and the central organisation are becoming fundamentally different in many companies.

In principle, it seems clear that area sales managers should be concerned with selling the product and making adequate arrangements for its distribution over their area. Those parts of the responsibilities which once were concerned with the collection and transmission of statistics to headquarters have in many cases been planned out of the area managers' work by a central marketing organisation using mechanical and computer methods to give historical results, and estimates based on them, far more rapidly and far more accurately than the area managers were able to do. Such statistics are: the total potential of users in the area, the frequency of calls relative to the amount of orders collected, the cost of each call continuously recorded, the likely frequency of orders based on statistical information, the optimum order and frequency of calling calculated from the order potential, and all other statistical information relating to salesmen's performance, incentives and rewards. The whole statistical operation has as its aim the assessment of the investment in this area and a running record of the return on that investment.

When these questions of calculation are taken away from the area manager, he has more time and energy to devote to the business of selling and planning the growth of sales—his true function.

CO-ORDINATING TECHNIQUES

The factor which distinguishes marketing since 1950 from previous eras of selling is the great speed of change and the rapid destruction which can overtake products unless the marketing manager in charge of them is constantly aware of economic and technological changes. The introduction and maintenance of vitality in the marketing department is therefore one of the main preoccupations of the marketing executive. The success of the business will depend largely on his ability to sustain alertness and interest and get a collective and immediate response to the necessity for change. Various devices have been suggested and used from time to time.

Reviews of the day-to-day business. A case has been quoted[1] of a company which still had on the pay-roll inspectors at railways goods yards many years after the company had abandoned their traditional method of transporting goods by rail in favour of road transport. Anomalies of this kind grow up very rapidly inside an organisation.

1. J. D. Mathews, R. B. Buzzell, T. Levitt, R. E. Frank, *Marketing*, op. cit., page 487.

Committees. Committees have proved themselves to be an extremely dangerous form of decision making since the responsibility is shared so widely as to dissipate into nullity. Working parties, however, especially in times of pressure and crisis, drawn from each specialist branch of the organisation and given a time limit for report and recommendation, can frequently perform extremely useful work. In addition to the particular material in hand, a great deal of ground outside the specific problem is covered simultaneously.

Consultancy. Some industrial marketing organisations find it profitable to call in industrial consultancy organisations almost at specified intervals, between three and five years, to analyse the success of co-ordination, recommend changes and, most important, to follow through the implementation of those changes as part of the assignment. In this way, it is frequently possible to dissolve persistent traditional attitudes which have grown up over the years until parts of the company's activities have become the 'private province' of individuals with long service or with overpowering personalities. These are often to be found in the 'specialist' departments such as research and advertising. Such situations, if violently disturbed from the inside, can upset a marketing organisation quite disproportionately and if the 'private province' cannot be usefully employed by the marketing manager in charge, it is far easier to 'expropriate' it through an outside consultant who is, in the eyes of the affected staff, far less biased.

New product development. New product development has been set out at length in Chapters 3 and 4 but within the context of co-ordinating marketing functions it is important to realise that this can be the most powerful catalyst for the fusion of any marketing team. A key operation here is the immediate appointment of a project leader who can be taken from any department. Whether a marketing, finance or production man, his operations will finally be judged by the return on the investment he initiates. The project leader has to be acknowledged as the most competent all-rounder by every individual member of the new product team. Timing is most critical and the importance of an accepted and fully understood time-table cannot be overstated. Formulation of a time-table is one of the best studies for a working party made up of the managers who will be called upon, in turn or simultaneously, to make decisions and act in the period before the start of production and sales. In this respect the application of network analysis can be particularly useful in devising realistic time-tables and subsequently checking the progress.[1]

A great deal of the preparation and launching of a new product is an act of mutual trust. The background for the marketing team is that, for example, purchasing will be efficiently and economically put through with-

1. L. J. Rawle, 'The Right Order of Things—network analysis', *Progress No. 3.* Unilever Limited (London, 1964).

out excessive yield losses or reject production. There will be an understanding that the profit-forecasting, budgeting and the historical accounting section, with responsibility for argument-proof apportionment of controversial charges like general administration, is effective and beyond reasonable criticism.

As soon as this is accepted, the operation depends on the sales forecasts for its initiation. It proceeds from the obligation of the marketing research department to establish the size of a potential market, its accessibility to a new supplier, and the proportion of the market such a supplier could reasonably hope to gain. Then come estimates of the gross profit margins likely to be obtainable in relation to the estimated cost of manufacture.

The result from the marketing working party may read something like this. Here is a total market of 50,000 tons in which it is likely that in five years this company could obtain 20,000 tons provided it could make a product with an outline specification capable of definition, to sell at a price not exceeding X at a production cost not exceeding Y.

The whole team has been at work to make this forecast. The specialists in advertising, promotion and statistics have been called in; the field sales manager and area managers will have made their estimates and proposals; the marketing researchers will not have been carrying out investigations in a vacuum but will have been working continuously with the actual people who are going to do the job. Under the project manager they will have been working as a team to present their joint recommendation to the marketing director, namely, that if the product is to the specification agreed, at the cost agreed, at the price agreed, the team believes that the company can sell 20,000 tons a year profitably.

It is at this point that the marketing director presents the estimates and the forecasts for approval to the representatives of the board of the company, and the team work begins again at many levels and in many different places within the company.

As a rule, the formal acceptance of a project is not difficult. The difficulties crowd in when action begins. Every company is well acquainted with the delays which supervene while a project revolves around departments for months on end and it is for this reason that the project leader must have complete authority to control the plan and force through the time-table after those concerned have agreed to its details. This plan is the summary of the time-tables compiled by the working party setting out contributions by day, week and month from each of its members. If the expertise is available, critical path analysis may very profitably be called in from the start for objective checking and control both of the overall plan and of individual manager's contribution to it.[1]

1. Ibid.

A great deal of emphasis is rightly placed on the qualifications and talents of specialists in marketing organisations and their obligations to the executive manager. It is perhaps useful that the man at the top, the co-ordinator, should from time to time examine his obligations and relations towards those he is co-ordinating. How, for example, does he propose to maintain his own vitality and to impart it to the others? He is, by virtue of his position, a professional man, and thus committed to keeping in touch with new techniques. Is he still abreast of the world marketing development? How much time is he prepared to give to his staff? Will he accept mistakes from them if this freedom contributes to the marketing initiative and daring which he once encouraged? How powerful is his desire for stability in the organisation he controls, set against the belief he certainly once possessed that successful entrepreneurship implies risks and change? What are the strongest incentives he has created for his team; ambition, pride, jealousy, power, money or interest? How far have increases in the size of the marketing organisation cushioned it against the shock of external stimuli, competitors and new products?

One test of the vitality he has retained is the study of his project book, that is, new work of any kind, new schemes and new outlets contemplated. This connects in turn with the sense of urgency generated and his belief in the superiority of his organisation.

It is his periodic function, perhaps even a day-to-day preoccupation, to make judgements on new ideas, to graft the new on to the old or make drastic changes, conscious that his competitors outside are equally concerned with the new and knowing that finally the new will always dictate its own position and force old organisations to adapt or perish. It is the executive marketing manager's responsibility to be the first to innovate, to integrate and to ensure survival.

17

Marketing within the Total Corporate Complex

PETER C. T. CLARK

INTRODUCING THE PROBLEM

'One of the major purposes in any system of organisation is co-ordination of the various tasks to be carried out. Co-ordination is especially important —and especially difficult—in marketing.'[1]

How much more difficult is it, therefore, to effect a co-ordination between marketing and the complex of jarring or warring elements and functions which make up the total organisation? Only in companies which have accepted and successfully operate the marketing concept (and perhaps in those which have rejected it completely) has the problem of friction and bad communication been squarely faced. In the majority of companies which typify the present stage of marketing development in industry, the emergence of marketing as an important function has set up new areas of disagreement, opposition and hostility within the firm, and the effects of unco-ordinated activity have become increasingly dangerous.

I believe one has adopted the marketing concept when one ceases saying we make excellent products, why do not all the users buy them, and starts saying what do our customers need which we can profitably make and sell?

The marketing concept does not elevate marketing to the sort of dominant role to which 'production' and 'research and development' have each in their turn elevated themselves. The marketing concept gives all the corporate functions equal prominence and no one function dominates. It is vital, however, in using the approach to business implicit in the marketing concept, that it should not get swollen and pompous with its own special jargon. The danger of this happening is implicit in the need to enlighten the people who claim that marketing is only a snob word for selling. A useful oversimplification is to suggest that marketing is the discernment of what the customer needs, whilst selling is the disposal of what the supplier has available.

1. J. D. Matthews, R. B. Buzzell, T. Levitt and R. E. Frank, *Marketing*, op. cit., page 483.

The democracy of the marketing concept requires that departments and functions shall co-operate as never before. It is easy to say this, but less easy to propound a method by which it can always be achieved. Firms are, after all, a collection of individuals of widely differing talents, energies, desires, emotions and personalities. Individuals will sometimes work better as a democracy, sometimes as an autocracy—and a medieval one at that. A great deal depends on the character and calibre of the team leader.

Thus, no idealised relationship of marketing with other functions exists. The outstandingly successful firm is likely to be characterised by its courage in allowing men of exceptional talent to operate in unorthodox ways. The mediocre firm will expect all to conform to the pattern of its own mediocrity.

There is, however, one inescapable truth, which is that acceptance of the marketing concept places an exceptional emphasis upon the leadership of the man at the top. In a truly marketing oriented ethos, all the departments and all the functions of the whole corporate complex are seen as services to the central commercial purpose of keeping the customer satisfied. If these departments or functions are led, as they increasingly must be, by men of outstanding calibre, they will not govern themselves effectively by mutual consent. Somebody has got to listen to, and understand, and adjudicate upon the inevitably divergent views of all these men.

In the absence of such a person in the chair, domination will pass to whichever of the departmental leaders has the most forceful personality. This might lead to an 'accountant domination' or a 'research domination', which could be even more unfortunate than the 'production domination' which many firms have inherited because the founder started the business from the workshop floor.

It has been said that many companies have achieved apparent success in spite of off-beat departmental orientations. Indeed they have, but almost invariably in the days when the rate of technological change was slow. Then, a good product fulfilling an established need could give a secure profitability subject only to competent procurement and manufacture. Today, in a quickening tempo of technological change, the business will go to the outstanding firms but within them the leaders have got to be led.

The first two questions a company must ask itself at its highest managerial level, as it moves towards acceptance of a true marketing concept, can be very briefly and clearly stated. First, are we sincerely prepared to allow our appointed leader to manage and to direct, and second, have we a man in that position prepared and able to do so?

If the answer to either or both of these questions is other than an unqualified affirmative, the appropriate action must be taken at top board level before chaos turns into confusion worse confounded at lower levels.

The managing director's function is to manage and to direct, to be the chief executive, to direct the management. Do his terms of reference encompass these things, and is he in fact committed to this necessarily intimate involvement with the problems of his departmental leaders; or is he in fact more of an industrial philosopher, whose most effective contribution would come from the less intimately involved position of executive chairman? Conversely, is the executive chairman in fact doing so much of the managing director's job that the latter is in fact no more than his own sales manager? It is not always possible to give men the titles which really fit their jobs, or the jobs which fit their titles, so one is told. But let us at least recognise the facts as they are, and not delude ourselves that things are as they are not. Somebody, whatever his title, must be given the clearly defined mandate to lead.

PURPOSEFUL ORGANISATION

Let us assume that our hypothetical organisation now has a leader empowered and willing to lead towards the new mental attitudes involved in adopting a marketing approach. He will at an early stage need to determine what methods of co-ordination can be adopted to ensure the proper functioning of the total activities of the firm and to devise organisational structures which operate smoothly and efficiently within an ethos in which marketing is neither inferior nor superior to other activities of the firm.

The primary task of organisation is to divide different tasks in some orderly fashion, so as to provide for their effective performance. The basic problem involved in specialisation is to group together similar tasks or activities. This has been termed 'the principle of functional homogeneity'.[1] For example, it is generally believed that the tasks of selling different products are more similar than tasks of selling a product and writing advertising copy for it. Not only is the field selling done in a different place from the copywriting but the skills required are generally believed to be different for the two jobs. Hence it is common to find salesmen selling two or more products, but uncommon to find the same man making sales calls and writing advertisements for a product. But tasks may be similar in all manner of different respects, including the skills or experience required and the time and place at which they must be executed. Moreover, adoption of the marketing approach within a total organisational structure brings with it new problems of requirements which seem to contradict orthodox theory. Organisation is intended to group together the tasks which contain elements of similarity, but what to do is vitally dependent on what is meant by 'similarity'.

The principle of functional homogeneity, unless one is very careful, may become a syndrome of 'integromania'. Accountants appear to be particuarly prone to this malady. It demands that all functions of even superficial similarity must needs be gathered together into one functional department well insulated and isolated from contact with the needs of those who seek to make use of the services involved.

The marketing concept tends to impose an entirely different interpreta-

1. Ralph C. Davis, *The Fundamentals of Top Management*, Harper and Row (New York, 1951), page 248.

tion of the word 'similarity', whereby the total needs of a particular customer industry must be looked after, in our model company, by what may be called a trade manager, responsible for all aspects of service to his appointed industry or group of industries. This could well lead to this man or even to a field salesman writing his own advertising copy, and indeed to a whole concept of 'similarity' which bears no relationships at all to functional homogeneity.

Acceptance of the marketing concept means acceptance of situations which would, traditionally, have been regarded as unacceptable and unworkable. A trade manager responsible for all aspects of service to the particular industry he covers requires the effective collaboration of many functions over which he can have no direct line authority whatsoever. Furthermore, he must 'require' that collaboration in two senses of the word. He 'requires' it in the sense that he needs it. He also 'requires' it in the sense that, as of right, he calls for it to be provided. This dual interpretation of the word requirement may be accepted quite readily by departments traditionally regarded as service departments, such as, for example, Costing. It is less readily acceptable by departments such as Manufacturing which may hitherto have been regarded as basic in their own right.

A second general goal of organisation is co-ordination. By this is meant attaining a consistent standard and proper timing of all the various tasks involved in a firm's activities. The need for co-ordination is paramount because customers perceive a company's activities as a whole, not as a series of separate and distinct operations. A customer purchasing a machine tool or an electronic component is interested in and influenced by the product itself, the promotional backing it receives, the salesman who introduces and explains it, the services that go with it, the financial terms offered and a whole host of unquantifiable factors which make up the total image of the firm. All of these factors he will compare with alternatives offered and all will work in combination to determine the success or failure of the firm. Obviously each factor is more effective if it is reinforced by others and equally obviously, a poor performance in one area infects the firm's total effort and appearance to its customers.

Thus the purpose of co-ordination in this respect is to ensure not only that the elements of the marketing strategy and activity reinforce each other, as has been explained in the previous chapter, but also that the total corporate activity is in harmony and is directed towards the overall goals of the company.

The third purpose of organisation is to provide a definite assignment of activity and responsibility. Organisation charts, such as those given in Figures A and B, attempt to specify those who have the authority to make a decision and, further, indicate their responsibility for results. The importance of providing a balance of authority with responsibility may be seen in the confusion that often results from failure to do so. In particular many firms suffer from a noticeable lack of leadership in new product planning. Because this activity involves production, finance and marketing, responsibility is often divided or not clearly defined at all.

The responsible trade manager of tomorrow (who is needed today) will insist upon being properly served by manufacturing, finance and administration services, no less than by the marketing people whom he directly controls. He will thus increasingly learn to understand the total problems of at least a sector of the business, and succession problems in top management will be reduced thereby. The fact that this 'three-dimensional' sort of situation is extremely difficult to portray on a two-dimensional organisation chart should not be allowed to defer top management from attempting to bring it about.

ACHIEVING CO-ORDINATION

The sheer size and complexity of modern business organisation creates new problems of co-ordination both within marketing and with other departments, particularly for large corporations but to a lesser degree for most medium-sized and smaller firms as well. The need for co-ordination in smaller business is less apparent and, therefore, frequently ignored. The proportionately higher cost of such shortcomings is particularly ironic because effective co-ordination in a smaller firm can often be achieved at a relatively low cost but with spectacular results. Experiences suggest that despite smoothly working informal personal relationships within the smaller firm, few organisations would not benefit from an intelligent approach to a more formal network of communication.

The relationships set forth in organisation charts reflect the formal organisational structure of a group and, therefore, the formal points of co-ordination. It should be recognised, however, that in all firms there is a system of informal relationships which is seldom fully known and much less charted. The formal structures are considered first.

A current and typical management structure is shown in Figure A. If one could get behind the scenes and examine the facts more closely, it might become apparent that the so-called marketing manager is no such

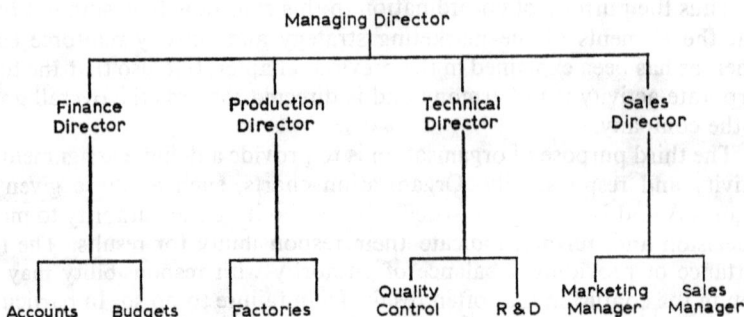

Fig. A

thing at all but only a sort of a staff assistant to the sales director, handling publicity, public relations, advertising and maybe a little marketing research—in other words of all the things regarded as ancillary services supporting the main job of selling. This type of organisation exists in cases where the marketing manager's job was created in order to keep up with the Joneses, without really changing in scope from the day when it commanded half the salary and was called marketing assistant.

Similarly, the marketing manager and the sales manager (who may likewise be little more than another staff assistant to the sales director, controlling the field sales force) are shown to be equal and parallel. Their precise relationship to each other may be ill-defined, or scarcely defined at all beyond vague indications that the marketing man is supposed in some way to be more strategic in function and the sales manager more tactical.

Organisations which are in fact like this rarely work well at board level, the departmental heads finding it hard to exchange their departmental responsibilities for the broader strategic requirements of their directorial function. Furthermore, when the managing director eventually retires exhausted, his successor will almost inevitably be one of the four departmental heads—the one with the strongest personality or the best concealed distaste for flattering his superiors. The company will then charge off on another round of illogical departmental domination the same as or different from that which was suffered before, depending upon the department from which the retiring managing director came.

An unfortunate method, not unknown in major industrial groups, of ensuring that this imperfect sort of organisation structure works even less well, is to deprive it of an effective whole-time managing director, and to give it instead merely the part time services of a senior officer from elsewhere in the group.

This man will generally not have the detailed knowledge of departmental problems required for effective adjudication nor will he have time to learn. The result is the ultimate end-point of ineffectual stagnation, since no controversial decision of any magnitude is ever likely to get taken by common consent.

A type of organisation which perhaps better meets the needs of a marketing approach is shown in Figure B.

Readers will note that the title marketing manager has disappeared and so has that of sales director, but the marketing responsibility now rests very squarely where it belongs, namely upon the shoulders of the men who answer to the managing director for the company's performance and profitability in a named sector of its activity. I have called them Commercial Directors 'A' and 'B'.

This organisation chart is circular, which is not just a 'gimmick' for the sake of novelty, but a serious attempt to illustrate that all departments and functions are servants of the central commercial aim of giving satisfaction to the customer. To ensure that this is done, both now and in the future, is the managing director's special responsibility: thus he, and his function are at the centre of the circle.

If an organisation cannot be drawn in circular plan, as in Figure B, the probability is that, like yeast, it needs to divide in order to multiply. If the managing director has more people answerable to him than he can effectively lead, then the answer is not to interpose one or more assistant

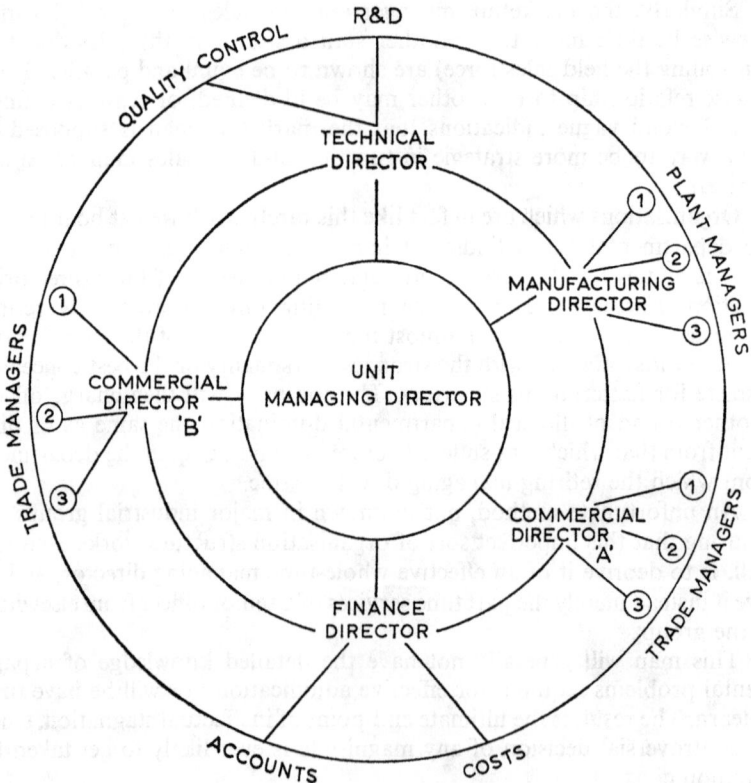

Fig. B

managing directors to whom some of the people rather ambiguously half-answer. It is far better to delegate total responsibility, for stated sectors of the business, to two or more deputy managing directors—or, going the whole hog, to create two or more unit managing directors answerable to an executive chairman. This is what, in effect, the managing director himself has now become. In this way, the desirable practice of 'getting it right at the top' is carried forward, and the company can continue to grow without smothering itself.

It also becomes possible, within a 'circular' organisation, for a trade manager in the course of his duties to move freely around the outer circle seeking the collaboration he needs, whereas under the old regime his only line of contact with another department may have been up through the head of his own department and thence down again (garbled) through the head of the other department. Similarly, at director level there can be informal movement around the inner circle, seeking personal views or more bluntly 'lobbying' before a proposal is submitted by the same people in formal session with the managing director. The circular chart is in fact an attempt to combine the best of both worlds, with a formal organisation structure which admits and condones the existence of informal contact points.

JOB WRITE-UPS

It has already been said that organisations are composed of the individuals who operate them and, therefore, a formal organisation cannot ignore the human aspects. If the formal structure is not to be meaningless then it is vital that each person should have an accurate and up-to-date job write-up. Without this and without clear demarcation lines and areas of responsibility, co-ordination is impossible.

Who does the write-ups at lower levels is very much a question for the individual organisation, but there is always a *prima facie* case for the managing director to do it himself for all who serve with him at director level. He must also closely scrutinise, and understand, the job write-ups which should between them cover the total work requirement down to middle management level.

Job write-ups are sometimes said to benefit the writers more than the recipients. This is probably true, but in any case, it is the company which really benefits. When things are not going too well in some sector, and somebody is about to get the blame, it makes sense to go through the job write-ups with all who are even obliquely concerned, to make sure that circumstances have not changed just sufficiently to make somebody's job impracticable.

A lot of patience is sometimes needed to elicit what a person really does, or what needs doing, as opposed to that person's interpretation of what it is thought the enquirer's wishes would be. Elegant exercises can be seen in which the total work requirement is beautifully stated and the individual job write-ups appear to dovetail into an impeccable interpretation of the whole. The only snag is that none of it has much relevance to the true nature of the problems confronting the company.

Many years ago an early Organisation and Method executive showed me a job analysis he had recently completed for a government department. There were thirty-six people involved in the performance of some hundreds of interrelated tasks. A few of these jobs had no ticks against them on the chart, indicating that nobody was consciously aware of being responsible for that particular job. A few other jobs had two or more ticks, indicating minor areas of overlap. It was not the uncovered jobs which caused trouble —somebody always had the good sense to do what obviously needed to be done—but the areas of overlap. These were a constant source of bickering, and often ended up by not getting done at all.

Fewer years ago, the managing director of a major concern stated that he did not believe in detailed job write-ups because they tended in his view to make people unwilling to step outside the narrow confines of what was written down, and thus unwilling to 'lend a hand at anything' when needed. Behind its façade it was notorious that this was a highly inefficient company and the morale in it was exceptionally low.

I consider job write-ups indispensable and I believe that their effective composition has a very real bearing upon morale and job-satisfaction—those two elusive requirements of a successful business which cannot be bought by money alone.

THE HUMANE USE OF HUMAN BEINGS

A wise company exerts its ingenuity to make the most effective possible use of the people it has got. It does not waste too much time firing and hiring new talent in restless and endless search for an ideal team which, if in fact it was ideal in the circumstances of today, would very rapidly cease to be ideal tomorrow.

A difference in attitudes to personnel between people who have seen active wartime service and those who have not, can often be observed. In the armed forces in wartime you could not fire your juniors and hire others, any more than your seniors could fire and replace you. Within the services great organisations were built by great leaders, and inferior ones by lesser men, but both from the fortuitously available personnel.

A great deal of the same can and should be done in industry, the major requirement for success being ingenuity and willingness to bend the system to suit the available men rather than rigid insistence that all men must conform to a standardised system. I can think of two highly successful sister companies, within a major group, which differ from each other in every conceivable way. Indeed, their only common features are same ownership and same success. This situation is indicative of an enlightened top management who allow their different enterprises to develop in different ways suitable to each.

But if somebody really cannot be made to fit, then let him go and let his going be short and sharp and generous. Most well-meaning companies end up creating more unhappiness for more people for a longer time than would be the case if they could bring themselves to be thoroughly beastly to a far smaller number of people just for once.

I believe there is a definite pattern that it is frustration, not overwork, which kills men off, literally or metaphorically, in their fifties. It is the passed-over lieutenant-commanders, not the captains of industry, who end their careers prematurely. Progressive companies attempting to improve the calibre of their personnel are, unfortunately, those most likely to find themselves creating frustrated 'has beens'.

In the late 1940's many companies recruited heavily from among university graduates. This was considered *de rigeur* in the industrial ethos of the time. They then lost the graduates again because the companies were not yet themselves attuned to the levels of leadership needed to retain the enthusiasm of top calibre men. In the early fifties these same companies recruited, less ambitiously, men of lower calibre than those of the previous period. By the mid-sixties the better of these companies have reached a point where the sort of talent that could not be contained in 1948–9 can now be effectively employed and is now in fact being successfully recruited. What is the right thing to do with the 'class of 1955'?

One day the reputable major companies, in taking men on to their permanent staff, will build a clause into the conditions of service whereby in the event of what is politely called 'redundancy', the company will underwrite their transfer to alternative employment without loss of face or cash.

BREADTH OF UNDERSTANDING

The management structure needed to implement a marketing approach will give more people a broader understanding of 'the total problem'—that is to say, of 'business'—than has ever been obtainable, in the past, in the line of everyday duty.

The suitable management structure will, of course, in itself provide the basic requirement for good inter-departmental functioning. But grafted on to this structure will be a number of specific co-ordination-inducing activities which will further help to clear the communication channels.

Bund and Carroll[1] suggest a number of approaches as being suitable for both large and small firms.

Mixing personnel with different backgrounds
Some firms deliberately add personnel with engineering or manufacturing backgrounds to the marketing team. However, the majority of firms do not believe this to be a constructive course except where engineering or manufacturing aspects are so important that marketing staff must include such specialists. The unnecessary use of engineers or manufacturing specialists in the marketing department can actually impede co-ordination and create suspicions of empire building. The exception might be the industrial marketing research department where the presence of technicians is in every way advantageous.

Cross attendance at departmental meetings
This is a technique used to broaden mutual understanding. It can be made into a feedback operation with research and development, engineering,

---

1. H. Bund and J. W. Carroll, 'The Changing Role of the Marketing Function', *Marketing for Executives Series No. 3.* American Marketing Association (Chicago, 1957), pages 48–51.

manufacturing, finance, personnel and marketing executives all partici-
pating at meetings other than those of their own department. Some companies hold sales meetings at the factory, facilitating attendance and participation by non-marketing personnel. Similarly non-marketing management meetings are held away from headquarters to boost the morale of
regional sales organisations and to foster active participation by field
executives.

Geographical concentration of top management

This is a desirable ingredient for smoother collaboration. It does, however,
run counter to the tendency by some companies over the last decade to
locate their main sales and marketing offices near the geographic centre of
their markets, leaving manufacturing operations on the original sites or
those most logical from the standpoint of raw materials, transportation
and manpower supply. Many companies are now finding it necessary to
locate top marketing personnel with the rest of corporate staff.

Joint experience projects

Some companies try to create synthetically better interdepartmental understanding. Such efforts must be 'sold' to all involved and justified by individual or departmental objectives. Thus, samples of new devices for field
testing are carried by a team of three men from Production, two from
Sales and one from Engineering. Other firms insist that every departmental
head spends a specified number of weeks each year in the field. 'He may not
necessarily be doing any selling but . . . talking to field managers . . . salesmen . . . going out on a few calls . . . so he keeps his perspective and
understands his job depends upon sales.'[1]

Nevertheless, this is a somewhat one-sided and autocratic approach
and in clumsy hands might create antagonism and resistance, with its
implied suggestion that only the marketing people have any real insight
into what business is all about.

Heavier reliance on committees

This is said to be still a growing trend despite general and often well
founded reservations on the committee type of management. For entirely
practical reasons, some companies increasingly look to committees to
expedite collaboration between departments. The committees are the means
for exchange of information and views. Each of the major functions or
divisions of the company is typically represented. The top committee
usually reviews, approves or vetos plans of individual departments.

Parallel committees at lower levels increasingly assume decision
making, subject to their immediate superiors. There is often a partial
exchange of membership. For example, a factory's 'planning and scheduling groups' and the sales department's 'production requirements group'
have common members. There is admittedly wastage in the committee

1. Ibid.

approach but their continued use indicates a legitimate function without adequate substitute.

Two other approaches have in my experience proved outstandingly effective co-ordination inducers.

The first, sending people from all over the company to courses organised privately for the company under competent instructors. At these courses groups of say fifteen to twenty men meet for an hour a week perhaps ten times, and a remarkably lasting camaderie grows up as they make assessments of themselves and each other. The victims may or may not be better informed and they may or may not thereby become more directly valuable to the company, but a bond of friendship is created which continues for a long time and perhaps inexplicably helps to surmount departmental business problems.

Secondly, setting up small teams (within a department) charged with presenting by a named date action recommendations on a subject of such a nature as will compel them to seek and obtain multi-departmental collaboration in considerable depth.

Special co-ordinating functions

A further important step in welding together the separate elements of a successful total operation is the setting up of co-ordinating responsibilities such as stock control or product planning and development.

Many companies still give manufacturing departments complete and final responsibility for planning and maintaining the finished goods stock. The marketing departments contribute to this control indirectly by making available its detailed forecasts and keeping them up to date with any changes in sales plans and new orders received. However, stock control is increasingly conducted co-operatively, or its main responsibility is placed in marketing, or it is set up as an independent function. The right course to take in a given case might better be judged against the detailed background of physical distribution set out in Chapter 11.

In the area of new product planning, a number of factors tend to pull in opposite directions, turning what ought to be a co-ordination inducing function into just the opposite. First, the sheer speed of industrial growth has produced repeated realignments of management structure and not necessarily well conceived ones. Secondly, there have been mounting pressures for new products, without in some cases a very clear idea of what product the company needs to seek.

Informal organisations

Many organisations work despite their formal structures because the executives within them maintain a separate system of informal communication and co-ordination that may possibly defy analysis.

To the extent that this merely means getting together in a congenial atmosphere to discuss things which might become contentious in the office, this is to be encouraged. If it means that people waste time keeping illicit and unofficial data and records because the organisation and methods or work study departments have organised them out of receiving data they vitally need, then informal organisations are bad and should be rendered unnecessary as quickly as possible.

Unfortunately, the informal contacts tend to run along lines where the formal communication is pretty good anyway. Regular interdepartmental luncheons, informal in nature but formal to the extent of being arranged for specific dates and with invitations issued, may help to extend these groups. Top management can help too, by inviting various groups to luncheon on a somewhat more formal basis. They should, in particular, avoid the disproportionately morale-destroying effect of appearing to bestow favoured-nation treatment on some individuals or departments, and of rubbing the noses of lesser mortals in this fact every day. Some top managements are quite unbelievably insensitive in this respect, and cannot see that they themselves are responsible for low-middle level management morale being poor.

Smaller companies tend to believe that a small staff working at close quarters automatically develops adequate communication and co-ordination. The experience of many people who have had the opportunity of observing the management of small companies from outside is that some of these firms in fact fail to communicate at all, largely because they do not see that the problem exists. The circumstances are such that a great deal of benefit might be obtained from the adoption of the more formal techniques used in large companies, to obtain better co-operation between marketing and other activities of the smaller firm.

CONCLUSION

Manufacturers of industrial goods have passed through, and it is to be hoped are now emerging from, a period of great confusion in their marketing beliefs. Some have been seeking an answer to their problems of maintaining profit growth by developing product lines in order to secure maximum plant utilisation. Others have begun to realise that the key to a more lastingly effective solution is to find out what the customer needs. Confusion between these two fundamentally different concepts has impeded the use of other companies' experience in mapping future progress, because the management structure needed for the new industry-wise orientation is itself different from that which sufficed for the old product-wise thinking.

Intelligent marketing is the key to survival in industry. This applies to large and small firms alike with the rider that in large firms more resources and more products are at stake. In the smaller firm the management can at least focus its attention on a small volume of output, while in the larger firms this is no longer possible without the necessary focal mechanism. Common to both, however, is the need to co-ordinate all the activities of the company, and this need is no less urgent in the smaller firms even if their problems are within a narrower spectrum.

Co-ordination between marketing and the other functions may be achieved whether it is sought for consciously or not. Accidental achievement of such co-ordination is, however, more likely to reflect the quality of the individuals and the ethos of a firm than any state of affairs which could be relied on under all circumstances and at all times. Understanding the problems of, and the techniques for, co-ordination is therefore a fundamental requirement for planned success.

18

Marketing Myopia[1]

THEODORE LEVITT, Ph.D., B.A.

Every major industry was once a growth industry. But some that are now riding a wave of growth enthusiasm are very much in the shadow of decline. Others which are thought of as seasoned growth industries have actually stopped growing. In every case the reason growth is threatened, slowed or stopped is *not* because the market is saturated. It is because there has been a failure of management.

FATEFUL PURPOSES

The failure is at the top. The executives responsible for it, in the last analysis, are those who deal with broad aims and policies. Thus:

The railroads did not stop growing because the need for passenger and freight transportation declined. That grew. The railroads are in trouble today not because the need was filled by others (cars, trucks, aeroplanes, even telephones), but because it was *not* filled by the railroads themselves. They let others take customers away from them because they assumed themselves to be in the railroad business rather than in the transportation business. The reason they defined their industry incorrectly was because they were railroad-oriented instead of transportation-oriented; they were product-oriented instead of customer-oriented.

Hollywood barely escaped being totally ravished by television. Actually, all the established film companies went through drastic reorganisations. Some simply disappeared. All of them got into trouble not because of TV's inroads but because of their own myopia. As with the railroads, Hollywood defined its business incorrectly. It thought it was the movie business. 'Movies' implied a specific, limited product. This produced a fatuous contentment which from the beginning led producers to view TV as a threat. Hollywood scorned and rejected TV when it should have welcomed it as an opportunity—an opportunity to expand the entertainment business.

Today TV is a bigger business than the old narrowly defined movie business ever was. Had Hollywood been customer-oriented (providing

---

1. Reprinted by permission of the publishers from the *Harvard Business Review*, (Cambridge, Mass., U.S.A., July/August 1960).

entertainment), rather than product-oriented (making movies), would it have gone through the fiscal purgatory that it did? I doubt it. What ultimately saved Hollywood and accounts for its recent resurgence was the wave of new young writers, producers and directors whose previous successes in television had decimated the old movie companies and toppled the big movie moguls.

There are other less obvious examples of industries that have been and are now endangering their futures by improperly defining their purposes. I shall discuss some in detail later and analyse the kind of policies that lead to trouble. Right now it may help to show what a thoroughly customer-oriented management *can* do to keep a growth industry growing, even after the obvious opportunities have been exhausted; and here there are two examples that have been around for a long time. They are nylon and glass —specifically, E. I. duPont de Nemours & Company and Corning Glass Works.

Both companies have great technical competence. Their product orientation is unquestioned. But this alone does not explain their success. After all, who was more pridefully product-oriented and product-conscious than the erstwhile New England textile companies that have been so thoroughly massacred? The DuPonts and the Cornings have succeeded not primarily because of their product or research orientation but because they have been thoroughly customer-oriented also. It is constant watchfulness for opportunities to apply their technical know-how to the creation of customer-satisfying uses which accounts for their prodigious output of successful new products. Without a very sophisticated eye on the customer, most of their new products might have been wrong, their sales methods useless.

Aluminium has also continued to be a growth industry, thanks to the efforts of two wartime-created companies which deliberately set about creating new customer-satisfying uses. Without Kaiser Aluminium & Chemical Corporation and Reynolds Metals Company, the total demand for aluminium today would be vastly less than it is.

ERROR OF ANALYSIS

Some may argue that it is foolish to set the railroads off against aluminium or the movies off against glass. Are not aluminium and glass naturally so versatile that the industries are bound to have more growth opportunities than the railroads and movies? This view commits precisely the error I have been talking about. It defines an industry, or a product, or a cluster of know-how so narrowly as to guarantee its premature senescence. When we mention 'railroads', we should make sure we mean 'transportation'. As transporters, the railroads still have a good chance for very considerable growth. They are not limited to the railroad business as such (though in my opinion rail transportation is potentially a much stronger transportation medium than is generally believed).

What the railroads lack is not opportunity, but some of the same managerial imaginativeness and audacity that made them great. Even an amateur like Jacques Barzun can see what is lacking when he says:

'I grieve to see the most advanced physical and social organisation of the last century go down in shabby disgrace for lack of the same comprehensive imagination that built it up. [What is lacking is] the will of the companies to survive and to satisfy the public by inventiveness and skill.'[1]

SHADOW OF OBSOLESCENCE

It is impossible to mention a single major industry that did not at one time qualify for the magic appellation of 'growth industry'. In each case its assumed strength lay in the apparently unchallenged superiority of its product. There appeared to be no effective substitute for it. It was itself a runaway substitute for the product it so triumphantly replaced. Yet one after another of these celebrated industries has come under a shadow. Let us look briefly at a few more of them, this time taking examples that have so far received a little less attention.

Dry cleaning. This was once a growth industry with lavish prospects. In an age of wool garments, imagine being finally able to get them safely and easily clean. The boom was on.

Yet here we are thirty years after the boom started and the industry is in trouble. Where has the competition come from? From a better way of cleaning? No. It has come from synthetic fibres and chemical additives that have cut the need for dry cleaning. But this is only the beginning. Lurking in the wings and ready to make chemical dry cleaning totally obsolescent is that powerful magician, ultrasonics.

Electric utilities. This is another one of those supposedly 'no-substitute' products that has been enthroned on a pedestal of invincible growth. When the incandescent lamp came along, kerosene lights were finished. Later the water wheel and the steam engine were cut to ribbons by the flexibility, reliability, simplicity, and just plain easy availability of electric motors. The prosperity of electric utilities continues to wax extravagant as the home is converted into a museum of electric gadgetry. How can anybody miss by investing in utilities, with no competition, nothing but growth ahead?

But a second look is not quite so comforting. A score of non-utility companies are well advanced towards developing a powerful chemical fuel cell which could sit in some hidden closet of every home silently ticking off electric power. The electric lines that vulgarise so many neighbourhoods will be eliminated. So will the endless demolition of streets and service interruptions during storms. Also on the horizon is solar energy, again pioneered by non-utility companies.

1. Jacques Barzun, 'Trains and the Mind of Man', *Holiday*, Curtiss Publishing Company (Philadelphia, February 1960), page 21.

Who says that the utilities have no competition? They may be natural monopolies now, but tomorrow they may be natural deaths. To avoid this prospect, they too will have to develop fuel cells, solar energy, and other power sources. To survive, they themselves will have to plot the obsolescence of what now produces their livelihood.

Grocery stores. Many people find it hard to realise that there ever was a thriving establishment known as the 'corner grocery store'. The supermarket has taken over with a powerful effectiveness. Yet the big food chains of the 1930's narrowly escaped being completely wiped out by the aggressive expansion of independent supermarkets. The first genuine supermarket was opened in 1930, in Jamaica, Long Island. By 1933 supermarkets were thriving in California, Ohio, Pennsylvania, and elsewhere. Yet the established chains pompously ignored them. When they chose to notice them, it was with such derisive descriptions as 'cheapy', 'horse-and-buggy', 'cracker-barrel storekeeping' and 'unethical opportunists'.

The executive of one big chain announced at the time that he found it 'hard to believe that people will drive for miles to shop for foods and sacrifice the personal service chains have perfected and to which Mrs. Consumer is accustomed'.[1] As late as 1936 the National Wholesale Grocers convention and the New Jersey Retail Grocers Association said there was nothing to fear. They said that the supers' narrow appeal to the price buyer limited the size of their market. They had to draw from miles around. When imitators came, there would be wholesale liquidations as volume fell. The current high sales of the supers was said to be partly due to their novelty. Basically people wanted convenient neighbourhood grocers. If the neighbourhood stores 'co-operate with their suppliers, pay attention to their costs, and improve their service' they would be able to weather the competition until it blew over.[2]

It never blew over. The chains discovered that survival required going into the supermarket business. This meant the wholesale destruction of their huge investments in corner store sites and in established distribution and merchandising methods. The companies with 'the courage of their convictions' resolutely stuck to the corner store philosophy. They kept their pride but lost their shirts.

SELF-DECEIVING CYCLE

But memories are short. For example, it is hard for people who today confidently hail the twin messiahs of electronics and chemicals to see how things could possibly go wrong with these galloping industries. They probably also cannot see how a reasonably sensible business man could have been as myopic as the famous Boston millionaire who fifty years ago

1. For more details see M. M. Zimmerman, *The Super Market: A Revolution in Distribution*, McGraw-Hill Book Company, Inc. (New York, 1955), page 48.
   2. Ibid., pages 45–7.

unintentionally sentenced his heirs to poverty by stipulating that his entire estate be for ever invested exclusively in electric streetcar securities. His posthumous declaration, 'There will always be a big demand for efficient urban transportation', is no consolation to his heirs who sustain life by pumping gasoline at automobile filling stations.

Yet, in a casual survey I recently took among a group of intelligent business executives, nearly half agreed that it would be hard to hurt their heirs by tying their estates for ever to the electronics industry. When I then confronted them with the Boston streetcar example, they chorused unanimously, 'That's different!' But is it? Is not the basic situation identical?

In truth *there is no such thing* as a growth industry, I believe. There are only companies organised and operated to create and capitalise on growth opportunities. Industries that assume themselves to be riding some automatic growth escalator invariably descend into stagnation. The history of every dead and dying 'growth' industry shows a self-deceiving cycle of bountiful expansion and undetected decay. There are four conditions which usually guarantee this cycle:

1. The belief that growth is assured by an expanding and more affluent population.
2. The belief that there is no competitive substitute for the industry's major product.
3. Too much faith in mass production and in the advantages of rapidly declining unit costs as output rises.
4. Preoccupation with a product that lends itself to carefully controlled scientific experimentation, improvement, and manufacturing cost reduction.

I should like now to begin examining each of these conditions in some detail. To build my case as boldly as possible, I shall illustrate the points with reference to three industries—petroleum, automobiles and electronics —particularly petroleum, because it spans more years and more vicissitudes. Not only do these three have excellent reputations with the general public and also enjoy the confidence of sophisticated investors, but their managements have become known for progressive thinking in areas like financial control, product research, and management training. If obsolescence can cripple even these industries, it can happen anywhere.

POPULATION MYTH

The belief that profits are assured by an expanding and more affluent population is dear to the heart of every industry. It takes the edge off the apprehensions everybody understandably feels about the future. If consumers are multiplying and also buying more of your product or service, you can face the future with considerably more comfort than if the market is shrinking. An expanding market keeps the manufacturer from having to think very hard or imaginatively. If thinking is an intellectual response to a problem, then the absence of a problem leads to the absence of thinking. If your product has an automatically expanding market, then you will not give much thought to how to expand it.

One of the most interesting examples of this is provided by the petroleum industry. Probably our oldest growth industry, it has an enviable record. While there are some current apprehensions about its growth rate, the industry itself tends to be optimistic. But I believe it can be demonstrated that it is undergoing a fundamental yet typical change. It is not only ceasing to be a growth industry, but may actually be a declining one, relative to other business. Although there is widespread unawareness of it, I believe that within twenty-five years the oil industry may find itself in much the same position of retrospective glory that the railroads are now in. Despite its pioneering work in developing and applying the present value method of investment evaluation, in employee relations and in working with backward countries, the petroleum business is a distressing example of how complacency and wrongheadedness can stubbornly convert opportunity into near disaster.

One of the characteristics of this and other industries that have believed very strongly in the beneficial consequences of an expanding population, while at the same time being industries with a generic product for which there has appeared to be no competitive substitute, is that the individual companies have sought to outdo their competitors by improving on what they are already doing. This makes sense, of course, if one assumes that sales are tied to the country's population strings, because the customer can compare products only on a feature-by-feature basis. I believe it is significant, for example, that not since John D. Rockefeller sent free kerosene lamps to China has the oil industry done anything really outstanding to create a demand for its product. Not even in product improvement has it showered itself with eminence. The greatest single improvement, namely, the development of tetraethyl lead, came from outside the industry, specifically from General Motors and Du Pont. The big contributions made by the industry itself are confined to the technology of oil exploration, production and refining.

ASKING FOR TROUBLE

In other words, the industry's efforts have focused on improving the *efficiency* of getting and making its product, not really on improving the generic product or its marketing. Moreover, its chief product has continuously been defined in the narrowest possible terms, namely, gasoline, not energy, fuel or transportation.

This attitude has helped assure that major improvements in gasoline quality tend not to originate in the oil industry. Also, the development of superior alternative fuels comes from outside the oil industry, as will be shown later.

Major innovations in automobile fuel marketing are originated by small new oil companies that are not primarily preoccupied with production or refining. These are the companies that have been responsible for the rapidly expanding multipump gasoline stations, with their successful emphasis on large and clean layouts, rapid and efficient driveway service, and quality gasoline at low prices.

Thus, the oil industry is asking for trouble from outsiders. Sooner or later, in this land of hungry inventors and entrepreneurs, a threat is sure to come. The possibilities of this will become more apparent when we turn to the next dangerous belief of many managements. For the sake of continuity, because this second belief is tied closely to the first, I shall continue with the same example.

IDEA OF INDISPENSABILITY

The petroleum industry is pretty much persuaded that there is no competitive substitute for its major product, gasoline—or if there is, that it will continue to be a derivative of crude oil, such as diesel fuel or kerosene jet fuel.

There is a lot of automatic wishful thinking in this assumption. The trouble is that most refining companies own huge amounts of crude oil reserves. These have value only if there is a market for products into which oil can be converted—hence the tenacious belief in the continuing competitive superiority of automobile fuels made from crude oil.

This idea persists despite all historic evidence against it. The evidence not only shows that oil has never been a superior product for any purpose for very long, but it also shows that the oil industry has never really been a growth industry. It has been a succession of different businesses that have gone through the usual historic cycles of growth, maturity and decay. Its overall survival is owed to a series of miraculous escapes from total obsolescence, of last-minute and unexpected reprieves from total disaster reminiscent of the *Perils of Pauline*.

PERILS OF PETROLEUM

I shall sketch in only the main episodes:

First, crude oil was largely a patent medicine. But even before that fad ran out, demand was greatly expanded by the use of oil in kerosene lamps. The prospect of lighting the world's lamps gave rise to an extravagant promise of growth. The prospects were similar to those the industry now holds for gasoline in other parts of the world. It can hardly wait for the underdeveloped nations to get a car in every garage.

In the days of the kerosene lamp, the oil companies competed with each other and against gaslight by trying to improve the illuminating characteristics of kerosene. Then suddenly the impossible happened. Edison invented a light which was totally nondependent on crude oil. Had it not been for the growing use of kerosene in space heaters, the incandescent lamp would have completely finished oil as a growth industry at that time. Oil would have been good for little else than axle grease.

Then disaster and reprieve struck again. Two great innovations occurred, neither originating in the oil industry. The successful development of coal-burning domestic central-heating systems made the space heater obsolescent. While the industry reeled, along came its most magnificent boost yet—the internal combustion engine, also invented by outsiders. Then when the prodigious expansion for gasoline finally began to level off in the 1920's, along came the miraculous escape of a central oil heater. Once again, the escape was provided by an outsider's invention and development. And when that market weakened, wartime demand for aviation fuel came to the rescue. After the war the expansion of civilian aviation, the dieselisation of railroads and the explosive demand for cars and trucks kept the industry's growth in high gear.

Meanwhile centralised oil heating—whose boom potential had only recently been proclaimed—ran into severe competition from natural gas. While the oil companies themselves owned the gas that now competed with their oil, the industry did not originate the natural gas revolution, nor has it to this day greatly profited from its gas ownership. The gas revolution was made by newly formed transmission companies that marketed the product with an aggressive ardour. They started a magnificent new industry, first against the advice and then against the resistance of the oil companies.

By all the logic of the situation, the oil companies themselves should have made the gas revolution. They not only owned the gas; they also were the only people experienced in handling, scrubbing and using it, the only people experienced in pipeline technology and transmission, and they understood heating problems. But, partly because they knew that natural gas would compete with their own sale of heating oil, the oil companies pooh-poohed the potentials of gas.

The revolution was finally started by oil pipeline executives who, unable to persuade their own companies to go into gas, quit and organised the spectacularly successful gas transmission companies. Even after their success became painfully evident to the oil companies, the latter did not go into gas transmission. The multibillion dollar business which should have been theirs went to others. As in the past, the industry was blinded by its narrow preoccupation with a specific product and the value of its reserves. It paid little or no attention to its customers' basic needs and preferences.

The postwar years have not witnessed any change. Immediately after World War II the oil industry was greatly encouraged about its future by the rapid expansion of demand for its traditional line of products. In 1950 most companies projected annual rates of domestic expansion of around 6 per cent through at least to 1975. Though the ratio of crude oil reserves to demand in the Free World was about 20 to 1, with 10 to 1 being usually considered a reasonable working ratio in the United States, booming demand sent oil men searching for more without sufficient regard to what the future really promised. In 1952 they 'hit' in the Middle East; the ratio skyrocketed to 42 to 1. If gross additions to reserves continue at the average rate of the past five years (thirty-seven billion barrels annually), then by 1970 the reserve ratio will be up to 45 to 1. This abundance of oil has weakened crude and product prices all over the world.

UNCERTAIN FUTURE

Management cannot find much consolation today in the rapidly expanding petrochemical industry, another oil-using idea that did not originate in the leading firms. The total United States' production of petrochemicals is equivalent to about 2 per cent (by volume) of the demand for all petroleum products. Although the petrochemical industry is now expected to grow by about 10 per cent per year, this will not offset other drains on the growth of crude oil consumption. Furthermore, while petrochemical products are many and growing, it is well to remember that there are non-petroleum sources of the basic raw material, such as coal. Besides, a lot of plastics can be produced with relatively little oil. A fifty-thousand-barrel-per-day oil refinery is now considered the absolute minimum size for efficiency. But a five-thousand-barrel-per-day chemical plant is a giant operation.

Oil has never been a continuously strong growth industry. It has grown by fits and starts, always miraculously saved by innovations and developments not of its own making. The reason it has not grown in a smooth progression is that each time it thought it had a superior product safe from the possibility of competitive substitutes, the product turned out to be inferior and notoriously subject to obsolescence. Until now, gasoline (for motor fuel, anyhow) has escaped this fate. But, as we shall see later, it too may be on its last legs.

The point of all this is that there is no guarantee against product obsolescence. If a company's own research does not make it obsolete, another's will. Unless an industry is especially lucky, as oil has been until now, it can easily go down in a sea of red figures—just as the railroads have, as the buggy whip manufacturers have, as the corner grocery chains have, as most of the big movie companies have and indeed as many other industries have.

The best way for a firm to be lucky is to make its own luck. That requires knowing what makes a business successful. One of the greatest enemies of this knowledge is mass production.

PRODUCTION PRESSURES

Mass-production industries are impelled by a great drive to produce all they can. The prospect of steeply declining unit costs as output rises is more than most companies can usually resist. The profit possibilities look spectacular. All effort focuses on production. The result is that marketing gets neglected.

John Kenneth Galbraith contends that just the opposite occurs.[1] Output is so prodigious that all effort concentrates on trying to get rid of it. He says this accounts for singing commercials, desecration of the countryside with advertising signs and other wasteful and vulgar practices. Galbraith has a finger on something real, but he misses the strategic point. Mass production does indeed generate great pressure to 'move' the product. But what usually gets emphasised is selling, not marketing. Marketing, being a more sophisticated and complex process, gets ignored.

The difference between marketing and selling is more than semantic. Selling focuses on the needs of the seller, marketing on the needs of the buyer. Selling is preoccupied with the seller's need to convert his product into cash; marketing with the idea of satisfying the needs of the customer by means of the product and the whole cluster of things associated with creating, delivering, and finally consuming it.

In some industries the enticements of full mass production have been so powerful that for many years top management in effect has told the sales departments, 'You get rid of it; we'll worry about profits'. By contrast a truly marketing-minded firm tries to create value-satisfying goods and services that consumers will want to buy. What it offers for sale includes not only the generic product or service, but also how it is made available to the customer, in what form, when, under what conditions and at what terms of trade. Most important, what it offers for sale is determined not by the seller but by the buyer. The seller takes his cues from the buyer in such a way that the product becomes a consequence of the marketing effort, not vice versa.

LAG IN DETROIT

This may sound like an elementary rule of business, but that does not keep it from being violated wholesale. It is certainly more violated than honoured. Take the automobile industry.

Here mass production is most famous, most honoured and has the greatest impact on the entire society. The industry has hitched its fortune to the relentless requirements of the annual model change, a policy that makes customer orientation an especially urgent necessity. Consequently the auto companies annually spend millions of dollars on consumer research. But the fact that the new compact cars are selling so well in their first year indicates that Detroit's vast researches have for a long time failed to reveal what the customer really wanted. Detroit was not persuaded that he wanted anything different from what he had been getting until it lost millions of customers to other small car manufacturers.

How could this unbelievable lag behind consumer wants have been perpetuated so long? Why did not research reveal consumer preferences before consumers' buying decisions themselves revealed the facts? Is that not what consumer research is for—to find out before the fact what is

1. J. K. Galbraith, *The Affluent Society*, Houghton Mifflin Company (Boston, 1958) pages 152–60.

going to happen? The answer is that Detroit never really researched the customer's wants. It only researched his preferences between the kinds of things which it had already decided to offer him. For Detroit is mainly product-oriented, not customer-oriented. To the extent that the customer is recognised as having needs that the manufacturer should try to satisfy, Detroit usually acts as if the job can be done entirely by product changes. Occasionally attention gets paid to financing, too, but that is done more in order to sell than to enable the customer to buy.

As for taking care of other customer needs, there is not enough being done to write about. The areas of the greatest unsatisfied needs are ignored, or at best get stepchild attention. These are at the point of sale and on the matter of automotive repair and maintenance. Detroit views these problem areas as being of secondary importance. That is underscored by the fact that the retailing and servicing ends of this industry are neither owned and operated nor controlled by the manufacturers. Once the car is produced, things are pretty much in the dealer's inadequate hands. Illustrative of Detroit's arm's-length attitude is the fact that, while servicing holds enormous sales-stimulating, profit-building opportunities, only fifty-seven of Chevrolet's seven thousand dealers provide night maintenance service.

Motorists repeatedly express their dissatisfaction with servicing and their apprehensions about buying cars under the present selling setup. The anxieties and problems they encounter during the auto buying and maintenance processes are probably more intense and widespread today than thirty years ago. Yet the automobile companies do not seem to listen to or take their cues from the anguished consumer. If they do listen, it must be through the filter of their own preoccupation with production. The marketing effort is still viewed as a necessary consequence of the product, not vice versa, as it should be. That is the legacy of mass production, with its parochial view that profit resides essentially in low-cost full production.

WHAT FORD PUT FIRST

The profit lure of mass production obviously has a place in the plans and strategy of business management, but it must always *follow* hard thinking about the customer. This is one of the most important lessons that we can learn from the contradictory behaviour of Henry Ford. In a sense Ford was both the most brilliant and the most senseless marketer in American history. He was senseless because he refused to give the customer anything but a black car. He was brilliant because he fashioned a production system designed to fit market needs. We habitually celebrate him for the wrong reason, his production genius. His real genius was marketing. We think he was able to cut his selling price and therefore sell millions of $500 cars because his invention of the assembly line had reduced the costs. Actually he invented the assembly line because he had concluded that at $500 he could sell millions of cars. Mass production was the *result* not the cause of his low prices.

Ford repeatedly emphasised this point, but a nation of production-oriented business managers refuses to hear the great lesson he taught. Here is his operating philosophy as he expressed it succinctly:

'Our policy is to reduce the price, extend the operations and improve the article. You will notice that the reduction of price comes first. We have never considered any costs as fixed. Therefore we first reduce the price to the point where we believe more sales will result. Then we go ahead and try to make the prices. We do not bother about the costs. The new price forces the costs down. The more usual way is to take the costs and then determine the price, and although that method may be scientific in the narrow sense; it is not scientific in the broad sense, because what earthly use is it to know the cost if it tells you that you cannot manufacture at a price at which the article can be sold? But more to the point is the fact that, although one may calculate what a cost is, and of course all of our costs are carefully calculated, no one knows what a cost ought to be. One of the ways of discovering . . . is to name a price so low as to force everybody in the place to the highest point of efficiency. The low price makes everybody dig for profits. We make more discoveries concerning manufacturing and selling under this forced method than by any method of leisurely investigation.'[1]

PRODUCT PROVINCIALISM

The tantalising profit possibilities of low unit production costs may be the most seriously self-deceiving attitude that can afflict a company, particularly a 'growth' company where an apparently assured expansion of demand already tends to undermine a proper concern for the importance of marketing and the customer.

The usual result of this narrow preoccupation with so-called concrete matters is that instead of growing, the industry declines. It usually means that the product fails to adapt to the constantly changing patterns of consumer needs and tastes, to new and modified marketing institutions and practices or to product developments in competing or complementary industries. The industry has its eyes so firmly on its own specific product that it does not see how it is being made obsolete.

The classical example of this is the buggy whip industry. No amount of product improvement could stave off its death sentence. But had the industry defined itself as being in the transportation business rather than the buggy whip business, it might have survived. It would have done what survival always entails, that is, changing. Even if it had only defined its business as providing a stimulant or catalyst to an energy source, it might have survived by becoming a manufacturer of, say, fanbelts or air cleaners.

What may some day be a still more classical example is, again, the oil industry. Having let others steal marvelous opportunities from it (for example, natural gas, as already mentioned, missile fuels and jet engine

1. Henry Ford, *My Life and Work*, Doubleday, Page & Company (New York, 1923), pages 146–7.

lubricants), one would expect it to have taken steps never to let that happen again. But this is not the case. We are now getting extraordinary new developments in fuel systems specifically designed to power automobiles. Not only are these developments concentrated in firms outside the petroleum industry, but petroleum is almost systematically ignoring them, securely content in its wedded bliss to oil. It is the story of the kerosene lamp versus the incandescent lamp all over again. Oil is trying to improve hydrocarbon fuels rather than to develop *any* fuels best suited to the needs of their users, whether or not made in different ways and with different raw materials from oil.

Here are some of the things which non-petroleum companies are working on.

Over a dozen such firms now have advanced working models of energy systems which, when perfected, will replace the internal combustion engine and eliminate the demand for gasoline. The superior merit of each of these systems is their elimination of frequent, time-consuming, and irritating refuelling stops. Most of these systems are fuel cells designed to create electrical energy directly from chemicals without combustion. Most of them use chemicals that are not derived from oil, generally hydrogen and oxygen.

Several other companies have advanced models of electric storage batteries designed to power automobiles. One of these is an aircraft producer that is working jointly with several electric utility companies. The latter hope to use off-peak generating capacity to supply overnight, plug-in battery regeneration. Another company, also using the battery approach, is a medium-size electronics firm with extensive small-battery experience that it developed in connection with its work on hearing aids. It is collaborating with an automobile manufacturer. Recent improvements arising from the need for high-powered miniature power storage plants in rockets have put us within reach of a relatively small battery capable of withstanding great overloads or surges of power. Germanium diode applications and batteries using sintered-plate and nickel-cadmium techniques promise to make a revolution in our energy sources.

Solar energy conversion systems are also getting increasing attention. One usually cautious Detroit auto executive recently ventured that solar-powered cars might be common by 1980.

As for the oil companies, they are more or less 'watching developments', as one research director put it to me. A few are doing a bit of research on fuel cells, but almost always confined to developing cells powered by hydrocarbon chemicals. None of them are enthusiastically researching fuel cells, batteries or solar power plants. None of them are spending a fraction as much on research in these profoundly important areas as they are on the usual run-of-the-mill things like reducing combustion chamber deposit in gasoline engines. One major integrated petroleum company recently took a tentative look at the fuel cell and concluded that although 'the companies actively working on it indicate a belief in ultimate success . . . the timing and magnitude of its impact are too remote to warrant recognition in our forecasts'.

One might, of course, ask: Why should the oil companies do anything different? Would not chemical fuel cells, batteries or solar energy kill the present product lines? The answer is that they would indeed, and that is precisely the reason for the oil firms having to develop these power units before their competitors, so they will not be companies without an industry.

Management might be more likely to do what is needed for its own preservation if it thought of itself as being in the energy business. But even that would not be enough if it persists in imprisoning itself in the narrow grip of its tight product orientation. It has to think of itself as taking care of customer needs, not finding, refining or even selling oil. Once it genuinely thinks of its business as taking care of people's transportation needs, nothing can stop it from creating its own extravagantly profitable growth.

'CREATIVE DESTRUCTION'

Since words are cheap and deeds are dear, it may be appropriate to indicate what this kind of thinking involves and leads to. Let us start at the beginning—the customer. It can be shown that motorists strongly dislike the bother, delay and experience of buying gasoline. People actually do not buy gasoline. They cannot see it, taste it, feel it, appreciate it or really test it. What they buy is the right to continue driving their cars. The gas station is like a tax collector to whom people are compelled to pay a periodic toll as the price of using their cars. This makes the gas station a basically unpopular institution. It can never be made popular or pleasant, only less unpopular, less unpleasant.

To reduce its unpopularity completely means eliminating it. Nobody likes a tax collector, not even a pleasantly cheerful one. Nobody likes to interrupt a trip to buy a phantom product, not even from a handsome Adonis or a seductive Venus. Hence, companies that are working on exotic fuel substitutes which will eliminate the need for frequent refuelling are heading directly into the outstretched arms of the irritated motorist. They are riding a wave of inevitability, not because they are creating something which is technologically superior or more sophisticated, but because they are satisfying a powerful customer need. They are also eliminating noxious odours and air pollution.

Once the petroleum companies recognise the customer satisfying logic of what another power system can do, they will see that they have no more choice about working on an efficient, long-lasting fuel (or some way of delivering present fuels without bothering the motorist) than the big food chains had a choice about going into the supermarket business, or the vacuum tube companies had a choice about making semiconductors. For their own good the oil firms will have to destroy their own highly profitable assets. No amount of wishful thinking can save them from the necessity of engaging in this form of 'creative destruction'.

I phrase the need as strongly as this because I think management must make quite an effort to break itself loose from conventional ways. It is all too easy in this day and age for a company or industry to let its sense of purpose become dominated by the economies of full production and to develop a dangerously lopsided product orientation. In short, if management lets itself drift, it invariably drifts in the direction of thinking of itself as producing goods and services, not customer satisfactions. While it probably will not descend to the depths of telling its salesmen, 'You get rid of it; we'll worry about profits', it can, without knowing it, be practising precisely that formula for withering decay. The historic fate of one growth industry after another has been its suicidal product provincialism.

DANGERS OF R & D

Another big danger to a firm's continued growth arises when top management is wholly transfixed by the profit possibilities of technical research and development. To illustrate I shall turn first to a new industry—electronics —and then return once more to the oil companies. By comparing a fresh example with a familiar one, I hope to emphasise the prevalence and insidiousness of a hazardous way of thinking.

MARKETING SHORTCHANGED

In the case of electronics, the greatest danger which faces the glamorous new companies in this field is not that they do not pay enough attention to research and development, but that they pay *too much* attention to it. And the fact that the fastest growing electronics firms owe their eminence to their heavy emphasis on technical research is completely beside the point. They have vaulted to affluence on a sudden crest of unusually strong general receptiveness to new technical ideas. Also, their success has been shaped in the virtually guaranteed market of military subsidies and by military orders that in many cases actually preceded the existence of facilities to make the products. Their expansion has, in other words, been almost totally devoid of marketing effort.

Thus, they are growing up under conditions that come dangerously close to creating the illusion that a superior product will sell itself. Having created a successful company by making a superior product, it is not surprising that management continues to be oriented towards the product rather than the people who consume it. It develops the philosophy that continued growth is a matter of continued product innovation and improvement.

A number of other factors tend to strengthen and sustain this belief:

1. Because electronic products are highly complex and sophisticated, managements become top-heavy with engineers and scientists. This creates a selective bias in favour of research and production at the expense of marketing. The organisation tends to view itself as making things rather than satisfying customer needs. Marketing gets treated as a residual

activity, 'something else' that must be done once the vital job of product creation and production is completed.

2. To this bias in favour of product research, development and production is added the bias in favour of dealing with controllable variables. Engineers and scientists are at home in the world of concrete things like machines, test tubes, production lines, and even balance sheets. The abstractions to which they feel kindly are those which are testable or manipulatable in the laboratory, or, if not testable, then functional, such as Euclid's axioms. In short, the managements of the new glamour-growth companies tend to favour those business activities which lend themselves to careful study, experimentation, and control—the hard, practical, realities of the lab, the shop, the books.

What gets shortchanged are the realities of the *market*. Consumers are unpredictable, varied, fickle, stupid, shortsighted, stubborn and generally bothersome. This is not what the engineer-managers say, but deep down in their consciousness it is what they believe. And this accounts for their concentrating on what they know and what they can control, namely, product research, engineering and production. The emphasis on production becomes particularly attractive when the product can be made at declining unit costs. There is no more inviting way of making money than by running the plant full blast.

Today the top-heavy science-engineering-production orientation of so many electronics companies works reasonably well because they are pushing into new frontiers in which the armed services have pioneered virtually assured markets. The companies are in the felicitous position of having to fill, not find, markets; of not having to discover what the customer needs and wants, but of having the customer voluntarily come forward with specific new product demands. If a team of consultants had been assigned specifically to design a business situation calculated to prevent the emergence and development of a customer-oriented marketing viewpoint, it could not have produced anything better than the conditions just described.

STEPCHILD TREATMENT

The oil industry is a stunning example of how science, technology, and mass production can divert an entire group of companies from their main task. To the extent the consumer is studied at all (which is not much), the focus is for ever on getting information which is designed to help the oil companies improve what they are now doing. They try to discover more convincing advertising themes, more effective sales promotional drives, what the market shares of the various companies are, what people like or dislike about service station dealers and oil companies, and so forth. Nobody seems as interested in probing deeply into the basic human needs that the industry might be trying to satisfy as in probing into the basic properties of the raw material that the companies work with in trying to deliver customer satisfactions.

Basic questions about customers and markets seldom get asked. The latter occupy a stepchild status. They are recognised as existing, as having to be taken care of, but not worth very much real thought or dedicated attention. Nobody gets as excited about the customers in his own backyard as about the oil in the Sahara Desert. Nothing illustrates better the neglect of marketing than its treatment in the industry press.

The centennial issue of the *American Petroleum Institute Quarterly*, published in 1959 to celebrate the discovery of oil in Titusville, Pennsylvania, contained twenty-one feature articles proclaiming the industry's greatness. Only one of these talked about its achievements in marketing, and that was only a pictorial record of how service station architecture has changed. The issue also contained a special section on 'New Horizons', which was devoted to showing the magnificent role oil would play in America's future. Every reference was ebulliently optimistic, never implying once that oil might have some hard competition. Even the reference to atomic energy was a cheerful catalogue of how oil would help make atomic energy a success. There was not a single apprehension that the oil industry's affluence might be threatened or a suggestion that one 'new horizon' might include new and better ways of serving oil's present customers.

But the most revealing example of the stepchild treatment that marketing gets was still another special series of short articles on 'The Revolutionary Potential of Electronics'. Under that heading this list of articles appeared in the table of contents: 'In the Search for Oil', 'In Production Operations', 'In Refinery Processes', 'In Pipeline Operations'.

Significantly, every one of the industry's major functional areas is listed, *except* marketing. Why? Either it is believed that electronics holds no revolutionary potential for petroleum marketing (which is palpably wrong), or the editors forgot to discuss marketing (which is more likely, and illustrates its stepchild status).

The order in which the four functional areas are listed also betrays the alienation of the oil industry from the consumer. The industry is implicitly defined as beginning with the search for oil and ending with its distribution from the refinery. But the truth is, it seems to me, that the industry begins with the needs of the customer for its products. From that primal position its definition moves steadily backstream to areas of progressively lesser importance, until it finally comes to rest at the 'search for oil'.

BEGINNING AND END

The view that an industry is a customer-satisfying process, not a goods-producing process, is vital for all business men to understand. An industry begins with the customer and his needs, not with a patent, a raw material or a selling skill. Given the customer's needs, the industry develops backwards, first concerning itself with the physical *delivery* of customer satisfactions. Then it moves back further to *creating* the things by which these satisfactions are in part achieved. How these materials are created is a matter of indifference to the customer, hence the particular form of manufacturing processing or what-have-you cannot be considered as a vital aspect of the industry. Finally, the industry moves back still further to *finding* the raw materials necessary for making its products.

The irony of some industries oriented towards technical research and development is that the scientists who occupy the high executive positions are totally unscientific when it comes to defining their companies' overall needs and purposes. They violate the first two rules of the scientific method —being aware of and defining their companies' problems, and then developing testable hypotheses about solving them. They are scientific only about the convenient things, such as laboratory and product experiments. The reason that the customer (and the satisfaction of his deepest needs) is not considered as being 'the problem' is not because there is any certain belief that no such problem exists, but because an organisational lifetime has conditioned management to look in the opposite direction. Marketing is a stepchild.

I do not mean that selling is ignored. Far from it. But selling, again, is not marketing. As already pointed out, selling concerns itself with the tricks and techniques of getting people to exchange their cash for your product. It is not concerned with the values that the exchange is all about. And it does not, as marketing invariably does, view the entire business process as consisting of a tightly integrated effort to discover, create, arouse and satisfy customer needs. The customer is somebody 'out there' who, with proper cunning, can be separated from his loose change.

Actually, not even selling gets much attention in some technologically minded firms. Because there is a virtually guaranteed market for the abundant flow of their new products, they do not actually know what a real market is. It is as if they lived in a planned economy, moving their products routinely from factory to retail outlet. Their successful concentration on products tends to convince them of the soundness of what they have been doing, and they fail to see the gathering clouds over the market.

CONCLUSIONS

Less than seventy-five years ago American railroads enjoyed a fierce loyalty among astute Wall Streeters. European monarchs invested in them heavily. Eternal wealth was thought to be the benediction for anybody who could scrape a few thousand dollars together to put into rail stocks. No other form of transportation could compete with the railroads in speed, flexibility, durability, economy and growth potentials. As Jacques Barzun put it, 'By the turn of the century it was an institution, an image of man, a tradition, a code of honour, a source of poetry, a nursery of boyhood desires, a sublimest of toys, and the most solemn machine—next to the funeral hearse—that marks the epochs in man's life.'[1]

Even after the advent of automobiles, trucks and aeroplanes, the railroad

1. Op. cit., page 20.

tycoons remained imperturbably self-confident. If you had told them sixty years ago that in thirty years they would be flat on their backs, broke, and pleading for government subsidies, they would have thought you totally demented. Such a future was simply not considered possible. It was not even a discussible subject, or an askable question, or a matter which any sane person would consider worth speculating about. The very thought was insane. Yet a lot of insane notions now have matter-of-fact acceptance—for example, the idea of 100-ton tubes of metal moving smoothly through the air 20,000 feet above the earth, loaded with 100 sane and solid citizens casually drinking martinis—and they have dealt cruel blows to the railroads.

What specifically must other companies do to avoid this fate? What does customer orientation involve? These questions have in part been answered by the preceding examples and analysis. It would take another article to show in detail what is required for specific industries. In any case, it should be obvious that building an effective customer-oriented company involves far more than good intentions or promotional tricks; it involves profound matters of human organisation and leadership. For the present, let me merely suggest what appear to be some general requirements.

VISCERAL FEEL OF GREATNESS

Obviously the company has to do what survival demands. It has to adapt to the requirements of the market, and it has to do it sooner rather than later. But mere survival is a so-so aspiration. Anybody can survive in some way or other, even the skid-row bum. The trick is to survive gallantly, to feel the surging impulse of commercial mastery; not just to experience the sweet smell of success, but to have the visceral feel of entrepreneurial greatness.

No organisation can achieve greatness without a vigorous leader who is driven onward by his own pulsating *will to succeed.* He has to have a vision of grandeur, a vision that can produce eager followers in vast numbers. In business, the followers are the customers. To produce these customers, the entire corporation must be viewed as a customer-creating and customer-satisfying organism. Management must think of itself not as producing products but as providing customer-creating value satisfactions. It must push this idea (and everything it means and requires) into every nook and cranny of the organisation. It has to do this continuously and with the kind of flair that excites and stimulates the people in it. Otherwise, the company will be merely a series of pigeonholed parts, with no consolidating sense of purpose or direction.

In short, the organisation must learn to think of itself not as producing goods or services but as *buying customers,* as doing the things that will make people *want* to do business with it. And the chief executive himself has the inescapable responsibility for creating this environment, this viewpoint, this attitude, this aspiration. He himself must set the company's style, its direction and its goals. This means he has to know precisely where he himself wants to go, and to make sure the whole organisation is enthusiastically aware of where that is. This is a first requisite of leadership, for *unless he knows where he is going, any road will take him there.*

If any road is okay, the chief executive might as well pack his attaché case and go fishing. If an organisation does not know or care where it is going, it does not need to advertise that fact with a ceremonial figurehead. Everybody will notice it soon enough.

Industrial Marketing in the Next Decade

AUBREY WILSON

This book has not perhaps answered the question of whether industrial marketing is an art or a science. It is a subject which holds high place in business polemics. The distinction is a matter of emphasis since under a business regime holding either viewpoint the practice of marketing varies little. What does matter is that marketing practice should be purposeful, dynamic, forward looking and based upon sound information.

Marketing personnel have increasingly taken to using the term 'scientific marketing' which has led to very great differences of opinion on precisely what in marketing can be scientific. To a large extent these differences of opinion are generated because everyone wants to use the term 'scientific' with its favourable connotations, in connection with their own field of activity and, at the same time, to demote as many other activities as possible to a lower 'unscientific' plane. By doing so it has been pointed out 'the individual hopes to raise himself and his special field of study in public esteem'.[1]

Marketing is not a science. Marketing is primarily an area for the application of findings from the sciences, perhaps especially the behavioural sciences. This does not mean, however, that marketing cannot adopt a more scientific approach. The first two rules of scientific method quoted in the previous chapter—being aware of and defining the problem and then developing hypotheses which can be tested to solve them—are well within the capability of the scope of the new methods of marketing.

Marketing in industry is now on the verge of a new era; an era in which its fundamental purpose of satisfying industrial buyers' wants through goods and services can be greatly advanced.

The need for a more scientific approach to marketing has been a theme common to every chapter of this book while its purpose has been to show some of the methods how this might be achieved. The scientific approach to marketing will turn tomorrow's business activities into a systematic, planned and controlled process. The attitude still pervades management—

1. Harper W. Boyd and Ralph Westfall, *Marketing Research—Text and Cases*, Richard D. Irwin, Homewood (Illinois, U.S.A. 1964), page 45.

and particularly industrial management—that unlike production, the elements of marketing are unpredictable, inexact and incapable of being measured and handled with precision. Unpredictable factors will un-questionably continue to exist for many years but with the advent of new tools to measure its elements, marketing is evolving a firm base.

From this foundation a new respect for, and approach to, marketing will develop in the next few years. Executives of the future will manage the marketing aspects of business as production is managed today; on a basis of scientifically predicted results. The plotting of specific and attainable goals conceived on a total corporate strategy and plan will at last be possible.

The concept of scientific marketing is not merely an idealised fantasy of marketing men who at present are struggling in a sea of immeasurable variants. It is an attainable objective that will be reached within the business life of the majority of today's senior executives.

It is reasonable to predict that powerful trends will force management to accelerated efforts to adopt scientific methods in marketing during the next ten years. The most important of them are the continuing squeeze on profits due to the difficulty of cutting production costs, the rising costs of marketing, the competitive trend towards product diversification, the flood of new products, the expense of developing or retaining markets among the uncommitted and under-endowed nations and the challenge of the new trading groups such as those emerging in Europe, South America and Africa. Together these will provide the background and impetus for improved marketing in the next decade.

The next ten years will be a 'take-off' period preceding the drive to marketing maturity in the late seventies. The take off will certainly be the result of the efforts of a few companies (regrettably, very few concerned with *industrial* products) which in the future will pioneer the scientific approach to marketing even more assiduously than at present.

In prognosticating the pattern of marketing in the seventies, I have chosen a number of areas of activity and a number of marketing functions and aspects of the marketing concept as illustrations of this change. Broadly these are: the technical skills of marketing, the structural changes in marketing, personnel aspects and marketing philosophy.

TECHNICAL CHANGES IN MARKETING SKILLS

Perhaps the most obvious of the developments which will add to the precision with which marketing tools can be used are the now ubiquitous electronic calculators and computers. Punch card systems already find one of their principal uses in sales and stock analysis. It is now practical to test many propositions that have been treated as only academic and marginal possibilities before the development of the data processing capacity of modern electronic machines.

Within the next few years there will not only be an increasing number of large companies with their own computers which have their sales fore-casts programmed for electronic processing but medium sized firms will also be using such facilities. The new generation of small and relatively cheap computers is rapidly closing the 'planning gap' between big and medium sized companies. Even the small firm without computer facilities will be at no disadvantage to their larger competitors. Computer time can be bought and in some respects the firm which buys time will have the advantage over the computer owning firm in that it will have access to the very latest and fastest machines and the broadest knowledge of computer use which the computer service centres can offer.

It will also be possible, before half the decade has passed, to regularly test models of marketing strategies on computers in a way now being developed for capital budgeting. Indeed, even more complex information for new product justification than Margot Newlands described in Chapter 4, will be commonplace and will play a vital role in new product development.

In all areas of decision making in management, the computer will have its impact. Without subscribing to the 'science fiction' school of prediction, in which the traditional managerial tasks will be usurped by the 'black box', there is no question but that marketing decisions will become more incisive and more accurate by the introduction of electronic data processing systems. Such systems permit the analysis and review of more and more complex data within time spans that are operationally feasible.

There is now ample evidence that mathematical techniques, in combi-nation with computers, can handle some types of decision making assign-ments better than human managers using experience, simple data hand calculations and judgement to reach solutions. Perhaps one of the best examples of this is in the problems of pricing and price strategy set out by Leon Smulian in Chapter 12. The superiority of the new techniques will certainly be exploited and it is equally certain that there will be vigorous efforts within the progressive firms to extend the reach of the new techniques into many areas—particularly marketing.

During the next ten years in marketing an early result of the computer control will be an upward shift of the organisational boundary between planning and performance which means that some planning responsibilities will be removed from middle-level managers. Further, a reversal of the trend of the 1950's towards decentralised operations, with top management suitably eulogised, taking on a much larger share of the innovating, plan-ning and creative functions can be envisaged. Another change will be that radical re-organisation of middle-management structure will be necessary with changes in status and importance in certain classes of jobs. Finally, the appearance of a sharper and perhaps more impenetrable demarcation between different levels of the organisational structure will come about.

These changes will affect the total management structure of organisa-tion but marketing management, traditionally dynamic, can respond more readily to such changes. They will be able to take advantage of the new alignments and responsibilities with perhaps greater speed and less difficulty than other sections of management which have longstanding traditions and loyalties to existing methods and concepts.

The question of the future of the marketing manager—absolute or obsolete—has been posed. The ability to set up simulation models for certain management problems and to solve these problems by computers does raise the question as to whether there is a future for the marketing manager. The answer for the next decade must be that there is no future for the marketing manager who does not recognise and actively work for the implementation of advanced decision making methods in his department. The most obvious change that marketing will produce in the next decade will be the fall from power of the marketing team that depends for its success solely on the personality of its members, push, intuition, experience and social graces.

Another important addition to marketing skills is the development of long-range planning techniques. Long-range planning is the only really new technique left to management that can give a company a major competitive advantage. Looking back it can be seen how technical and managerial superiority, marketing research and selling and sales promotion innovations have, in the past, given firms an important lead on their competitors. Looking forward, long-range planning is another business technique that will spell the difference between success and mediocrity in the profit and loss account as indeed David Burns makes so clear in Chapter 15.

The task of long-range planning is to pose certain basic questions. Where is the company going to be ten to fifteen years from now? What products should the company be selling in 1975 or 1980? What is the plan of action to accomplish these goals?

Long-range planning has been limited in the past not only by a lack of understanding of the techniques which contribute to planning but also because long-range thinking assignments have usually been given to the wrong people—to executives whose rank is equal to the issues which are the subject of planning. But regular duties are time consuming and require onerous day-to-day operating responsibilities which, in turn, require steady and mature habits of thought and action. It is asking a great deal from such executives to transform themselves periodically into philosophers and forecasters to deal with theoretical long range propositions. Their very training in executive methods and techniques, necessary for daily routine tasks, tends to handicap them in contemplating the problems of the future.

In planning, a scientific approach will help decide what the overall corporate objectives must be. Planners must, moreover, meet the challenge of devising the means to reach the goal. Plans will be increasingly specific as to methods and responsibilities and more types of plans will become essential to the total marketing job, as prediction accuracy gains steadily but slowly over the next decade.

What will be seen, as we progress through the sixties into the seventies, is the development by the large firms of planning teams, selected as a task force from executives who are known for their imagination, audacity, originality, creativity and for their cosmopolitan approach to business problems—and all this regardless of their position in the management hierarchy. On to this task force, created from within the business, will be grafted outside consultant specialists, divorced from the pressure of everyday business activity of the company and approaching the question of forward planning objectively. The task force will develop as an arm of management and, ultimately, as its importance and effectiveness becomes known, all other business functions will work with it to evolve long-range planning methods and objectives.

The third, and perhaps the most exotic, of the technical changes that will occur in marketing in the next decade, which Max Adler refers to in Chapter 6, is the development of a new marketing research technique for the industrial goods sector of the economy. The use of the behavioural sciences for investigating markets and attitudes is not new in the consumer goods field. They have influenced a growing number of investigations aimed at discerning motivational patterns—psychological needs, cultural and inter-personal influences, economic, material and situational factors as determinants of buying behaviour. In the industrial field these methods will be developed to achieve a high level of accuracy.

The most important contribution to be made from the behavioural sciences are their theories and the knowledge of the nature of man and how he lives. In the words of Jacqueline Marrian in Chapter 2, these disciplines offer concepts which marketing has needed for viewing the acts of buying and consumption not as isolated acts, but as part of a general pattern of human behaviour.

The paramount consideration in the purchase of industrial products has always been stated as the possibility of profitable use rather than personal gratification. Factors such as the cost and safety of operations are all measurable through increased revenues or decreased costs. It is said that because these factors can be quantified that rational buying motives prevail. This view of the buying situation in which the wits of the buyer are pitted against those of the seller to secure the most favourable terms is deceptively oversimplified and primitive. The use of the techniques of the behavioural sciences is now revealing new and unsuspected motivational dimensions in buying decisions. In fact, they are showing that the industrial buyer is a human being even though at times he might not seem so to the salesman. The industrial buyer has the same psychological drives, desires, ambitions, urges and biological needs as the consumer, and, after all, he is, in another capacity, also a consumer. The classical conception of industrial buying as being wholly rational will be abandoned in the next few years in the face of a growing volume of new information to the contrary which is being revealed by observation and research.

The behavioural sciences will make the most important single contribution to marketing research advances, and thus to marketing, during the next decade. This impact will be greatest and most sensational in the industrial field which still clings tenaciously to the old concepts and it is in the industrial field where the great prizes of the future lie.

STRUCTURAL ADJUSTMENTS

The second group chosen for this prognostication into the shape and direction of marketing in the next decade, is the structural aspects of marketing. It is obvious that if the great changes forecast in marketing responsibilities and techniques are to take place there must be many adjustments in the marketing structure of companies. Not the least of these will be the change in status of the marketing man in the management hierarchy.

Currently the number of responsibilities devolving on the marketing director or manager, aggravated by misleading and partly misinformed opinions, has retarded their adoption of the broad sweep of the marketing concept. Implementation of this wider concept does not require supermen but round men. What will emerge will be the marketing man with total marketing orientation as opposed to the purely selling-minded line executive. It is clear from Anthony Lever's contribution in Chapter 14 that the next generation, if not the current generation, of marketing executives will have had experience in both staff and line work, and often in other parts of the firm too.

The emergence of a new type of marketing executive will bring with it an unaccustomed and far higher level of co-ordination between the specialist skills which the sheer size and complexity of future marketing will demand. Line and staff personnel in marketing face similar problems and work towards the same goal, but departmental barriers tend to create distance between them. The new generation of marketing managers, having themselves had both line and staff experience, will be able to overthrow such traditional and restricting demarcations. They will bring about a more task-oriented integration of different specialists, which will be furthered as up-and-coming executives move between line and staff experience during their development and progress through the organisation.

In the large firm the marketing executive will be primarily concerned with matters of strategy, planning and control and their role in the top management team. Operating decisions will be delegated to sales, advertising and distribution managers and, eventually, technical planning and research decisions will also become the area of specialist function decisions.

Integration, as Franklin Colborn notes in Chapter 16, between the marketing functions such as marketing research, advertising, selling, distributing and merchandising, will be produced by methods which are currently used—common training for line and staff, exchange of personnel, regularly scheduled marketing meetings, the creation of marketing committees and, of course, the development of marketing executives without a parochial approach to their job. However, in the next ten years it is the integration between marketing and other functions which will achieve a new break-through. If a moral is to be sought from Peter Clark's Chapter 17 on integrating marketing into the total corporate complex, it is that *marketing cannot be effective if considered from a marketing viewpoint alone.* Just like war—it is too important a matter to be left to generals. Thus, with the wider horizons will be developed a new conceptual quality in viewing the operations of the firm—and indeed the industry—as a whole and integrated activity.

Reference has been made to the development of specialist skills and their integration into the marketing plan. This is another trend which has gathered strength and which will reach a new intensification in the late sixties. The business economist is now an accepted member of the management team. Michael Desoutter has shown in Chapter 8 and Harry Trigg in Chapter 9 that the advertising agency has gone from the mere space booker of the twenties to an agglomeration of specialist departments and the PR man from a company apologist and smoke screen to a counsellor and provider of important informational services. The market research department within firms is now commonplace and Gordon Brand notes in Chapter 5 that the marketing research agencies have developed to the point at which there has emerged highly specialised agencies concentrating on particular product groups or the use of particular research techniques.

The next ten years will see a sharp upturn in the activities of these and other specialists whose services will be called upon, not only by the large firms, but increasingly by the medium sized and small firms. If the service economy has arrived for the domestic consumer, it is only just round the corner for the industrialist who will be offered an ever widening range of technical services while, at the same time, being forced to offer a wide range of services himself of the type described by Dennis Rose in Chapter 10. Management consultancy, marketing research broken down into specialist divisions, management staff selection services, specialist advertising and public relations will all increase in use and will all improve their techniques and services to industry.

One other sector of industrial activity likely to undergo considerable change and thus likely to have an impact on the firm's structure, is the distributive system for industrial goods. If standardisation has become the cult of production then concentration is its counterpart in distribution. According to one American marketeer a distributor can do an excellent job of promoting one or two lines, a fair job of selling three but with one more added he is just handling orders. Many progressive industrial distributors, forced to justify their position in the industrial pipelines in the face of increasing direct sales by producers, are now tending to concentrate purchasing with a few suppliers. The progressive distributor in the sixties will find his place in carrying out an efficient job of warehousing, stock-holding, credit provision and selling for a limited number of manufacturers so that they will find it more economic to distribute through him, than round him.

This trend has an important implication in it for all industrial goods producers who use distributors. The days are passing when the distributor considered his role to be that of an industrial 'universal provider' to his customer, to be able to meet any order for any brand or product. Stock in depth but not a fathomless stock, will be the policy for the future.

For manufacturers dealing with these outlets, this trend means that manufacturers must themselves offer complete and well promoted lines or else risk having to use other, and probably less progressive, distributors. Selectivity in both stocks and distributors will be the need of the seventies.

Changes in methods of industrial distribution will be paralleled by a new insight into the problems of physical distribution as they apply to the manufacturer. In physical distribution, policies tend to be empiric rather than designed. It is here where opportunities for advancement in techniques and economy in operations exist. John Aylott has shown in Chapter 11 the many areas in which new thinking is required and new methods needed in order to keep distribution in line with advances made elsewhere in the marketing complex.

PERSONNEL ASPECTS

The third group in which changes in the next ten years can be forecast is that concerned with personnel. The role of the marketing director or manager, it has already been suggested will change and so will the skills required to fulfil this role. There are basically three skills involved— *technical skill*—proficiency in the use of specific methods, processes, procedures or techniques; *human skill*—proficiency in operating as a member of a group, especially as the leader who induces superiors and subordinates to work effectively as a team and, *conceptual skill*—proficiency in visualising what the enterprise really is and what it is supposed to do.

Perhaps one of the most striking developments in marketing in the last decade has been the effort to reduce the emphasis on human skill while increasing the emphasis on technical skill. This change has been the concomitant of the development of sales analysis, distribution cost analysis, marketing research and other marketing tools.

It is, however, the third skill—conceptual—which is destined for further development and emphasis in the next decade. If management wants to establish effective controls of marketing it must start by deciding what particular combination of operations and forces it is trying to control. There is now evidence that business is beginning to give thought to this conceptual problem, if only in the recognition that all aspects of marketing operations are intimately inter-related.

Highly creative people are found among the many specialist consultants to business and in design and production technologies but they are found less frequently within corporate staffs, probably because originality is rarely consistent with the demands made on the organisation man. There are, of course, significant exceptions, but recognising that the conceptual qualities in marketing are vital, management in the next decade must direct its efforts to stimulating it within the firm. Once again the behavioural sciences will make their contribution by designating the conditions under which creative thinking can be stimulated and the climate wherein it will flourish. It will be management's task to create the conditions and climate within the firm.

The preferment of thinking men, the relief from the pressure of operational duties and organised group efforts will together produce the psychological and environmental conditions for new conceptual approaches in marketing. Management's other task will be to identify both line and staff personnel who possess the technical and human skills and can be encouraged in the development of their conceptual qualities. These executives, by reason of their age, are at this moment most likely to be at the lowest or lower levels of the middle-management structure, and their thinking not yet fully conditioned by the organisation. There are only a very few of them and they will be very fortunate indeed if their careers have taken them into a firm where management is willing to invest in company personnel by this approach. Those companies who will not, or cannot, invest in this way will seek originality and creativity by consulting outside agencies.

Innovation is vital to market leadership. This factor will be the force motivating firms towards the realisation of the conceptual abilities of their executives. A new high level of creative marketing will be achieved in the years to come but only slowly and only towards the end of the period under review. The lack of any progress will stem not only from the shortage of personnel with the required latent skills but from the possible shortcomings of management in stimulating a flow of original thinking.

MARKETING PHILOSOPHY

Finally, in the discussion of those aspects of marketing which will undergo change in the next decade that of the philosophy of marketing requires comment.

The marketing arm of a business organisation has traditionally been the sales department. In recent years many companies have changed from reliance primarily on a sales organisation charged with selling the products turned out by the company to a co-ordinated operation. This begins with the study of market needs and potential and proceeds to the planning and manufacturing of products to meet these needs. It then determines the most effective method of gaining acceptance of these products and distributing them. Sales management achieved a high state of effectiveness long before the present broader concept of marketing developed. But the principles of sales management outlined in texts on the subject written today vary very little from those issued twenty-five years ago, while the marketing concept, although spanning a far shorter period, has already changed considerably and will change even more fundamentally before

1975. The need for selling to adjust itself to its new role within the broader marketing concept has been illustrated by David Rowe in Chapter 7.

The growth of marketing knowledge has, surprisingly, brought about a new awareness of how much those in marketing—industrial and consumer —have still to learn about the nature of purchasing and consumption. To understand the opportunities that lie ahead a new and long look is being taken at the most fundamental of all marketing principles—knowledge of buyer wants—which is basic to planning. The satisfaction of wants is the rationale for marketing and it is important to know what these wants are. The marketing research function which is only one of the tools of marketing will thus rise to a new position of dominance in the 'marketing mix' and it is the research function that is moving fastest towards the idea of the new and expanded role of marketing. Product planning and development may eventually overtake marketing research in importance but this is not likely to occur before the end of the decade. Certainly if it is to do so, a more selective and reliable approach will be needed perhaps along the lines suggested in Chapter 3 by Mary Griffin.

Because of the preoccupation of day-to-day business with gathering unrelated facts, marketing research has often been out of phase with other marketing operations. The key to the crucial role that marketing research will play in the future is the fact that while marketing will embrace and control the research function, in its long term objectives it will be oriented by, and responsive to, the research findings to a degree never hitherto achieved. Marketing attitudes are about to undergo a very considerable re-positioning in which research and researchers cease to be ugly ducklings of the marketing mix and become the proud swan.

For the final look at marketing in the next decade there is no more exciting area to be examined than the most fundamental of all the marketing concepts—the marketing approach that asks simply 'What business are we in?' Theodore Levitt's much quoted 'Marketing Myopia', reprinted as Chapter 18 of this book, has made perhaps the most important of all contributions to wider management thinking which is now taking place and which will broaden even further in the period under review. It is no accident that Levitt should have been quoted quite independently by so many of the other contributors of this book.

There are many industries other than those Theodore Levitt quotes, to which the same story of decline and fall has applied, is applying and, more important, will apply in the future.

Business philosophies and activities which are based upon a production orientation will be those most strongly attacked in the next decade—and they will be superseded. Similarly the dominance of the home market in managements' thinking and the parochial view that an export market is only an extension of the home market, will change under the impact of increasing internationalisation of business and the cosmopolitan outlook of the new marketing managers. This is the clear inference of Fred Davies' contribution in Chapter 13.

Thus, for the next ten years, the most important and far reaching of all developments will be neither methods nor skills but the changes in men's minds and their attitudes towards business and to marketing. The new marketing concept of a customer creating and customer satisfying organism is a challenging adjustment for all firms to achieve as was made very clear in the opening chapter by Clive Barwell. Those firms which do succeed in making the adjustment will reap rewards such as have rarely been offered to industry since the early years of the industrial revolution.

Further Reading

CHAPTER 1

THE MARKETING CONCEPT

Theodore Levitt, *Innovation in Marketing*, McGraw-Hill (New York, 1962)
E. C. Bursk and J. F. Chapman (Eds.), *Modern Marketing Strategy*, Harvard University Press (Cambridge, Mass., 1964)
R. Bartels, *Development of Marketing Thought*, Richard D. Irwin (Homewood, Ill., 1962)

CHAPTER 2

MARKETING CHARACTERISTICS OF INDUSTRIAL GOODS AND BUYERS

R. S. Alexander, J. S. Cross and R. M. Cunningham, *Industrial Marketing* (Revised Edition, 1961) Richard D. Irwin (Homewood, Ill.), especially chapters 1, 3, 4, 15
Perry Bliss (Ed.), *Marketing and the Behavioural Sciences*, Allyn and Bacon (Boston, 1963), especially chapters 19, 25, 27, 29
John A. Howard, *Marketing: Executive and Buyer Behaviour*, Columbia University Press (New York, 1963), especially chapters 1, 4, 5
P. D. Converse, H. W. Huegy and R. V. Mitchell, *Elements of Marketing* (6th Edition, 1958), Pitman (London), especially chapters 7, 21, 22
D. A. Revzan, *Wholesaling in Marketing Organisation*, John Wiley (New York, 1961), especially chapters 12, 13, 14

CHAPTER 3

GENERATION OF NEW PRODUCT IDEAS

P. Hilton, *Handbook of New Product Development*, Prentice-Hall (Englewood Cliffs, New Jersey, 1961), especially chapters 2, 3, 4
D. W. Karger, *The New Product*, Industrial Press (New York, 1960), especially chapters 2, 3

Developing a Product Strategy, American Management Association (New York, 1959), especially parts 1, 2, 3

Nicholas A. H. Stacey and Aubrey Wilson *Industrial Marketing Research—Management and Technique*, Hutchinson (London, 1963), especially chapter 14

T. L. Berg and A. Shuchman, *Product Strategy and Management*, Holt, Rinehard and Winston (New York, 1963), especially Part 3

CHAPTER 4

ORGANISATION OF NEW PRODUCT DEVELOPMENT

A. J. Merrett and A. Sykes, *Finance and Analysis of Capital Projects*, Longmans, Green (London, 1962)

Science and the City, Papers prepared for a conference sponsored by Hambros Bank and the *New Scientist, New Scientist* (London, 1963)

T. L. Berg and A. Shuchman, *Product Strategy and Management*, Holt, Rinehart and Winston (New York, 1963), especially parts 2, 4

Stanley S. Miller, *Management Problems of Diversification*, John Wiley (New York, 1963)

CHAPTER 5

INDUSTRIAL MARKETING RESEARCH—MANAGEMENT ASPECTS

R. S. Alexander, J. S. Cross and R. M. Cunningham, *Industrial Marketing* (Revised Edition, 1961), Richard D. Irwin (Homewood, Ill.), especially Chapter 5

John A. Howard, *Marketing Management: Analysis and Decision*, Richard D. Irwin (Homewood, Ill., 1957)

J. S. Bain, *Industrial Organisation*, John Wiley (New York, 1959)

Nicholas A. H. Stacey and Aubrey Wilson, *Industrial Marketing Research—Management and Technique*, Hutchinson (London, 1963), especially chapters 1, 5, 6

CHAPTER 6

INDUSTRIAL MARKETING RESEARCH TECHNIQUES

Nicholas A. H. Stacey and Aubrey Wilson, *Industrial Marketing Research—Management and Technique*, Hutchinson (London, 1963), especially chapters 7, 8, 9, 10

R. A. Fisher, *Statistical Methods for Research Workers*, Oliver and Boyd (Edinburgh, 1950)

W. E. Deming, *Some Theory of Sampling*, John Wiley (New York, 1950)

A. Stuart, *Basic Ideas of Scientific Sampling*, Griffin (London, 1962)

W. J. Walford (Ed.), *Guide to Reference Material*, Library Association, (London 1963)

CHAPTER 7

INDUSTRIAL SELLING

Elizabeth Marting (Ed.), *The Marketing Job*, American Management Association (New York, 1961)

Perry Bliss, (Ed.), *Marketing and the Behavioural Sciences—Selected Readings*, Allyn and Bacon (Boston, Mass., 1963)

Robert T. Davies, *Performance and Development of Field Sales Managers*, Harvard University Press (Cambridge, Mass., 1957)

J. B. Matthews, R. D. Buzzell, T. Levitt, R. E. Frank, *Marketing—An Introductory Analysis*, McGraw-Hill (New York, 1964)

Theodore Levitt, *Innovation in Marketing*, McGraw-Hill (New York, 1962)

A Committee of the Institute of Marketing and Sales Management, *A Manual of Sales Management*, Pitman (London, 1961)

CHAPTER 8

INDUSTRIAL ADVERTISING

Fred R. Messner, *Industrial Advertising*, McGraw-Hill (New York, 1963)

Pre-Testing Advertising, Studies in Business Policy No. 109, National Industrial Conference Board (New York, 1963)

S. Watson Dunn, *International Handbook of Advertising*, McGraw-Hill (New York, 1964)

D. B. Lucas and S. H. Britt, *Measuring Advertising Effectiveness*, McGraw-Hill (New York, 1963)

CHAPTER 9

INDUSTRIAL PUBLIC RELATIONS

Sam Black, *Practical Public Relations*, Pitman (London, 1962)

Nigel Ellis and Pat Bowman (Eds.), *The Hand-Book of Public Relations*, George Harrap (London, 1963)

James Derriman, *Public Relations in Business Management*, University of London Press (London, 1964)

CHAPTER 10

SERVICE ELEMENT IN ADDED VALUE

R. S. Alexander, J. S. Cross and R. M. Cunningham, *Industrial Marketing* (Revised Edition, 1961), Richard D. Irwin (Homewood, Ill.), especially Part VI

E. Raymond Corey, *Industrial Marketing—Cases and Concepts*, Prentice-Hall (Englewood Cliffs, New Jersey, 1962), especially Section 4

Developing a Product Strategy, American Management Association (New York, 1959), especially Part 5

P. D. Converse, H. W. Huegy and R. V. Mitchell, *Elements of Marketing* (6th Edition, 1958), Pitman (London) especially Chapter 21

CHAPTER 11

PHYSICAL DISTRIBUTION

R. S. Alexander, J. S. Cross and R. M. Cunningham, *Industrial Marketing* (Revised Edition, 1961), Richard D. Irwin (Homewood, Ill.), especially parts III, VI

G. W. Aljian, *Purchasing Handbook*, McGraw-Hill (New York, 1958)

A. Battersby, *A Guide to Stock Control*, Pitman (London, 1962)

J. R. Immer, *Materials Handling*, McGraw-Hill (New York, 1953)

Nicholas A. H. Stacey and Aubrey Wilson, *The Changing Pattern of Distribution*, Pergamon (Revised Edition, 1965), (Oxford)

William M. Diamond, *Distribution Channels for Industrial Goods*, Ohio State University (Columbus, Ohio, 1963)

CHAPTER 12

PRICING IN INDUSTRIAL MARKETING

R. S. Alexander, J. S. Cross and R. M. Cunningham, *Industrial Marketing* (Revised Edition, 1961), Richard D. Irwin (Homewood, Ill.), especially Part IV

W. Brown and E. Jacques, *Product Analysis Pricing*, Heinemann (London, 1964)

E. C. Bursk and J. R. Chapman (Eds.), *Modern Marketing Strategy*, Harvard University Press (Cambridge, Mass., 1964), especially chapters 16, 17, 18

E. Raymond Corey, *Industrial Marketing—Cases and Concepts*, Prentice-Hall (Englewood Cliffs, New Jersey, 1962), especially Section 3

CHAPTER 13

INTERNATIONAL MARKETING

H. Mynt, *The Economics of Developing Countries*, Hutchinson (London, 1964)

Firms and Their Exports, P.E.P. (London, November 1964)

Max K. Adler, *A Short Guide to Market Research in Europe*, Crosby Lockwood (London, 1962)

James Derriman, *Public Relations in Business Management*, University of London Press (London, 1964), especially Chapter 9

S. Watson Dunn, *International Handbook of Advertising*, McGraw-Hill (New York, 1964)

CHAPTER 14

MARKETING MANAGERS AND THEIR DEVELOPMENT

H. Lazo and A. Corbin, *Management in Marketing*, McGraw-Hill (New York, 1961)

E. F. L. Brech (Ed.), *Principles and Practice of Management*, Longmans, Green (London, 1963)

J. H. Westing and G. Albaum (Ed.), *Modern Marketing Thought*, Macmillan (New York, 1964)

S. J. Shaw and C. McGittringer, *Marketing in Business Management*, Macmillan (New York, 1963)

M. Zober, *Marketing Management*, John Wiley (New York, 1964)

A. Corbin and G. Blagowidow, *Decision Exercises in Marketing*, McGraw-Hill (New York, 1964)

CHAPTER 15

FINANCIAL CONTROL OF THE MARKETING FUNCTION

M. Schiff and M. Mellman, *Financial Management of the Marketing Function*, Financial Executives Research Foundation (New York 1962)

R. S. Alexander, J. S. Cross and R. M. Cunningham, *Industrial Marketing* (Revised Edition, 1961), Richard D. Irwin (Homewood Ill.), especially Chapter 16

E. Raymond Corey, *Industrial Marketing—Cases and Concepts*, Prentice-Hall (New York, 1962)

P. D. Converse, H. W. Huegy and R. V. Mitchell, *Elements of Marketing* (6th Edition, 1958), Pitman (London), especially Chapter 30

How to Read a Financial Report, Merrill Lynch, Pierce, Fenner and Smith, Inc. (New York, 1962)

CHAPTER 16

INTEGRATING THE MARKETING FUNCTIONS

M. P. McNair and H. L. Hansen, *Readings in Marketing*, McGraw-Hill (New York, 1956)

J. D. Matthews, R. B. Buzzell, T. Levitt and R. E. Frank, *Marketing—An Introductory Analysis*, McGraw-Hill (New York, 1964), especially Part 5

E. J. McCarthy, *Basic Marketing*, Richard D. Irwin (Homewood, Ill., 1964)

W. Alderson and P. E. Green, *Planning and Problem Solving in Marketing*, Richard D. Irwin (Homewood, Ill., 1964)

W. J. Stanton, *Fundamentals of Marketing*, McGraw-Hill (New York, 1964)

CHAPTER 17

MARKETING WITHIN THE TOTAL
CORPORATE COMPLEX

P. D. Converse, H. W. Huegy and R. V. Mitchell, *Elements of Marketing* (6th Edition, 1958), Pitman (London)

R. S. Alexander, J. S. Cross and R. M. Cunningham, *Industrial Marketing* (Revised Edition, 1961), Richard D. Irwin (Homewood, Ill.)

E. A. Duddy and D. A. Revzan, *Marketing*, McGraw-Hill (New York, 1953), especially Part 8

CHAPTER 18

MARKETING MYOPIA

Theodore Levitt, *Innovation in Marketing*, McGraw-Hill (New York, 1962)

E. Raymond Corey, *The Developments of Markets for New Materials*, Bureau of Research, Harvard University Graduate School of Business Administration (Boston, 1956)

Seymour Banks, *Experimentation in Marketing*, McGraw-Hill (New York, 1965)

Bertil Liander and Staff of Marketing Science Institute, *Marketing Development in the European Economic Community*, McGraw-Hill (New York, 1965)

CHAPTER 19

INDUSTRIAL MARKETING IN THE NEXT DECADE

Theodore Levitt, *Innovation in Marketing*, McGraw-Hill (New York, 1962)

R. Bartels, *The Development of Marketing Thought*, Richard D. Irwin (Homewood, Ill., 1962)

Perry Bliss (Ed.), *Marketing and the Behavioural Sciences*, Allyn and Bacon (Boston, Mass., 1963), especially Part X

R. Ferber and H. G. Wales (Eds.), *Motivation and Market Behaviour*, Richard D. Irwin (Homewood, Ill., 1958), especially Part I

John A. Howard, *Marketing: Executive and Buying Behaviour*, Columbia University Press (New York, 1962), especially Part II

Leslie W. Rodger, *Marketing in a Competitive Economy*, Hutchinson (London, 1965)

Index

For Product Safety Concerns and Information please contact our EU
representative GPSR@taylorandfrancis.com
Taylor & Francis Verlag GmbH, Kaufingerstraße 24, 80331 München, Germany

www.ingramcontent.com/pod-product-compliance
Lightning Source LLC
Chambersburg PA
CBHW061139220326
41599CB00025B/4291